Goliath's Groove, Stanage, ALPHA CLUB MASS SOLO ASCENT

For my wife Pauline,
and my daughter Lucy

Alpha Males
The Story of the Alpha Mountaineering Club

– AL PARKER –

FASTPRINT PUBLISHING
PETERBOROUGH, ENGLAND

www.fast-print.net/store.php

Alpha Males
Copyright © Al Parker 2010

ISBN 978-184426-906-8

First published 2010 by
FASTPRINT PUBLISHING
Peterborough, England.

An environmentally friendly book printed and bound in England by
www.printondemand-worldwide.com

Mixed Sources
Product group from well-managed
forests, and other controlled sources
www.fsc.org Cert no. TT-COC-002641
© 1996 Forest Stewardship Council

PEFC Certified
This product is
from sustainably
managed forests
and controlled
sources
www.pefc.org
PEFC/16-33-415

This book is made entirely of chain-of-custody materials

Contents

Acknowledgements

I want to thank various people for their help and the time they have spared for me.
Thanks to Steve Dean for his advice and encouragement, Geoff Milburn for the same. Thanks to Pete Bamfield, Les Brown, Eddie Birch, John Smith, Steve Barber and Barry Chopping for photographs.
A Special thanks to Val Johnson for correcting my punctuation etc.
Thanks to Brian (Bill) Bowker for letting me use information from his article about the Bonatti Pillar and thanks to Ray Wegrzyn for his help on the computer.
Thanks also go out to the members of The Alpha who have supplied invaluable information about their past lives and climbs, especially Alan McHardy. And finally to my parents who supplied me with the genes to appreciate the hills, I wish they could have lived to see this book.

Illustrations

Introduction

I first conceived the idea of writing a book about the Alpha Club after reading inaccurate accounts about it; one stated that Martin Boysen was a founder member, when in actual fact Martin joined five years after the club's inception. Another error described Pete Bamfield and Bob Brayshaw as Sheffielders, whereas Bob came from Manchester and Pete from Stockport. In fact the Alpha was a Manchester-based club at the beginning and remained so until Paul Nunn went to Sheffield University four years later; then others from Sheffield became members.

Another article, about the various climbing clubs and the impact of their contributions to the course of British climbing history, surprisingly, did not include the Alpha in its list.

After at first ignoring this kind of inaccuracy, I began to think that perhaps it was time for someone to write a history of the Alpha club - the true story, so to speak! Being a founder member and having climbed with most of the characters involved, I decided to take on the task of setting things straight.

This book is written from my own perspective, so for descriptions of those events where I wasn't actually present, I have relied on the testimony of those who were.

Also, as I never kept diaries or journals, I have been dependent on my 70 year-old memory, fortunately a good one, and the memories and journals of others, but if ever accounts differed, I have opted for what I remembered as the true version.

The result is, I hope, an accurate account of the activities and antics of the Alpha lads, from the founding of the club in 1956 to the present day. To paraphrase the words of Eric Morecambe, "The events about which I write, Sunshine, are all true, but not necessarily in the right order;" although some things have been censored to protect the guilty.

I know that by the standards of today and considering the achievements of the leading modern climbers, the exploits of the Alpha club may seem tame in comparison, but it was a different time with different attitudes, dangers and conditions.

Over a period of about ten years the Alpha club was at the forefront of exploration in Derbyshire, the Lakes and Wales; amongst its members were some of the country's most talented climbers. A major contribution was the discovery and opening up of Gogarth by Barry Ingle and Martin Boysen and elsewhere important new routes at the top standard were done by many Alpha members particularly on gritstone and in north Wales. They were the main group involved in breaking down the Rock and Ice myth and raising the general standard by producing new routes at least equal to, if not harder than, the climbs of the Brown / Whillans era. This is not meant to suggest that Brown and Whillans had been superseded, but that younger climbers, mainly from the Alpha Club had raised their own standards to the same level, thus setting the scene for further development.

Members of the Alpha accomplished early ascents of some of the harder Alpine climbs, both in the western and eastern Alps, later graduating to the Himalayas. In the late 1960s Richard McHardy was at the forefront of the new trend of soloing extreme climbs, with solo ascents of Vector, Woubits and the Overhanging Arete finish to the Grooves along with many other hard climbs of the day.

The Alpha was never a club in the true sense of the word; it was a group of like-minded individuals (which never exceeded thirty-five in number) who gravitated together through friendship and a shared love of mountains and the outdoors. There were some at the beginning who tried to introduce subscriptions, but very few would pay them and organised club meets shared the same fate with few turning up; later on, a membership card and club badge were introduced but were eventually consigned to the re-cycle bin never to be resurrected.

Casual arrangements were more the norm with various small groups within the Alpha feeling free to follow their own plans and preferences for different areas. This anarchic approach worked well as quite often everyone finished up at the same place anyway, without the feeling of having been organised.

The only organised event was the annual club dinner, and this was only in the respect that a set number of dinners were ordered at an acceptable venue, for a set number of people. Everything else about it usually descended into chaos!

I have tried to capture the spirit of the time and to convey the personalities of the characters involved and their journey from young, sometimes daft, youths, to perhaps more sensible old men who can still act daft on occasion. Club dinners, which were always boozy and wild occasions, are now, when they take place, more akin to a war veterans' reunion, with talk of past glories and comparisons of old injuries, along with current illnesses and operations. Discussion of the latest state-of-the-art equipment is usually confined to the best walking sticks, knee supports and hearing aids etc.

Just think, some of these guys are still climbing and imagining they're as good as they used to be (although with modern gear, some of them are better). The rest have either given up altogether or have become keen hill walkers or twitchers.

"Tempus doesn't part fugit," and like most Alpha males they must at some time give way to the next generations. Though there are still some, but not many, amongst them, who prefer to fight on to the bitter end.

These climbers have seen many changes - in attitudes, training, techniques and equipment as well as vast changes to the climbing environment. For instance, the path up to Stanage in 1957 was all but non-existent and in summer months was hidden in the bracken! Today, as every climber knows, it resembles a motorway.

Back then, there was no necessity for car parks at the crags as few could afford cars; transport was by train, pushbike / motorbike or hitch-hiking.

The climbs on Stanage numbered about 250 and there was a lot of unclimbed rock. It was usual to travel to the crags on either Friday nights or Saturday mornings and, once there, either camp or sleep rough in any place that could provide shelter from the elements. There was no such thing as jumping in the car to go home for the night. There was camaraderie between various groups and clubs and a certain amount of rivalry. Everybody knew everybody else!

Because of the lack of transport and an old fashioned road system with no motorways, trips to Wales or the Lakes and Scotland were major events and at first restricted mainly to long weekends or summer holidays. The Derbyshire gritstone edges were popular on most weekends except during national holidays, when almost all gritstone climbers went further afield; then, there was practically no one there. Bob Brayshaw and I went to Stanage at Whit 1959 and were the only ones on the crag, and that in sunny weather too!

Some of the traditional moorland crags such as Laddow and those of the Chew valley and Kinder areas were more popular during this period owing to their proximity to Manchester but seem to have fallen out of favour with the passing of time.

Equipment was primitive: hawser-laid hemp or nylon ropes which were tied direct on to the waist, foot wear was Kletterschuh, rubber pumps or big boots. Very few people had rock boots; PAs were just coming in but had to be brought in from France. Chalk and climbing walls were 20 years away. The most modern protection was homemade machined-out nuts on slings, which were just taking over from natural chockstones, jammed knots and the occasional peg. The old rule that the leader must never fall off was of that time.

Any guidebooks that were available were usually years out of date and climbing magazines as such, didn't exist! It was quite possible to do a new route and to not see it in print for five years, so information was passed on by word of mouth.

Despite all this, hard new climbs even by today's standards were being done by various groups. The Craig Lough lads from the north east were active mainly in the Lake District, as were many Yorkshire climbers. The Manchester Gritstone Club, the Black and Tans and the Peak Climbing Club along with the MUMC and SUMC did many good new routes, mainly in Derbyshire.

The Alpha Club, a young and keen group of up and coming climbers, followed in the footsteps of the Rock and Ice by pioneering routes on Derbyshire gritstone; and after acquiring their own transport, which at first was motorbikes and then later Morris 1000 vans, they regularly did the same in Wales and the Lake District, with the occasional foray into Creagh Dhu territory. They spearheaded the new wave of exploration.

Admittedly the big jump in climbing standards came later with a new generation. This was mainly due to changes in climbing gear and training facilities and the desire to do new routes. To achieve this advancement meant that training had become almost mandatory; until then doing a few press-ups and pull-ups at home and a lot of climbing on the crags regardless of the weather had been sufficient.

The hardest climbs of the day were all graded the same, Extreme, which covered climbs which nowadays would probably be E1 to E3. Then, they were either mild Extreme or Hard Extreme and there were no technical grades. This eventually necessitated a revision of the grading system at the top end.

Then along came harnesses, belay plates, chalk, sticky boots, Wires and Friends; indoor climbing walls provided safe all-weather training and the standards went up accordingly and have continued to do so to this day.

It used to be said of impossible looking lines, "Leave that for future generations." We looked, we sometimes tried them and then that's what we did, we left them for today's climbers and most of them have now been climbed!

Where will it end? Have we reached the point where anti-gravity boots will soon become necessary? Or will interest in climbing fade away? That too we shall have to leave for future generations.

In addition to the climbing history of the Alpha Club, I have included many anecdotes and travel stories which I hope give an insight to the overall activities of the club and which the reader will find interesting.

Finally, if in this book I have missed out anyone, or any event considered by others to be important, I apologise. As I said earlier, I have been dependent on my memory, the memories of others and the memories of some who can't remember anything at all!

Al Parker 2010

Chapter 1
Early Days

"Come to Edale next weekend, we're going to start a club." Three young climbers extended this invitation to Ralph Harris and me at the foot of Yellowslacks crag when we were both about 17 years of age. This invitation was to change our lives and although we didn't know it at the time, would influence in no small way the course of British climbing and our share in its history.

It all began about five years earlier, in 1951 when two of us, myself and Ralph, a neighbour and school friend of mine from our home town of Hyde, decided we would like to take up hill-walking. Our interest had been fired by a trip to the hills of Derbyshire with a teacher from our school and was meant as a reward for doing well in class. On that day, we had our first view of Kinder Scout (Derbyshire's highest hill) from the rocks of Cown Edge, high above the village of Charlesworth. Kinder and the nearby moors of Bleaklow seemed to us then, to be mysterious places, exciting unknown territory, like a "Lost World" calling out to be explored.

My parents had been keen walkers in their younger days and used to take me and my two sisters, Joan and Hilary, to the Derbyshire Dales. My mother's two sisters and their husbands were keen hill walkers and had been on many rambling holidays to North Wales and the Lake District. I was brought up on tales of Helvellyn and Tryfan and couldn't wait for the time when I would climb those mountains with the magical sounding names. One of my uncles had even taken part in the mass trespass on Kinder in the 1930s; so I felt that the hills were in my blood. Ralph and I began to go out every weekend, hiking for miles over the moors of the Dark Peak. Ralph was a good companion, a lad of medium build with dark ginger hair and a dry, subtle sense of humour. Having briefly been a boy scout he knew about map reading and compass work and during weekday evenings at his house or mine, planning our walks for the coming weekend, Ralph would instruct me in the use of map and compass, the art of which until then had been alien to me. Both he and I were about the same age and on leaving junior school, Ralph went to Grammar school and after a brief spell at a secondary modern, I started at technical school in nearby Stockport.

Over the next couple of years, we went out every Sunday, taking the bus to Glossop or the train from Hyde to Hayfield. We joined the local library and read everything we could lay our hands on about rambling and mountaineering in general, favourites being books by our hero Frank Smythe.I used to ask my uncle Fred about places to go and he would tell me about Black Hill and the Marsden- Edale or the Derwent watersheds walks. He knew the Dark Peak area very well and during the war, whilst a member of the Homeguard, he had made a relief map mounted on a board, to assist in the instruction of the soldiers at the Crowden barracks. That map still exists today.

When I was 16 years old, I left school and began work in 1955 as an apprentice fitter at The National Gas & Oil Engine Company in Ashton-U-Lyne. During that year Ralph and I continued with our weekend rambling and even tried our hand at some easy rock-scrambling. On one occasion at Laddow Rocks, some climbers asked if we would like to have a go on a rope. We did Straight Chimney (moderate) and Green Gully (mod) but it was only later that we learned these names. Ralph seemed keen to take up climbing but I wasn't so sure. We decided to go along to see what a local climbing club had to offer; this was the Black and Tans climbing club, who met every week at a pub not far from where we lived. So one Wednesday evening, full of expectations at the prospect of meeting some real climbers, we went to the Hare and Hounds on Werneth Low in Hyde. The climbers were in a back room, and we found that most of them were much older than us except for a lad who went to the same school as Ralph. His name was John Gosling.

The conversation that evening was all about cars and motor bikes, not climbing as we had hoped. Ralph and I sat without drinks, listening to these older men who more or less ignored us. Not being old enough to drink or drive, we spent what to us was a very boring evening. When we eventually got up to leave, they invited us to return the following week. We thanked them, bade them good-night and walked home vowing never to go back!

At Easter the following year, Ralph and I caught the train to Preston where we had planned to meet my cousin Barry (the son of my uncle

Les, of Kinder Trespass fame).Barry lived in Preston and as we were to change trains there he joined us at the station. We all three boarded a connection which took us to Windermere, then after a short bus journey we arrived at our final destination, Ambleside. As it was Easter, the Youth Hostel was full, so having booked into a b&b for the princely sum of ten shillings per night, 50p in today's currency, the rest of the evening was spent looking around Ambleside, before turning in early as we had a big day planned for the morrow.

Next day we were up early. It was Good Friday 1956. After breakfast we boarded a bus to Grasmere and disembarked at the Swan Hotel. Little did we know then, that in a few years time, Barry's parents would move to Grasmere to live at Forest Side Cottage and Barry would live and work in Keswick.

The day was very hot for the time of year, the sky a deep blue with not a cloud in sight. It was turning out to be one those rare Easter weekends more like summer, but with cold frosty nights. Setting off with heavy sacks and light hearts, we turned off the road and plodded up Tongue Gill to Grisedale Tarn where we rested in the sun. Above us we could see what looked like a conga chain of walkers ascending the zigzags to Dollywagon Pike. Barry had been up here before, to the top of Helvellyn with his parents and his sister Valerie; when they were both quite young. But for Ralph and me, this was a great adventure. After a long and arduous slog, punctuated by many rests, we collapsed on the summit of Helvellyn, glad to shed our heavy sacks.

After a bite to eat, taking in the magnificent views all around, we set off again following the path down along past Browncove Crags to Thirlspot. On the way, whilst running downhill, I plunged up to my waist in a bog and had to be hauled out by the lads, much to their amusement.

At Thirlspot Farm, we bought a glass of cold milk each, which tasted delicious and seemed to put some strength back into our weary bodies. Jumping on a bus to Keswick and trying without success to get in at the YHA, we again had to break into our hard earned cash to stay at a B&B in the centre of town. We bought fish and chips and ate them on the shores of Derwentwater at Friars Crag, then spent the rest of the evening messing about by the lake before heading back to our digs for an early night.

Saturday was again sunny and hot, so after a good breakfast we set off to walk down Borrowdale along the shores of the lake. At the Bowder Stone, we played around on this large boulder for a while, pretending to be climbers. Pushing on to Rosthwaite and again failing to get in at the youth hostel, we at last realised that we should have booked in advance. After cooking a meal down by the river we got talking with some local girls in Rosthwaite village, who told us of a good barn to sleep in. After dark, we sneaked into the barn and only having YHA sheet sleeping bags, covered ourselves with hay for extra warmth. The night was cold and very frosty. Around midnight, Barry woke us up in alarm saying he was being eaten alive by something. Shining a torch, we discovered that we were all crawling with what the Cumbrians call "Red Biddies", minute red lice. Throwing off the hay we spent the rest of the night shivering!

Dawn saw us back down by the river cooking our breakfast of sausage and beans. After this culinary masterpiece cooked by our chef Ralph, we made a brew, packed the sacks and were then ready for anything.

It was another clear blue day and by the time we reached Seathwaite, it was scorching hot. Setting off up Grains Gill we saw a climber with a rope and some slings and karabiners draped around his neck. Ralph said he wouldn't mind taking up rock-climbing seriously to which Barry and I said, "You must be mad".

Halfway up Grains Gill, stopping for a rest and a drink from the stream, we lay there sun bathing. Looking up at Seathwaite Fell above us (not on our route,) Barry said to Ralph, who was renowned for being tight," Would you walk up that hill for three pence?" Ralph's reply was to take off his sack and set off up the fell. Lying there in the sun watching him disappear over the horizon, Barry said "We'll have a laugh when he gets back". Sometime later Ralph came staggering back, hoping to collect his reward. Barry asked him if he had taken a photo of the summit. "How could I?" said Ralph. "I don't have a camera." Barry said that without photographic proof of the ascent he wasn't obliged to pay. Ralph was very angry to be done out of the price of a bag of chips and a fight ensued, but this didn't come to much. What annoyed Ralph more than his failure to collect the princely sum, were the taunts of "Sucker" from his "friends," but like all the pranks we played on each other, this episode was soon forgotten. We resumed our upward journey via Esk Hause to Great End then past Broad Crag to Scafell Pike; England's highest mountain. We lay on the summit in the hot sun, drinking in the view. After a while, I wandered away a little from the lads to take a photo of Great Gable. When I returned, I found them laughing about something. On enquiring what was so funny, Barry told me a joke and we all laughed together. I thought how great this is: the mountains, the weather and the company of two good and amusing friends.

Preparing to move on again, I picked up my sack and with great difficulty and help from Barry, managed to get it on to my shoulders. "Phew," I said" That's heavy, I'm sure it's got heavier." "Mine too," said Barry. Ralph said the same so I assumed that the heat had weakened us making our loads appear a lot heavier than before. Retracing our steps to Esk Hause I had to rest frequently before carrying on past Angle Tarn to the top of Rosset Gill. The scenery was magnificent but I was too tired to appreciate it. The other two seemed OK and quite fit but I had aching shoulders and needed to rest every few hundred yards. Eventually, below the Langdale Pikes and somewhere along Mickleden, stopping for yet another rest, Barry said to Ralph," Shall we tell him?" "OK," said Ralph. "Tell me what?" said I. Barry looked nervously at me and said, "You know when you were taking that picture of Gable from the top of Scafell Pike and you asked why we were laughing?" "Yes," I replied." Well," said Barry, "we put a big rock in your sack and you've carried it all this way." I pondered his claim. If I was to look in my sack and there wasn't a rock, I would be a sucker, but if I didn't look in the sack and there really was a rock in there, I would be a very tired sucker by the end of the day. I made my decision. The lads took off like frightened deer. Opening the sack I stared in disbelief. There before my eyes was the cause of my fatigue, a rock as big as a football. It must have weighed at least ten pounds. I chased after the jokers, anger fuelling my speed. The whole episode finished with a wrestling match and honour was restored.

That night we slept in an empty railway carriage at Windermere Station, and the next day we went home; the end of a great adventure!

Back home, we were soon in the old routine of weekend walking. Ralph again expressed his desire to start rock-climbing but I wasn't keen. I enjoyed our days out walking and thought that climbing would interfere with it. We eventually compromised and decided to alternate between climbing one weekend and walking the next. We bought a rope between us, our first very own rope, 100 feet long half weight hemp about half an inch in diameter, alright for holding a second but probably useless for a leader fall. Hence the old maxim "The leader must never fall off." With a couple of nylon slings and two ex- army karabiners, we felt really well equipped! We chose Laddow Rocks for our first venture onto the crags. Cycling to Crowden we left our bikes in some bushes and walked up to the crag. As we approached, the cliff seemed to grow in height before our eyes. By the time we got there it looked enormous and we were beginning to have second thoughts but taking the bull by the horns attempted our first climb, Waterfall Climb, which although graded difficult, was up a series of large ledges in a gully with very little exposure. Two climbers who were doing the route next to us showed us how to belay with the rope and told us the name and grade of our climb. Confident to try something more daring, we wandered along under the crag looking for something that appealed to us. After much deliberation we decided on a steep looking chimney in the middle of the upper face. Ralph led up the wall to the foot of the chimney and as he took in the rope, I climbed up to him. We pooled our brains and remembered how to belay. Feeling secure I led on, but in reality without runners on the upper section a fall would have been serious. We later learned that we had done Straight Chimney again. We thought it seemed familiar. As we walked back down the valley, talking of the climbs that we had done, I had to admit to Ralph that I had really enjoyed the experience. We decided there and then to go climbing again the following weekend and miss out the walking.

From then on we climbed every weekend, usually on a Sunday, going to Yellowslacks, Kinder Downfall or Laddow Rocks, walking there after taking the bus or train to Glossop or Hayfield. Many a time we got soaked to the skin, and thought nothing of walking 14 miles as well as climbing 10 routes in the same day. By this time, I was the proud owner of a pair of size 10 nailed boots. My dad had advised me to get them big as they were expensive and it would be a shame to grow out of them quickly, I took size 8s at the time and still do to this day! At that time there was a debate amongst climbers as to which was better on wet rock, nails or the new rubber Commando soles, the forerunners of Vibrams. Being traditionalists, Ralph and I went for nails but used rubber pumps from Woolworths for the harder climbs. My uncle nailed the big boots for me, fixing clinkers round the edges of the soles and heels with studs on the bottom; a year or so later I had them re-soled with Vibrams! That year, 1956, we bumbled along not really knowing what we were doing as we didn't have any guide books. In fact, up-to-date guides were rare things indeed. As we learned rope techniques from library books or from other climbers that we sometimes met, it was a miracle that we survived those early days.

That summer we planned to go to Wales and as I needed some new equipment I visited Ellis Brigham's shop in Manchester to buy it. Bob

Brigham was the proprietor along with his younger brother Ellis. When their father Ellis senior died, Bob at the age of 19 had taken over the running of the family business; at that time Ellis junior was only a young boy. The shop was very small and was situated on Conran St. in Harpurhey. That first time at Brigham's, I thought," This is great". There were boxes everywhere, stacked almost up to the ceiling, filled with boots and other outdoor equipment. It looked chaotic. I asked Bob if he had any corduroy climbing breeches. He knew just where to look and after moving a pile of boxes, he found a pair of brown cord breeks for me. Next thing on my list was an ice axe, an Aschenbrenner with a wooden shaft. Bob couldn't understand why I wanted the axe when I was only going to Wales and particularly as it was August. I bought it anyway thinking it would come into its own the following winter. After all, we were mountaineers and mountaineers have ice axes! I left the shop with a bag full of socks, maps, a compass and my first guidebook, a Climbers Club guide to Tryfan and Glyder Fach, by Colin Kirkus.

Over the next few years, Bob Brigham started to build up his business and he became a good friend to me and my friends.

When our summer holidays arrived, off we went to Wales having booked two weeks full board at a hill farm on the slopes of Moel Siabod near to Capel Curig this was in 1956.

Travelling by train to Bettws-y-Coed and then by bus, we were dropped at the bottom of the lane which led up steeply to the farm. "Cae Gwegi" was owned by Mr and Mrs Williams and was a typical Welsh hill farm, mainly sheep but also a few cows in the meadows below, where the river Llugwy flowed down from Capel Curig.Mr Williams and his wife were quite elderly and had been host to my aunts and uncles some years previously when they were all young. Ralph and I shared a large double bed and each morning we washed in cold water from the wash stand in our room. The WC was outside at the back of the farm. This might sound a bit spartan, but there was always a good fire in the living room, giving it a cosy atmosphere when the weather was cold and wet. Mrs Williams was an excellent cook, providing a good breakfast every day, a packed lunch for our outings and a substantial dinner in the evenings. We felt that it was fit for a king and all for £4 each per week. After our evening meal, sitting by the fire, listening to the ticking of the grandfather clock, either reading or talking of the events of the day, we felt that life was very good.

Our first morning at Cae Gwegi, we breakfasted early then walked through the woods to Capel. Following the track from behind the Post

Office to the foot of Little Tryfan (the slabby little sibling of Tryfan) in the Nant Francon valley, we climbed the left hand arête, [moderate] our first climb in Wales! From the top of the climb we walked to the Eastern Terrace of Tryfan and made our way to the summit, where we performed the obligatory ritual of jumping from Adam to Eve. These two monoliths, which can be seen from the road far below, are the summit stones of Tryfan and stand about 4ft apart above the East face; to jump and miss one's footing could result in a nasty fall. Leaving the summit we scrambled up the Bristly Ridge to Glyder Fach. Our return route was along the ridge, over Y Foel Goch back to Capel Curig and Cae Gwegi. This had been a long tiring walk and we were so pleased to get back in time for dinner and a well-earned early night.

The next few days, we walked in the Carnedds, did the Snowdon Horseshoe and climbed on the Bochlywd Buttress and the Gribin Facet.

All that first week, it either blew rained or was misty; sometimes we got the lot together. Our room at the farm was in the attic and had a skylight and most days we awoke to the sound of rain drumming on the glass, but being young and keen we went out every day. We always walked to the mountains, even to Snowdon, but while we nearly always walked back as well from the mountains in the Ogwen valley, we succumbed to taking the bus back from Snowdon.

The high spot of the holiday came during the second week. It was a beautiful morning as we walked again along the Ogwen valley. All the mountains were clearly visible for the first time and we felt on top of the world. As we approached Cwm Idwal, the slabs came into view appearing enormous to us and we felt a little overawed. Leaving our sacks at the foot of the crag, we climbed Idwal Buttress, a 300ft moderate, the longest climb we had ever done! Afterwards whilst eating our lunch at the foot of the slabs we got talking to a group of older climbers.

They had been watching us and one of the group an American named John, who was 6' 6" tall, told us he was a guide from Colorado. He said he had climbed with the famous Joe Brown, so we thought,"He must be good!"

John's friends didn't want to climb, saying that they had been doing hard routes all week and they were tired. John asked if we would like to do the classic Tennis Shoe, a 460ft climb up delicate slabs graded Severe with him in the lead of course. We enjoyed the climb enormously and after descending the ordinary route and saying goodbye to John and his friends who said they had to leave Ralph and I decided to try another Idwal classic slab climb. We set off up a V-Diff called Charity, but after only 140ft it started to rain heavily, so retreating quickly we walked back to Ogwen cottage and for once caught the bus back to Capel Curig.

We never saw John again and I have often wondered over the years, who he was and what happened to him.

The rest of the holiday was taken up with walks and easy climbs and then it was home to the old routine of work and looking forward to weekends in the hills.

We improved in our climbing very rapidly, and most weekends we cycled the nine miles from Hyde, where we both lived, to Crowden in Longdendale. Then after hiding the bikes we'd walk up to one of the crags, sometimes Torside where we did our first new route, the Lower Girdle of Castle Buttress VS, or Lad's Leap, but our favourite was Laddow. Occasionally we would climb on the crags of Kinder. This was in the days when the trains ran to Hayfield. I remember once going to the Downfall and meeting Keith Sutcliffe for the first time. He was climbing alone and was wearing a blue boiler suit. We thought this must be the climbing plumber, Joe Brown, but were too overawed to ask his name. A few weeks later we saw him again, this time in the company of two other climbers Ronnie Hughes and Ernie Thornhill who had a good laugh when we asked if Keith was Joe Brown. Ernie said that he himself was a member of the Rock & Ice club and that he knew Joe Brown and Don Whillans. We were very impressed!

Weeks went by and we climbed as often as possible mainly in Longdendale or the Kinder area, not having heard of Stanage or any of the Derbyshire edges at that time. One Sunday Ralph and I were at Yellowslacks, when Ronnie Hughes and some friends from the Manchester Gritstone club arrived. They began trying a climb called Nose Crack, one of many good climbs which disappeared a few years later when the local farmer blew up the crag in an effort to discourage climbing there.

Ron and his friends were having a struggle and not making much headway. Ralph and I sat on a rock watching them. Eventually when they were about to give up, I asked if I could have a go. I received looks which said "How does a kid of your age expect to succeed when we have failed?" Nevertheless they handed me the rope and grinned at one another. I was told "Help yourself, we don't mind holding your rope for you." I tied on and set off up the crack and although very scared, I didn't let it show. Before I knew it, I had climbed the route. Everyone was amazed, including me. Ralph came up next, followed in turn by Ron and his mates. Ron said to us," I can see that you two are going to make a name for yourselves as rock gymnasts." He meant this as a compliment, but for us, he couldn't have said anything worse. "Rock gymnasts!" we exclaimed." We are going to be mountaineers in the tradition of Frank Smythe. " "We'll see," said Ron. Years later, Ron Hughes had a bad accident whilst climbing at Dovestones Quarry with Graham West. They pulled away some loose rock and he suffered severe head injuries which I believe put an end to his climbing days.

We were now beginning to lead VS, mainly in rubber pumps, but sometimes in big boots depending on how we were feeling. As stated earlier, my boots were very big and nailed and very bendy. One day at Laddow Rocks, with a friend named Peter who was out climbing for the first time, we sat watching a group of climbers trying the first problem moves of Tower Face, the classic VS of the crag. A stocky, strong looking lad managed to do the moves then traversed off to the left. When he rejoined the group, I heard him say that he would like to do the whole route, if anyone would care to join him. "I'll do it with you," I said. He looked me up and down and said, "OK, you lead." Me and my big mouth! I had done the first moves before, so knew what to expect but the rest of the climb was unknown to me. In those days, before the advent of harnesses, we either tied directly onto the rope, or clipped the rope with a karabiner to a length of nylon cord tied around the waist. I was using the latter method.

I set off in my bendy boots carrying one sling and karabiner to belay at the top of the climb. About halfway up there was a ledge and a good belay, so I took a stance there, below the final crack. The lad I was climbing with was Stan Wroe, a member of the Manchester Gritstone club. Stan was slightly older than me and probably more experienced. He moved quickly up the lower section and soon joined me on the ledge. The plan was for Stan to lead the upper crack which he approached cautiously. I sat on my ledge watching him intently. When he was about 20 ft above me, he announced that he was about to fall off! This was something new for me. I'd never seen anyone fall off before. I said, "OK, jump for the ledge." He did and just caught the edge of it with his heels before falling over backwards and somersaulting down the crag. I was using a waist belay - that is, the rope ran round my back at waist level through both hands and was wrapped around my right wrist. Suddenly there was a tremendous weight on the rope and a searing pain as it burned into my flesh. I wanted to let go but I knew I had to try to hold on. I managed to stop Stan a few feet from the ground but he had broken a toe, probably when jumping for the ledge. I lowered him to the foot of the climb, then traversed into a nearby chimney and descended to Stan and the group of onlookers. It was only on reaching the ground that I started to feel the pain in my hands. They were burnt to the bone and my injuries kept me off work and from climbing for several weeks. This episode taught me not to use a nylon waist length in conjunction with a nylon rope when using a waist belay. The friction of the rope round my waist had burned almost through the waist length. One more strand and I would have been pulled off the ledge, either to fall to my death or at the very least to sustain serious injury. It was this type of event that led to the invention of the climbing harness.

My friend Peter never came out climbing again!

It was now November 1956 and one Sunday, Ralph and I took the train to Glossop and walked through Manor Park and up to one of our favourite crags, Yellowslacks. There, we met a lad from Hyde whom we had climbed with before whose name was Tony Hunt. He was with two friends, Peter Bamfield and Alan McHardy. They called themselves, rather grandly, the Pennine Rambling Club, and told us that they had two other members who were climbing elsewhere that day. Pete said they were planning to start a climbing club and were on the lookout for new members. They rented a barn at Upper Booth in the Edale valley and were in the process of converting it into a club hut. Tony Hunt was a small stocky lad who seemed to be full of nervous energy. Pete Bamfield was a strong looking character, who appeared to be very knowledgeable about climbing. He was very likeable with a ready laugh and a good sense of humour. The third member of their group was younger than the rest of us by about a year. His name was Alan McHardy. He said that he lived in Droylesden and that he was an apprentice joiner with Manchester Corporation Direct Works. He showed us an ice axe that he had made from an old fireman's axe. I don't think he ever used it on the hill but he was very enthusiastic about it. Not wanting to be unkind, we said it was a fine looking tool, which seemed to please him, although Pete was killing himself laughing. Alan was a lad of medium height, broad shouldered and slightly plump. He was very friendly and we took to him straight away.

This was the day that they invited us to join them the following weekend at their "club hut" in Edale. We all walked back to Glossop together where we went our separate ways, promising to meet up at the barn on the next Saturday afternoon.

Chapter 2
The Young Alpha

Ralph and I took the train to Hayfield arriving there at Saturday lunch time. We took the path up past Tunstead Farm and by the time we reached Edale Cross the rain was pouring steadily. Descending Jacob's ladder we reached the barn, or hut, as the lads called it, just as it was going dark. Situated in the middle of a field at Upper Booth in the Edale valley it was in reality an old barn, but the lads had worked to make it comfortable. At one end a fireplace provided the warmth, while at the opposite end, a rickety ladder led up to the sleeping area on a raised platform where there was a selection of single and double beds. Underneath the platform was the kitchen, equipped with an enamel bowl for a sink and an array of primus stoves on wooden tables. Ralph and I were very impressed by such 3-star accommodation. The whole building was about 45ft long but only two thirds of it were used for the hut. There were two outside doors, one opening into the kitchen the other to the living area. The other third of the building, the part nearest to the approach end, was a separate room with its own door and was obviously a shelter for sheep. It was full of sheep dung and a pungent smell of urine filled the air. When we first arrived Ralph and I had looked in and thought this was the hut. We were relieved when we heard voices coming from next door. Tony, Pete and Alan were there and seemed pleased to see us. They introduced us to the other two members, Keith Taylor, a bespectacled, broad-shouldered and strong-looking lad who we judged to be two or three years older than us and Dave Upton, a tall, seemingly nervous character. They too had brought along two new aspirant members, a pair whom they had met the previous weekend at Castle Naze, when one of the new lads, Pete Baldwin, had fallen off and almost landed on Keith's head. Baldwin was a tall, slim, tough-looking character with a wild gleam in his eyes. His climbing partner, Brian Barlow, was somewhat noisy and boisterous with a quick and sometimes cruel wit. So, this was the makings of our club, except for our invisible aspirant member, a friend of Pete and Brian who, they informed us was temporarily out of action due to a broken ankle sustained when he fell off "Valhalla," a VS crack on Stanage Edge. They said that their friend, who was called Les Brown, was a fantastic climber who had done such routes as Inverted Vee and Goliath's Groove at Stanage and even F Route on Gimmer Crag in Langdale. We were all impressed. Les apparently belonged to Manchester University Mountaineering Club and lived near Brian and Pete in Stockport. They had all been good friends for years and Les had told them that as soon as he was fit again, he would like to join us. Now the big problem, what to call ourselves? It would have to be good, something meaningful. Pete Bamfield came up with a name almost immediately. "The Alpha Mountaineering Club". "What does Alpha mean?" he was asked. "It means the first, superlatively good." "That's the name for us," we said, and so it was settled. Late November 1956 the Alpha club was born.

Those were happy days, all meeting at the barn on Saturday nights after spending the day climbing at various crags on Kinder, pooling our food to make a giant stew, then afterwards walking the two miles or so to the pub in Edale village. Of the two pubs there, we tended to favour the one near the station," The Church Inn," as they didn't ask too many questions about our ages. Baldwin and Barlow were old enough to drink alcohol, being a couple of years older than the rest of us, and boy could they drink! They both drank, smoked and swore like troopers. This was something Ralph and I weren't used to and at first we were quite shocked, but it didn't take long for us to be corrupted. During that first winter we enjoyed many Saturday nights at the pub but sometimes, if the weather was bad, we might stay at the barn and spend the evening talking and planning future climbs. It was always good fun with challenges as to who could traverse all the way round the inside walls, which were rough stone. Sometimes the outside wall was traversed as well, by the light of a Tilley lamp.

The barn had some good items of furniture: armchairs, tables, etc. and even an old piano. Keith Taylor was the pianist amongst us and his party piece was Malaguena. This was always requested when we were drinking at the Church Inn where there was also a piano. I think we probably thought it made us look intelligent to be seen appreciating such fine musicianship.

Baldwin had adopted Ralph as his medium for bringing out his own sadistic streak. He had renamed him Rastus, a name that he was stuck with from that day on. They had this game, where Baldwin would stroke Rastus's wiry hair and say, "Oh master, what is your command?" This would have the rest of us trembling in our boots because whatever Rastus said, Baldwin would do. He might say, "Al has a bad knee, can you treat it for him?" where upon Baldwin, assisted by Brian Barlow, wrestled me to the ground, sat on me and rubbed margarine into my knee, all the time thumping and jumping on it until Rastus ordered, "OK that's enough." The result was that no one complained about their ailments ever again.

Alan Mc Hardy by this time had also been re-christened by Baldwin who rather cruelly gave him the name Dick McThick. This was to distinguish him from any other Alan in the group, but gradually this got changed to Richard McThick and then eventually the McThick bit was dropped. Richard became the butt of Baldwin's Mickey taking and so-called fun. He had a hard time of it. I remember one Saturday night we were all sitting round the fire talking, except for Richard who had retired early to bed. Baldwin decided that he would like a brew. He demanded that I go outside to the trough for water, which I did, only to find that it had dried up. The only other source was the stream a quarter of a mile away but I refused to go; after all, it was almost midnight and pitch black outside and there was no way I was going for water without a torch to light my steps. Brian said, "Wake Richard, he can go." No sooner had he said this, than he and Baldwin started throwing anything they could lay their hands on in the direction of the sleeping area. Boots, pans, metal cups, anything that could be thrown was sent flying in Richard's direction. Eventually he got out of bed and said he would go for water, if someone else would light the Primus stove. Off he went into the night. A short time later, Baldwin decided that he didn't want a brew after all, saying that it was too much trouble to light the stove and that we should all go to bed. So whilst Richard was away at the stream, we bolted the doors, went to bed and turned off the lights. I felt really guilty for not standing up to Baldwin but was afraid to be the odd one out.

When Richard came back, he somehow managed to get inside. He was met by the sound of Baldwin's voice coming out of the darkness. None of us were able to see further than the ends of our noses, but Baldwin could see in the dark and proceeded to terrorise Richard. When he grew tired of this he started on the rest of us. A hand would shoot out of the darkness and grab someone. There would be a scream and a scuffle then another shout from the opposite side of the room as he moved about in the dark. The terror came from not knowing whether or not you were next, and was intensified by the scraping noises which Baldwin said was a yeti trying to get in. Only Brian Barlow and Rastus escaped. Despite all this, Pete Baldwin was well liked. We knew that if any of us was ever in trouble Pete could be relied upon to take our part and would always be a staunch friend.

In later years, Richard, through hard training and dedication, became one of the top rock-climbers in Britain. Along with this he acquired physical and mental strength and was never to be bullied again, although he did get into quite a few punch ups.

The weekends usually started on Friday evenings with us meeting up at Tiviot Dale station in Stockport to take the train to Edale. From Edale village we had two miles or so to walk to the barn, sometimes in pouring rain, and usually arrived around 10.30pm.

On one such occasion, Brian Barlow, Pete Baldwin and I arrived at the barn, had a brew and turned in early as we had a big day planned for Saturday.

The following morning, rising early, we breakfasted then set off up Crowden Clough to Kinder plateau.The sky was blue, the day hot and sunny and we walked to the Downfall and descended into the amphitheatre. Up until that day, Barlow and Baldwin had told us all about the routes that they had climbed and in turn they had heard about things that Ralph and I had done, but we had never actually seen each other climb, apart from easy stuff in the wet. I felt that I was in superior company and got the impression that they believed they were the better climbers too, because in the absence of Richard, I was coming in for a lot of Mickey taking. Pete naturally took the lead on the first climb, a chimney graded difficult on which he struggled. The next climb was "Zig Zag", v. diff led by Brian. When my turn arrived, we were at the foot of Great Chimney, a mild, VS with an awkward layback start. Pete said, "Are you sure you want to do this, Al?" I nodded, then, leading off, climbed all the way to the top of the crag in one pitch. Brian came up next then Pete and they informed me that it should have been done in two pitches. I pretended that I knew this but hadn't thought it necessary. It was after this, that I began to notice a marked change in attitude towards me. Instead of regarding me as inferior to them, they now began to treat me as an equal. This became more noticeable when

Pete failed to lead the second pitch of Mermaids Ridge and handed the lead over to me. I really enjoyed that climb!

My first visit to Stanage was in January 1957 with Pete Bamfield. Getting up early when the rest of the lads were still in bed recovering from a boozy Saturday night, we cooked our breakfast and left the barn at 8.30 a.m. Walking the two miles or so down the railway track to Edale station, we boarded the first train of the day to Hathersage. After a steep walk up the dale, Stanage Edge came into view. We had not seen anything like it before. The two of us stopped and stared in amazement, then, full of enthusiasm, hurried on toward the popular end of the crag. Pete said, "Look at that, it goes on forever. The lads will be really sick when we tell them what they've missed." Our first climbs that day were Plate Glass and Ground Glass slabs. It was a cold day with the odd shower of snow, but we were so pleased to be at this crag that we had heard so much about that we never really noticed the cold. We wandered along doing v. diffs and severes, and at one point, stopping below Flying Buttress, we watched a climber on an abseil rope removing a peg from the overhang. He was holding the rope in his teeth so that he could use both hands. It was Joe Brown! As we moved along to do another climb, Green Crack, we met our old friend, Ernie Thornhill. He told us that most of the Rock and Ice Club were there that day, and pointed out Ron Moseley. Later on at the café in Hathersage, Don Whillans and his wife Audrey arrived. We couldn't wait to get back to see the other lads to tell them about our great day.

January and February had seen us all attempting to climb an overhanging face at Nether Tor in Grindsbrook above Edale. Barlow and Baldwin had been the first to try it using pitons and etriers, and Pete Bamfield and I had also tried it, as had Keith Taylor and Dave Upton, all without success. We had given it the name "Funeral Face". I think it is a free climb these days and goes at about VS! During this period, I climbed a new route, at Grindsbrook Rocks with Pete Bamfield, an overhang which we christened "The Fiend VS." We used to go in for dramatic sounding names! Pete and I also did YoYo and The Shroud. Keith Taylor and Dave Upton produced Free Wall and Grave Crack HVS 5A.

There was a climber known to some of the lads who was called Stan Potter who was older than the rest of us but used to join us occasionally. Stan owned an Austin A35 van so he became quite popular. One weekend, six of us, Petes Baldwin and Bamfield, Rastus, Brian Barlow and myself with Stan driving all crammed into the van for a trip to Wales. We booked into the YHA at Ogwen and spent Saturday night drinking at Bethesda. The next morning, not so bright but early, we parked up below Tryfan and walked up to the Milestone Buttress. The day was very cold with a covering of wet snow on the rocks. We climbed in boots and all ascended the Direct Route before walking round to the Eastern Terrace, where we did Pinnacle Rib to the summit of Tryfan. We descended by the west face and walked round to Cwm Idwal where Ralph and I showed Pete Bamfield some of the routes that we had done the previous summer. After a brew at Ogwen cottage, we all crammed into the van again and drove home.

One time during this period, on one of our excursions to Nether Tor to attempt Funeral Face, we found ourselves at Upper Tor lower tier where Richard, who had never climbed much at all, seconded a moderate slab climb. He was really pleased with himself and promptly stood on a 15ft high boulder and announced, "Look here lads, I'm getting used to exposure." We all collapsed laughing, not realising that this was the beginning of an illustrious climbing career.

Gradually we started to venture further afield, Stanage being our new main haunt on most weekends, with occasional trips to Castle Naze and Roches.

Ralph and I had by now abandoned Longdendale in favour of these new found crags. We all started to work our way through the classic climbs on Stanage and Pete Bamfield and I became regular climbing partners.

Easter 1957 saw the newly formed Alpha Club down in Wales. We travelled by train and on our way to Stockport station were accosted by a newspaper reporter who was doing an article on holiday destinations. He took a group photo of us - fame at last! The following week, there we were in the local paper looking more like a group of escaped juvenile offenders than the hard climbers we imagined ourselves to be. We arrived at Bangor late that night and shared a taxi to Ogwen Cottage where we camped in the woods near the youth hostel. The next day, carrying all our gear up to Llyn Bochlwyd below Glyder Fach, we pitched camp there. As soon as the tents were up, we had a brew, then immediately set off to climb on Bochlwyd Buttress. As Brian Barlow and I were sharing a tent, we decided to climb together, and over the weekend did many good routes, the best for us being the Direct Route on Glyder Fach and Grooved Arete on Tryfan. Brian also led Marble Slab on Bochlwyd Buttress which was a really good effort!

I didn't sleep very well that holiday because of something under the groundsheet (or so I thought) that dug into my leg and kept me awake. Every morning I searched for the cause of my discomfort to no avail. On the last night, much to the amusement of the lads, I discovered, not a stone under me, but my penknife in my trouser pocket. Because of the very cold nights, we had been sleeping fully clothed and I must have overlooked my knife when emptying my pockets.

One day during that weekend, whilst the rest of us were climbing, Richard set off by himself to do the Bristly Ridge on Glyder Fach. We were all very worried for his safety and were relieved to see him return after a successful scramble. On Sunday morning, we awoke to the sound of heavy rain on the tent roof; so some of us decided to walk to Capel Curig to buy supplies. Walking along the road below the Milestone Buttress, Dave Upton took out his last ciggy and somehow managed to drop it on the wet tarmac. Quick as a flash, he reached down to retrieve it and Richard who was looking up at Tryfan at that moment, accidentally placed a size 8 boot right in the middle of Dave's hand squashing both it and the cigarette. The air was blue! I don't know what upset Dave the most, the pain in his hand or the loss of his last smoke. The rest of us had a good laugh and walked on with an added spring to our step. Events of this kind made wet days bearable.

All too soon the Easter holiday ended and it was back to work again.

Out at Stanage, Pete and I had just done Central Trinity, when a young bespectacled youth appeared. He had a mass of pitons clanking noisily at his waist and Baldwin asked the youth "What do you call those things?" "Picons," said the youth." You're a bloody piecan," said Pete. And that's how we met Malcolm Cundy, known henceforth as Piecan or Pike. He was probably only about 15 at the time and hailed from Sheffield, being the first of many from that city to join the Alpha club. Pike was a cheery lad, always eager to please and consequently taken advantage of by some of the other lads. Some of the treatment usually meted out to Richard eased off and was transferred to Pike. I remember one instance at the barn, when a rope was tied around his waist and the other end thrown over the beam in the roof. He was then hoisted up so that he could grab the beam to take the weight off his arms. He hung there until his strength ran out then fell down to hang on the rope which tightened on his chest, squeezing the air out of him. His pleas for mercy were eventually heeded and he was lowered to the ground where he promptly retied the rope more securely and said breathlessly, "OK, haul me up again.". As I said before, he was always eager to please.

Another time, at Nether Tor, Brian Barlow was leading a climb and asked Pike to hold his rope. Brian placed a runner below the crux overhang about 30ft above the ground then after asking Pike to watch him, he started to tackle the overhang. Looking down to see if his trusty second was paying attention, he noticed that Pike was dutifully holding the rope but at the opposite end of it. There was 120ft of slack between the pair of them. Brian let out a torrent of swear words, Pike got the message and learned immediately how to handle the rope! After this, whenever Brian related this tale he always referred to Pike as the Sheffield belay king.

An old friend of mine from secondary school days had recently become a member of the Alpha. His name was Brian Platt or Platty as he was known to us. He was a stocky lad probably about 5ft 4" and very strong. Brian was a somewhat nervous climber preferring to second rather than lead but on a motor bike he was absolutely fearless. He and I became firm friends, both of us coming from the same town. Other new members around this time were Stan (V S Goodwin) and his young brother Al, and a little later Andy Garvey, all from the Manchester area.

It was decided that to qualify for membership of the Alpha, aspirants had to knock about with the lads for as long as it took to be accepted, usually about six months to a year. Other conditions were a love of the hills, and to be liked by every other member or at least to have not been objected to by anyone. Les Brown now fully recovered from his broken ankle was a regular active member of the Alpha as well as being a member of the Manchester University Mountaineering Club (MUMC). Les introduced us to some good climbers from that club, the likes of Dave Sanders and Rodney Wilson and we would sometimes join them on MUMC club meets. On one such meet, we were all at Stanage. It was a cold day and snowing on and off. Les asked me if I had ever done Agony Crack, which I hadn't. He said Baldwin had recently done it and had declared it desperate. It must be remembered that in those days our only means of protection was either jammed chockstones or jammed knotted slings or slings over flakes. I approached the climb nervously and because of the coldness of the day, I was wearing a donkey jacket and climbing in big boots. To my surprise I found the climb OK and after belaying brought Les up. While coiling the rope, Les suggested I lead Goliath's Groove, a climb that he had done before and which he said was a classic route. First done by Peter Harding in 1947 Goliath's Groove had quite a reputation for being difficult and was graded "Exceptionally Severe." Les said that judging by the way I had done Agony crack, I shouldn't have any trouble. We wandered along the bottom of the crag to the foot of Goliath's where I tied on the rope and set off up the difficult bottom crack still wearing the donkey jacket etc. By now we had quite a big audience of Alpha and MUMC climbers. Arriving at the mid-way ledge, I tied into the chockstone and brought Les up, changing over belays. Les took my rope for the top bit. At the over- hang, I tried to get decent jams without success, as everything was full of snow and ice. I said, "I don't like the looks of this Les. I think you'd better lead it seeing as you have done it before". I descended quickly hoping he wouldn't object, and before he knew it, I was belayed and he was on the sharp end. Les climbed to the overhang. We could hear mutterings from the gathered throng below, things like "Les is climbing really safely since his broken ankle". I watched with interest as he tackled the icy bulge. There was a flurry of activity and snow as a determined Brown swung into a layback and disappeared upwards out of my view. "Well done, Les," I shouted. No sooner had the words left my mouth, than a 6ft 4" 11 stone windmill of arms and legs dived towards me. The feet hit first, in my lower back, then the knees in my neck and the next minute I was hanging down the lower groove from my too-long belay. Les was still travelling. I was using a waist belay and owing to the friction of the rope against my donkey jacket I managed to stop him about 3ft from the ground. There were gasps from the onlookers as Les's loose change flew out of his pockets. I don't think anyone had realised he was so wealthy. For weeks after this I couldn't walk upright, and had to employ the services of a Sherpa in the person of Pike to carry my rucksack for me. One positive thing to come out of this was that critics of the donkey jacket had to admit to the usefulness of this garment as a friction belay device.

Brian Barlow and Pete Baldwin used to have what they called prems on certain climbs. The word prem was short for premonition and meant thinking about a climb so much that every move on it became familiar, so that when it was eventually tried it seemed easy. None of the lads had done Rugosity Wall at Stanage. I had tried it and failed, so I decided to prem on it. One night I had a vivid dream about it and going to Stanage the next day, I did the climb with ease having rehearsed it already in my sleep. Sometimes, prems didn't work but this was usually if the climb in question was approached in too casual a manner. It was always best to be super psyched up, and then the climb would be easier than expected .On one occasion we all sat in Robin Hood's Cave and watched Pete Baldwin lead Cave Gully Wall. He placed a low thread runner and started up the steep wall above; every move was an epic." Watch me, I'm coming off, no I'm not, yes I am." None of us dared breathe. We willed him up the climb. It was only finger strength, fear and a streak of madness that got him up. He was like this on most of the climbs that he did, tackling things that were too hard for him and just scraping through on strength, guts and an unshakable belief in the power of prems!

One weekend Les, Brian Barlow, the two Pete's, Richard and I went to Stoney Middleton to try some limestone climbing. Camping in the trees near where the road turns up towards Eyam, we suffered very cold conditions only made bearable by a long session in the pub; our sleeping bags were only cheap ex-army surplus and the rest of our gear wasn't up to much either. That weekend we did a few routes which were probably first ascents because they were covered with Ivy and were very loose. There wasn't a guidebook to Stoney at that time and very little climbing had been done there apart from the odd aid route by the Rock and Ice. Not being very impressed, we were of the opinion that limestone climbing didn't have much of a future so we beat a quick retreat to our beloved grit. In retrospect, we were very short sighted and missed out on a lot of excellent new routes which were later done by members of the Cioch Club from Sheffield.

Richard and I would often hitch-hike over the Snake Pass on Saturday mornings, usually meeting at a café in Glossop where we drank tea and played the juke box (which always had an abundance of Elvis records) until we deemed it time to hit the road. There were always plenty of empty coal lorries on their way back to Rotherham from Manchester, so it was easy to get a lift and be dropped off at either Ladybower or Moscar Lodge. It was on one of these Saturdays, April 19th 1957, that we did our first new route at Stanage. This was "Aries" on the Blurter Buttress. Pete Bamfield who met us at the crag joined us on this climb. This whetted our appetites for first ascents, and early the next year, Pete and I did another one, "Mother's Day." This was done on Mothering Sunday 1958.

The summer of 1957 Les and Sanders went by train to the Dolomites arriving at the Cinque Torre after an epic journey. They did two routes then headed off to the Tre Cima to do the Dibona route on the Cima Grande. They then went by bus to the Sella Towers where they did the complete traverse before moving on to the Vajolett Towers to traverse those as well. They had only gone for three weeks and were either on a train or a bus, walking up to huts or sleeping or climbing the whole "holiday". After leaving the Vajolett they went back to the Tre Cima to do the Preuss Route and then the East Ridge on the Cima Ovest.

Back home, other Alpha members were heading north to the Isle of Skye; travelling by train from Manchester to Glasgow. The team consisted of Keith Taylor, Pete Bamfield, Ralph, Richard, Dave Upton, myself and an aspirant member, Stan Colclough.

From Glasgow, we continued by train to Mallaig on the West Highland Line via Fort William, I remember we were all very impressed by the scenery, in particular the wildness of Rannoch Moor.

At Mallaig, we asked around at the docks if any of the fishermen there would be prepared to ferry us over to Loch Brittle on Skye. Eventually we found a man who said that he would take us for ten shillings each, 50p in today's money. The trip took about two hours and as we were in an open boat, it was very cold. Richard sat in the bows of the boat looking longingly towards the Cuillins and the islands of Eigg, Rum and Canna. We joked that he imagined he was the young pretender and in a way that's what he eventually turned out to be. The afternoon was beautiful with a dramatic sky, clear blue to the west, great banks of cloud behind us over the mainland; we were thrilled to see a large whale surface away to our left. The sea was quite choppy and there was a bitter wind blowing so we were all forced to take shelter in the bottom of the boat behind the small wheelhouse. All that is except Richard, who we could see turning blue before our eyes. He just couldn't be persuaded to come in. He later told me that he felt he was returning to his spiritual home. When Pete heard this he said "what a load of cobblers."

We came ashore on the beach at Glen Brittle, paid the boatman and set off up the glen to the Youth hostel, a large wooden building with the feel of a Yukon gold rush saloon. There was a very big common room cum eating area with a kitchen at one end which felt warm and welcoming and had an Aga type stove with hot plates and a substantial oven.

The first morning there, Pete was making porridge; Richard was assisting him and absent mindedly put his plastic plate onto the top of the stove. The first we knew of this was when we heard Pete laugh out loud and say "You dozy bugger, look at your plate." Richard's plate had a section of it's circumference missing .From then on whenever porridge or any sloppy food was served up he had to tilt his plate so as not to lose most of his meal.

The weather was typical Skye, a little sunshine usually late in the afternoon and the rest of the time either showers or rain and more rain. Richard had developed a bad cold due to getting almost frozen on the boat, so the start to his holiday hadn't turned out very well for him. Unperturbed by the weather, we were out every day, being young and daft, we didn't mind getting wet. One day up on Sgurr Alasdair, Pete, Ralph, Richard and I did Collie's Route, a long and loose mountaineering climb which was graded about diff. We didn't even get a view it was thick mist all the way up. The climb is approached from the Alisdair Stone Shoot, which we all found very tiring necessitating frequent rests. After one of these rests, we resumed our upward progress and Ralph suddenly said "what's up with Richard?" Looking back down the scree to where Richard was still sitting motionless, Pete said "Perhaps he's dead; that cold of his is really bad. " "Hey, Richard" we all shouted but there was no movement. We shouted again but louder this time. To our relief, he moved." I must have fallen asleep" he said.

We didn't really think much of Collie's Climb and tended to agree with the sentiments expressed by some anonymous climber who had scratched on the rock at one point his opinion of the first ascensionist, which wasn't very complimentary. Keith, Dave and Stan Colclough did Window Buttress and then descended into Coire Lagan. On the way down the corrie, Stan slipped whilst crossing some boiler plate slabs and slid about 100ft. He came to rest at a point where it levelled out and although he had a badly grazed bum he suffered no further injury. That night he didn't sleep very well and next day he decided to go home. This ended his ambitions to become a member of the Alpha and I don't think we ever saw him again.

We all did the Inaccessible Pinnacle and Cioch West. Pete and I did the Direct route on Sron na Ciche and tried the Crack of Doom without success; possibly due to the fact that we were soaked to the skin and very cold. Another time Keith led the then unprotected Arrow Route which we all followed. We lunched on the Cioch block and admired the magnificent scenery.

During this period, Richard was still very much the novice. He was very keen and tried hard but was nervous and got little sympathy from the rest of us. The important thing was, he wanted to be a competent climber and although he had the Mickey taken out of him, he persevered. He probably didn't realise at the time how much the rest of us respected him for his courage and good humour.

During this holiday in Skye, we got in conversation with two young Scots climbers who were also staying at the hostel. They told us that they had climbed with Hamish MacInnes and had done some VS climbs in Glencoe. Their names were Robin Smith and Dougal Haston, later to become famous internationally.

One day Pete, Ralph, Richard and I paid to go by boat to Loch Coruisk. The plan was to do the slabs to the summit of Sgurr Dubh Beag and then to follow the ridge to the Great Stone Shoot and descend this to Coire Lagan and so back to the hostel at Glen Brittle. The sun was shining as we walked along the side of Loch Coruisk and we were all in high spirits, cheered by the good weather and the splendour of the scenery around us.

Unnoticed by the three of us, Richard had fallen a long way behind. Some way up the glen we came to an evil smelling red bog barring our progress. Ralph who was in the lead, tested it with his foot and left a large footprint, we decided that it wasn't safe to cross and detoured around it. A little further on we heard a terrified shout behind us and on turning round, saw Richard who appeared to have shrunk in height. He was waving frantically and swaying from side to side, it took us a minute or two to realise that he was up to his waist in the red bog. He had seen Ralph's footprint and had assumed that we had crossed at that spot. He was probably about 100 yards away but we could see him trying desperately to extricate himself from the glue like mud that held him. Before any of us could make a move to help him, he managed to free himself with a sort of swimming motion. We waited for him to catch up with us, then all except Richard, fell about laughing. He didn't seem to think it was at all funny. Looking back, it had probably been a potentially dangerous situation but all's well that ends well.

Reaching the foot of the Dubh slabs we decided to have a bite to eat. Richard was banished to sit alone a few yards away from us, as the odour of red bog didn't mix well with the delicious aroma of corned beef sandwiches. After our snack we set off to climb the 3000 or so feet of slabs to the summit of Sgurr Dubh Beag by which time we were enveloped in thick cloud. We followed the ridge over the summit of Sgurr Dubh Mor to Sgurr Dubh na Da Bheinn, at the junction with main ridge. We were now battling a gale force wind and in the thick cloud were having navigational difficulties i.e. two compasses pointing in opposite directions. Common sense should have told us, that as we had just ascended an east ridge, to go north we should turn right. But we were young, relatively inexperienced lads and somewhat lacking in the aforementioned quality. Then Pete had a brain wave. He reasoned that most people who climbed the Dubh ridge as we had done would then head north towards Glen Brittle; as was our intention. Bamfield's Law stated that all we had to do was follow the ridge which had the most scratches from nailed boots. We all thought this was brilliant, and luckily he was right, because fairly soon the yawning chasm of the Thearlaich Dubh Gap was barring our way. At this point Richard informed us that he didn't know how to abseil. After a quick lesson on how to descend the rope using the classic method of abseil we all descended into the gap. When trying to retrieve the rope we found it to be stuck fast. Ralph volunteered to solo back up to free it and then abseiled again to rejoin us. Looking up at the north-west wall of the gap our blood ran cold. The chimney that splits this wall looked smooth and holdless with a waterfall cascading down it. The wind was howling through the gap like through a wind tunnel. We were beginning to get worried, particularly me, as I had been elected by a majority of three to one to lead the 90ft unprotected looking fissure. I fought my way to the top by imagining that I was Hermann Buhl or Joe Brown. Soon we were all at the top of the Great Stone Shoot, where we ran quickly down the scree to Coire Lagan. Walking down the path to the hostel, we enthused to each other about our heroic and to our minds, competent escape from becoming benighted. We had all shared in our success; Pete's method of navigation, Richard had abseiled safely, Rastus had retrieved the rope by climbing back up for it when it got stuck and I had led the chimney out of the gap overcoming our last obstacle to safety. We were very pleased with ourselves. Back in the warmth of the hostel we related the events of our epic to the other lads and ate a good meal.

All good things must come to an end as did our holiday, and we all took separate routes home. Some went by train but Pete and I decided to hitch hike.

Richard said, "When I get home, I'll ask my Ma to make a bath full of spuds with a crust on it."

Two days later saw us at Piccadilly station in Manchester at midnight on Saturday, having missed the last train home. We spent the night in the waiting room with assorted drunks and down-and-outs for company. Next morning, we caught the first train home, Pete to Stockport me to Hyde. Then it was back to work on Monday.

Chapter 3
New Pastures, New Members, New Routes. 1957/58

We had by this time almost completely abandoned the barn at Edale and most weekends found us sleeping rough in the Hathersage area. We slept in sheds, bus shelters, the cricket pavilion, under bridges and Robin Hood's cave at Stanage, although the latter was considered inconvenient, because it was a long way from the pub and we didn't have transport.

It was also dangerous to sleep in the cave, because on occasion whilst staggering back from the pub it wasn't unknown to attempt routes like Flying Buttress or April Crack in the dark.

Richard had got hold of the book Nanga Parbat Pilgrimage, by the great Austrian mountaineer, Hermann Buhl, and was inspired by it. He turned up at Stanage one Saturday afternoon and to everyone's amazement led Mississippi Buttress Direct with practically no runners. This was a momentous occasion as I think this was his first VS lead and marked a turning point in Richard's climbing ability. I think that he identified with Hermann Buhl who had been the victim of bullying and ridicule by his contemporaries, and had, through dedication and mental strength, become one of the leading climbers of his generation. From then on, in Robin Hood's cave on Saturday nights, after the pub, we would lie in our sleeping bags and by the light of flickering candles, listen to Pete as he read aloud from Herman's book. He would read a different chapter each week and always finished by reading the title of the following chapter to keep us gripped. He would say, "And next week, THE NORTH FACE OF THE EIGER! " We couldn't wait for the next instalment, but try as we might we could neither persuade nor bribe Pete to read more than one chapter a week.

Then one weekend, whilst climbing at Stanage, Pete arrived with news that Hermann had been killed in the Himalaya; we couldn't believe it, our hero dead.

Richard's climbing, improved week by week and pretty soon he and I were climbing at the same standard. Around this time we got to know a group of climbers from the Rotherham area, some of whom were coal miners. They were a tough bunch with some good climbers in the group. One climber who was outstanding was Len Millsom, who later did the first ascent of Millsom's Minion at Stanage. When we first met them, Len climbed all manner of things in pit boots with metal studs in the soles. I remember he once traversed from Robin Hood's Cave to the Balcony Cave wearing pit boots and with a lighted primus stove in one hand! He was very strong with a wiry physique and was extremely good on gritstone.

Pete Baldwin had decided that drinking was more up his street than climbing, and had stopped coming out. This decision was probably prompted by a days climbing in Llanberis Pass with Brian Barlow and then the events of a weekend in Wales with Les Brown.

Brian and Pete had made their way to Carreg Wastad to try a climb that Les had recommended to them, Ribstone Crack. Pete was nominated as leader and all was going fine until Pete suddenly parted company with the rock. Somehow he managed to arrest his fall by grabbing a large flake. Unfazed by this little setback, Pete decided he would like to go to the Grochan to try Kaisergebirge Wall. It was pointed out to him that this was a grade harder than the climb he had just fallen off but he said he fancied it because it had a great name! He promptly fell off this as well, but was saved by the in situ peg which was just below the crux moves. Working on the theory of third time lucky, they decided to try Spectre, another hard climb. They fared no better on this as Pete fell off yet again. He was on the second pitch, on the bulge below the overhang, when he came off, landing in a Holly bush. Ouch! It was time to call it a day.

On another occasion in Wales, Baldwin and Les, arriving at the MUMC hut, went to collect the key at the farm, where they were told of a suicide at the hut the previous week. On top of this news, the electricity was off and they would have to use candles for lighting. They spent a nervous evening imagining all kinds of things about the tragic happening. As the night wore on, sitting in their sleeping bags next to a roaring fire, Les was suddenly alarmed to see Pete, eyes bulging and fear written all over his face; staring at the door. Pete announced that he had seen the door knob turn, and then slowly turn back again; they both sat there frozen in fear. To their relief, two MUMC climbers came through the door. On seeing our heroes' faces, they asked if there was anything wrong so the lads told them about the suicide. One of the newcomers said, "Enough of this, I'm going to make a brew," and headed for the kitchen. A minute later there was a terrified scream from that direction. Striking a match to light a candle he had seen his own reflection in a full length mirror next to the kitchen and thought it was someone standing there in the dark. The rest of the lads had a good laugh at his mistake and this broke the ice. The fear was gone. They all retired to their bunks early, to prepare for the more serious business of the following day.

The next morning, it was decided that they were ready for Cloggy. Clogwyn Du'r Arddu, to give it its proper name, is a big sombre cliff, situated high up on Snowdon. It is a steep north facing crag and in the shade most of the time, except for early mornings and late afternoons when the sun hits it if you're lucky. Some of the hardest climbs in Britain wend their way up its walls and slabs and to make things more difficult, it is very often damp. The crag is usually approached from Llanberis up the footpath which roughly follows the Snowdon Railway track. Just beyond the Halfway House (a refreshment shack) the path forks right and is fairly level for the rest of the way to the crag.

As neither had climbed on Cloggy before and Les was recovering from another broken ankle which he sustained from falling off Chequers Direct at Froggat Edge, it was agreed that Pete should lead. They decided that Chimney Route would be a good one to start with. When they reached the crux pitch, Les found himself belayed to a rusty old piton on a small ledge 170ft above the ground. He watched anxiously as Pete tried the hard moves on the overhang 30ft above him. The guidebook describes this overhang as being very unstable, but climbable by the brave or the foolish; Pete possessed both of these qualities. Les's anxiety changed to sheer fright as Baldwin did a little skip to change feet on a small slimy foothold and was suddenly hanging from one hand with both feet off the rock.

Pete later described it this way: he said, "I did a one arm pull up and when I got over the overhang, there was a hand-jamming crack, and I crawled right into the back of it. That Cloggy, the screes are vertical and the slabs are overhanging." He was really impressed. Anyway after that he gave up climbing for good and by that, I mean for the good of his climbing partners.

Easter 1958 found us camped near the Cromlech boulders in the Llanberis Pass where Pete Bamfield and I shared a tent and climbed together. Our old friends Ernie and Joe Thornhill were there with some of the Rock & Ice and they gave us some advice on which routes to try. During that Easter weekend, Hugh Banner and Les Brown made an ascent of Cemetery Gates on Dinas Cromlech and Whillans did the first ascent of Grond. Another historic event took place that weekend as well. The Scottish lad whom we had met the year before in Skye, Robin Smith, was also in the Pass mopping up every route in sight. He was literally running from crag to crag repeating as many Joe Brown routes as possible. That weekend showed the Sassenachs what was brewing north of the border. A new star was born.

That Easter also saw Hugh and Les do two new routes, The Link on Dinas Mot and Rackstone Crib on the Wastad.

Pete and I did routes like Wrinkle, Crackstone Rib and Trylon on the Wastad; and climbed The Cracks and Direct Route on the Nose of Dinas Mot.

At that time, I found the Direct Route hard as I didn't feel confident on what was then a long unprotected run out.

Another Scottish climber who we got to know quite well was Pat Walsh. Pat belonged to the Brown/Whillans generation and was a member of the Creagh Dhu, one of their top climbers. He had done many first ascents in Scotland where his routes were as legendary as anything south of the border. When he came to live in Manchester he had a house in Moss Side which was always filled with rent paying tenants from the climbing world, mainly Langdale lads and Scots.

Pat quickly showed how good he was by soloing the Right Unconquerable on Stanage, and when Whillans pointed him at Deadbay Groove on Curbar he soloed that as well. He had very bad eyesight and wore glasses with lenses like jam jar bottoms and it amazed us how he ever saw the holds.

Pat had a large motorcycle, (a Norton I think) and once when I was riding pillion on Brian Platt's bike on the way to Wales, and going down the hill into Ruthin round the sharp bends at speed, we were startled by a great noise; it was Pat overtaking us on a bad bend. He was like a character from a Biggles book, wearing an off white trench coat, leather flying helmet and large leather gauntlets. Over his specs he wore large goggles, a bit like the ones used by engineers when grinding metal, and after passing us on the hairpin bend he was soon out of sight. When we met up with him in Llanberis he denied all knowledge of the event. He either hadn't seen us or he was winding us up!

The Alpha started to take on new members. We had recently met a bespectacled, ginger haired youth by the name of Bob Brayshaw. Bob was a tall lad, well over 6ft and he and his friends Arthur (Nirk) Williams, Keith Froggat and Geoff Skitt were all into doing new routes. They came from the Manchester area and so it was natural for them to start coming along with us each weekend. Both Bob and Arthur later became members of our club.

Richard, climbing at the Roaches one weekend, met a young climber from Macclesfield, a 15 year-old schoolboy called Paul Nunn. Richard was impressed by Paul, who had done some good routes for such a young lad. He had led things like Bengal Buttress and Valkyrie on the Roaches; which was his local crag. Richard told Paul about the Alpha and invited him to meet up with us. Paul was very big for his age, over 6ft tall and heavily built, not fat, just a big strong lad. Platty immediately gave him the nickname Angus, because he said Paul reminded him of a wild highlander. Paul took it all in good part and we discovered that he also had a very hearty laugh. Paul would cycle out to the crags at weekends to wherever the lads were climbing and we would all sleep out somewhere, but when we awoke on Sunday mornings Paul would have disappeared only to reappear later on. This puzzled us at first because when we asked him where he had been, he would just laugh it off until one day he told us he had been going to morning Mass. Paul had been brought up in a Roman Catholic family and attended a Catholic school. When asked by us if he was religious he replied," It's good to keep a few lifelines open." Later in life Paul found out that he had been born in Ireland but was adopted and taken to live in Macclesfield by his adoptive parents. He later discovered and visited his natural family in Ireland where he met his parents and siblings and other relatives for the first time. This gave him tremendous pleasure.

Dave Peck was Paul's friend from Macclesfield. They had been at primary school together. Dave had been introduced to the hills at an early age by his Dad who was secretary of Macclesfield Rambling Club. Paul and he joined the scouts and started to go on long hikes and when passing the Roaches, Windgather or Castle Naze, they would do some scrambling; it all started from there. Dave was 11 and Paul a year older. Even then Paul was exceptionally strong and surprisingly graceful in his climbing despite his bulk. This was in 1955.

When the pair moved to the same grammar school in Manchester (Xaverian College) they used to do boulder problems on the school buildings and were joined in this by others who later became Alpha members, namely Dave Sandall, John Moss and Tony Riley.

The Alpha was growing fast. Other new members came along, some lads from Buxton, John Smith, Roy Fryer and Ian Hartle. The first two already knew Paul from climbing at the Roaches and were very good climbers. Roy was quite a gymnast and often amazed us by doing tricks like swallow diving over walls, somersaulting and landing on his feet. John Smith was, and still is, a sometimes serious person, yet at other times is outrageously funny with an infectious laugh and a good sense of humour. Both of these were good company and fitted in well. We had no sooner got to know John when he went off the scene for two years. Having decided not to apply for a deferment from national service, thinking it better to get it over with, he went off to join the army, which he hated. If he had hung on like the rest of us, he wouldn't have needed to go at all, as national service was scrapped a short time later. Pete Bamfield introduced us to a friend from technical college, Allan Ellison, who lived at Crewe in the flat grasslands of Cheshire. Allan was a tall slim lad and was rather quiet compared with some of the others, but he was a competent climber and good company. The club now had a considerable number of good climbers who were ticking off the hard climbs of the day and at the same time producing some good new routes. Others among the lads preferred to do easier classic climbs but also enjoyed seconding the harder ones. This meant that no matter who was out on any given weekend we could always make up compatible teams.

Transport was still mainly trains or buses for most of us. Platty had just bought a Triumph Tiger Cub 150cc motor bike which made him very popular and Brian Barlow had given up smoking to save up for a brand new 650cc BSA Roadrocket; this had taken him 12 weeks. Hugh Banner who had recently started to climb with the Alpha also owned a motor bike, a 1000cc Vincent Black Shadow, so our transport was improving, the only trouble being they drove so fast that sometimes we wished we had gone by bus! Hugh was the only climber around at that time who was repeating some of the harder Joe Brown & Don Whillans routes. He was older than the rest of us and had come from Liverpool to work and live in Manchester. At first he associated with the MUMC and through that club and the likes of Les Brown, Rodney Wilson and Dave Sanders, he was introduced to us. When we first met Hughie, we got to know some of his friends from Liverpool and Widnes area, namely Bob Beasley and Jim O'Neill who had done a lot of climbs at Frodsham and Helsby. Bob Beasley was also a keen motor cyclist and a member of the Vagabonds club but was soon adopted by the Alpha.

During 1958 we increased our output of new routes at Stanage and elsewhere on gritstone and took our holidays in Wales and the Lakes. Other favourite crags were Froggatt and Curbar, Roaches and Hen Cloud Burbage and Millstone Edge, the latter being mainly used for practising artificial climbing although quite a few free climbs were just starting to be done there. Pete Bamfield and I did the first free ascent of the Great Slab, which was a lot harder than it is today and was about HVS. At first, there used to be not many holds but gradually with more frequent ascents bits got broken off the slab and new holds appeared reducing the grade, but it is still a good route. We were also doing new routes on Dovestones quarry in the Chew valley area. Keith Taylor led Jericho Wall, Bob and I did Epitaph Corner, Dave Sanders and I did Waterfall Groove Direct and Pete Bamfield and Allan Ellison did the really good A-lu-te whatever that means! One time when climbing at Wimberry rocks, Richard fell off Blue Lights crack and went down the large crevasse at its base; he was very lucky not to get hurt! Bob Brayshaw and I were climbing together that day and had done most of the VS climbs on the crag, when we were brought to an abrupt halt with our attempt at the overhanging Freddie's Finale. John Smith summed it up by saying, "You'd have to be as strong as an ox and daft as a brush. Richard, where are you?"

Whenever we couldn't get lifts, we took the train to Hathersage from Stockport or Romiley and then walked up the hill to Stanage. We frequented a café at Station Road, Hathersage, which belonged to Mrs. Thomas, a widow who was originally from Cardiff and who was probably in her sixties. She used to fuss like an old hen but didn't stand for any nonsense from the lads. Richard and I were her favourites, particularly Richard, who I think she had earmarked as a future husband for her grand-daughter Elaine who was a waitress in the café at weekends. Elaine was a schoolgirl and although very nice, was far too young for any of us and we looked on her as more of a little sister - and anyway at that time we weren't interested in girls, only crags.

The food in the café was mainly beans or runny eggs on toast and greasy fried breakfasts. We would spend hours drinking endless cups of tea, sneaking in our own tea bags and topping up with pots of hot water from the kitchen. Ma Thomas's became a meeting place for climbers and eventually quite famous. We would see members of the Rock& Ice in there and got to know them quite well. Ray Greenall, Don Whillans and his wife Audrey were often there. Whillans must have only been in his twenties, but we thought of him as much older, probably because he was famous and was a heroic figure to us. At that time, Don was in his prime, fit and very strong. We watched him do his pendulum route on the edge of Black Slab at Stanage. He was soloing in boots and was leaning horizontally off a small flake with his left hand and had just reached a hold with his right hand when the small flake broke off. He swung across to his right on one hand and pulled up on to the slab, hence the name Whillan's Pendulum. It had been a case of up or off and his strength had saved him.

During June that year Rastus and Pete Bamfield took their holidays in Scotland, camping at Kinlochewe in the Torridon area. During two weeks they walked and climbed in all weathers and succeeded in producing four or five new climbs on the Triple buttresses of Ben Eighe, although these were probably never recorded.

August 1958, Richard, Dave Sanders and I went to the Pass for two week's holiday but the weather was very wet and quite cold. Richard who was in charge of the cooking, went grocery shopping and came back with a big bag of potatoes, a big bag of carrots, some onions and 7 tins of corned beef. He said, "That'll do for the first week, stew every night." We were staying in the cave under the enormous Cromlech boulders, next to the road; it was a real rat-hole, literally. We could hear them running about during the night and would throw cans in their general direction to scare them off. The cave was only three or four feet in height, not very wide and not very long. There was a stone wall on the side next to the road and on the opposite side the roof sloped down almost to the ground and became a narrow horizontal crack. This crack receded into the darkness of the bigger cave on the other side of the boulder, which, if it hadn't been used as a toilet over the years, would have made a better home for us. We were joined in our minus 3-star hotel by three Scots lads. They were members of the Creagh Dhu, a Glasgow climbing club which had a reputation for hard climbing and roguery. Their names were Andy Scott, who was a ski instructor, one was called Pete and the other was John McLean, a tall tough looking character, who later became one of Scotland's leading climbers.

The weather was terrible but we managed to do some routes between showers, Lion, Unicorn, Brant Direct, Sabre Cut and Ivy Sepulchre being memorable, and Hugh Banner and Bob Beesley did the first ascent of Karwendel Wall on the Grochan. Most of our time however was spent mooching around the Llanberis cafes and pubs. One day, Richard found this ladybird type beetle which was brownish in colour and which we all decided must be a Colorado beetle. We had seen a picture of one in the Post Office along with a notice offering a reward of £5 to anyone finding and handing in such a creature, dead or alive. Richard kept his beetle in a matchbox and we planned a big nosh-up on the proceeds. Next day to our dismay, we couldn't find the matchbox, home of the beetle. Asking the Scots lads if they had seen it, Big John said, "Och, I sent it for a wee ride down the river" (which was in spate). We never thought at the time, being naïve, but I now wonder if the Creagh Dhu lads stole it for the reward.

Big John had his heart set on Cenotaph Corner which at that time, was regarded as the big test piece of Welsh climbing, having had fewer than ten ascents. The weather had been so bad that the Corner was dripping wet right through the two weeks, so he was forced to leave it for another time. I have this memory of him setting off back to Glasgow from the Cromlech Boulders and saying, as he looked up at Cenotaph "I'll be back."

The following Christmas, Paul and Richard went to Wasdale Head. On Boxing Day, in search of more company, they set off for Langdale by way of the Styhead Pass. On the way, they met Rastus who was heading in the opposite direction. He persuaded them to turn around and accompany him back to the Wasdale Head, where they made up their beds in the barn next to the pub. They then went across to the bar, where they had a meal and in Rastus' words "proceeded to reduce the club funds to zero" (he being the club treasurer). Not all the rogues were in the Creagh Dhu!

My friend Ralph Harris used to keep a journal and I would like to include an entry from this describing a typical weekend for the young Alpha.

Saturday September 13th 1958.

Due to some accident, my alarm clock was an hour slow and I awoke late at 8.40am instead of 7.40am. This meant that I only had 10 minutes in which to get ready. After much running about, I left at 8.50am and met up with Al Parker, thence to the bus stop. At Mottram we caught the 9.33am to Crowden. Alan McHardy (Richard) was on board.

We walked up to Laddow where we met some of the lads. After cooking a meal in the cave, we decided it was about time we started climbing. We warmed up on Long Climb and then did North Wall, I found some of the moves on the first pitch a bit tricky although the overhang didn't seem as difficult as when I first did it. Keith arrived and with Richard and I did Sirens' Rock, Al and Brian did Vee Arete and then the Girdle Traverse with Pike who had also arrived by this time. Keith, Al and I did Route 1, Gallic Buttress and Pillar Ridge, the first time I had done the whole route. Dave arrived so I threw the rope down for him to do it also. Keith and I then did Vee Arête and Comedy Corner, me taking three attempts before final conquest.

Everyone went down to the George and Dragon excepting Keith, me and Dave. I went for the water for the brew, up Straight Chimney and returned via Long Chimney, a difficult climb in descent with a bucketful of water in one hand. I reached the bottom with about half a bucket left and was just in time to see Keith and Dave do North Wall. We made soup and cooked some steak, then set off down the hill to the road and along to the George and Dragon (a pub between Crowden and Woodhead long since demolished). The boys were in residence, engaged in a game of cheat. The evening developed into a rock and roll session with Platty doing his best to drive everyone out of the room with his rendering of Delilah Jones. By 10.45pm, Brian had drunk four double whiskies, a single ditto, five pints of lager and a Drambuie. Consequently, he was not his normal self and this was obvious by the unselfconscious manner with which he threw all the ash trays through the open window. I restrained him from throwing the slot machine out and we departed, leaving behind us what could have been mistaken for a battlefield. The drunkard gave us an exhibition of dancing in the car park then dived over a wall into a field and rolled down the hill. We left him where he came to rest, then Pike, Al, Richard and I, went to look at a hut behind the George but it was full of rat holes so we departed. We checked on Brian who was in a heap being sick. Placing him in his sleeping bag we set off up the road to look for Keith and Dave. Assuming they would have headed for a waterworks hut we knew of, we decided it would be a good place for us to spend the night also. Eventually reaching our destination, we found that it had been recently cleaned out and the walls were freshly whitewashed. There was no sign of Keith and Dave. After covering the windows, we lit a fire with some wood and coal that was there. Settling down into our sleeping bags, Al told us about the Dracula film that he and Brian had been to see that week.

We arose at 9.30am packed our sacks and left the hut. It was a fine sunny morning and walking down to the George car park, we met Keith, Brian and Dave. Keith related the events of the night before. After we had left them, together with Dave he had bedded down behind a wall. Then, unbeknown to Dave, Keith had got up again and walked down to the road and along it. In the dark and in his drunken condition, he had mistaken the reservoir overflow channel for another road as he could see car headlights reflected in it. Unthinkingly, he stepped in and to his dismay discovered his mistake. Roads aren't usually 5ft deep in water. He had managed to drag himself out and had stumbled back to the main road where he flagged down a car. The driver took him to Sheffield Infirmary where he was examined by a doctor, who declared him OK, but in need of a nights sleep to sober him up. The motorist kindly took Keith to his home and put him to bed. The next morning he provided Keith with dry clothes, and drove him back to the George & Dragon, where his car unfortunately broke down and he had to be towed away. What laughs we had when Keith told us of his nocturnal wanderings. That morning in the car park, there was a gathering of rally cars with the drivers all dressed smartly in cord slacks, cravats and cord caps. They were in sharp contrast to our bleary eyed and scruffy crew. After retiring to the café for a breakfast of coffee and chocolate biscuits we sat on the wall outside sunning ourselves, trying to decide which crag to go to. Al, Richard and Pike bestirred themselves to go up to Shining Clough whilst Dave, Platty and I thought about going up to Crowden Great Quarry. Walking down the road towards Crowden, we found Keith asleep under some trees and relieved him of a tin of salmon, a loaf and some biscuits. These goodies added to some Fryets that we cooked made a welcome repast, after which we took a short siesta. Feeling refreshed we walked to the lower quarry but found it to be dangerous due to the close proximity of some army sharpshooters. The slag heaps of the upper quarry were climbed and we were soon at the foot of the upper cliff, a hundred feet of vertical insecurity. Deterred by its awesome appearance, a not very ambitious route up a boulder strewn gully was climbed to the top the cliff. An amusing time was had trundling boulders over the edge then festering in the sun viewing the scenery. Later on returning to the road, we found a water trough, washed ourselves and our cooking equipment then caught the 5.45pm bus home.

Les, who by this time had finished at university, started work as a physicist at the Windscale nuclear power station in Cumbria (now called Sellafield). Here he met another climber, Pete Turnbull, a local lad whose parents ran the Royal Oak in Ambleside. Pete belonged to a group of climbers who were known as the Langdale lads and Les started to climb with them. He also met another group from Newcastle, the Craig Lough, who frequented Keswick. Geoff Oliver was a well known member of this club and he and Les did some routes together, Geoff later becoming an Alpha club member. Les was now a frequent Lakeland climber, but as his parents lived in Stockport, he made regular trips home to visit them and on these occasions usually managed to get out on gritstone or down to Wales

During November and December Pete Bamfield and I did Lusitania, Fina and Seranata, all new climbs on Stanage. These were all very good climbs but the one I really wanted to do was one to the right of Lusitania. I had been hesitant about trying it but was spurred on when Hugh Banner said that if I didn't hurry up and get it done, he would do it. So I led it and Hugh and Les Brown seconded me. We named it Titanic. Bob Brayshaw did the 1st ascent of Cleft Wing Superdirect.

Winter climbing for most of us had so far been limited to Derbyshire, with the odd gully in Wales or the Lakes. Les Brown, Pete Bamfield and I, had during one winter, climbed the gully on the face of Back Tor in Edale. The conditions were soft snow overlying frozen shale and rubble. The result was precarious unprotected climbing. This was before the advent of curved picks, twelve point crampons and ice pegs. In fact I don't recall any of us having crampons of any type at all. We did have an ice axe each but cutting steps in frozen shale left a lot to be desired.

Kinder Downfall was the favourite and usually in condition at some time during the winter. Rock pegs were used for protection in icy conditions but quite often the ledges were piled high with snow making it difficult to place them. Winter climbing of this type was masochistic, gloves were usually wet through, fingers were numb and if climbing second, long waits in the cold made even the keenest feel miserable. One of the best winter gully climbs was on Torside Clough in Longdendale, but this is rarely in condition nowadays with the milder winters.

None of us realised that avalanches could occur in the Peak District until 1962 when Graham West and Michael Roberts of the Manchester Gritstone club were killed in one. They were attempting a winter ascent of Wilderness Gully at Chew valley when they were suddenly buried under tons of snow. Before this tragedy, we were unaware of the danger, thinking it was confined to bigger hills, and consequently we probably put ourselves at risk of being avalanched.

One climb that had captured our imagination was the very loose face of Mam Tor above Castleton. It had already been climbed, but we were attracted to it; imagining it looked like the Eigerwand. It was best to wait for a hard frost when all the loose stuff, in other words all the face, would be glued together.

The day arrived, very cold with a smattering of snow. Pete Bamfield and I were roped together and tentatively made our way up the gully in the centre of the face. Even though the shale was frozen, our weight loosened the rock underfoot which cascaded down on to anyone climbing below us. Belays were typically loose pegs which when combined with large stances were the safest thing available. Bob and Paul also did this climb, followed closely by Richard and Stan. At one point Bob loosened a block but omitted to warn the pair below Stan was paying out the rope to Richard when suddenly the above mentioned block and Richard parted company with the face. It was fortunate that he wasn't wearing crampons as Stan felt the full force on his head as the diving Richard collided with him! It was also fortunate that Stan was on a good stance!

We all finished the route but I don't think any of us would like to go on that face again.

Chapter 4
A Golden Year 1959

Easter 1959 saw most of the Alpha in the Pass, once again camping on the Grochan field. The easier extremes such as Brant Direct, Kaisergebirge Wall and Spectre were ticked off. Hugh Banner and Bob Beesley did the first ascent of Ghecko Groove on Cloggy

This was to be a good year for the club and early in the summer, Les Brown did the tenth ascent of Cenotaph Corner (seconded by Paul Nunn) then went off to the Alps.

In Chamonix whilst doing the north ridge of the Peigne, Les dropped his sack which plummeted hundreds of feet losing all his gear and his camera. Back in the valley he decided to go home and was about to leave when he was asked to make up a team of four with Whillans, MacInnes and John Streetly. They were hoping to do the first British ascent of the Walker Spur. Les jumped at the chance but as most of his gear was either up on the Peigne or on its way home he decided to climb in his best suit. They moved fast, Les and Don climbing together and they could have completed the route in a day but for being held up by two very slow Czech climbers. At a couple of points Hamish had noticed various items which looked suspiciously like a British team had passed that way. Descending to Courmayeur they learned with great disappointment that Robin Smith and Gunn Clarke had done the route and finished it the day before, thus claiming the first British ascent.

During 1959 at Stanage, Pete Bamfield and I explored the Enclosure Buttresses area doing some good climbs there. Then I teamed up with various Alpha members to do a number of first ascents, namely Anniversary Arete, Surprise and Cosmic Crack, the latter two with Bob Brayshaw. Bob led Desperation, The Wedge, Blockhead Direct and Cue and Pete Bamfield joined me on Parallel Cracks, August Arete and

Traversity. Paul led me up Genesis whilst Richard led a big team up Exodus. I climbed a lot with Bob Brayshaw that year. He had this idea that we should try to do 1000ft of gritstone VS climbing every weekend until he had completed his 200th VS. We kept this up for seven weeks; boy was I glad when he achieved his goal!

Meanwhile on Kinder at Nether Tor Keith Taylor and Dave Upton did the first Girdle traverse of the Central Buttress, 170ft VS.

One weekend, I broke one of my own rules, I worked a Saturday. The reason for this was to earn enough money to buy my first pair of PAs. The following week Paul and I went to Wales where I broke in my magic boots on Munich Climb on Tryfan. What a difference good rock boots make. I immediately dumped my old Brigham's Kletterschuh!

During this period Paul, Richard, Bob and I would climb together changing partners regularly. If one pair did a particular climb the other team would do it soon after. There was a lot of friendly competition and I remember one time when Bob and I were teamed up we overheard Richard and Paul planning to do the Right Unconquerable the following Sunday. As none of us had done this test piece before, it promised to be a real plum. Bob and I did it on the Saturday both leading it, placing chockstones as runners.When Richard and Paul arrived that evening they were obviously upset by our treachery and vowed to put things right the following day. Sleeping in Robin Hood's Cave that night we heard the wind start to blow and the rain pouring down. Bob and I thought, that's it, they'll never do it now. The next morning it was still raining and very misty. Richard collected his gear and turning to Paul said, "Come on, we're going to do the Right Unconquerable." Everyone quickly got out of their sleeping bags and followed Richard and Paul to their chosen route. Richard looked up at the dripping slimy crack above him and taking the slings from around his neck, he dropped them on the ground saying, "I'm not going to have time to put those on." The rest of us lit up cigarettes and settled down to watch. He then proceeded to climb the Joe Brown classic in classic style. Paul quickly seconded him.

One Wednesday night at Richard's house, Paul, Bob, Richard and myself were faced with a difficult decision. We had been approached by a member of the Rock and Ice to see if we would like to join that club, as they were looking for young members. The big problem was, they only wanted the four of us.

We liked the idea of being club mates of Brown and Whillans and thought it would be a good opportunity to learn things from them, particularly about Alpinism. But, we didn't want to give up on the Alpha which was just beginning to show promise as a club. Neither did we want to desert our mates for the sake of climbing with some of the world's best climbers, so we decided to stay with the Alpha and build our own club.

Another group of climbers from the Hyde/ Manchester area was the Black and Tans. This was the same club that Ralph and I had rejected earlier but with a new and younger membership. John Gosling was their star climber who along with the likes of Mike Simkins, Tony Brooder, Dave Little, Pete Cowie and the Birch brothers were doing new routes in the Longdendale valley. This group became good friends and sometimes climbing partners with the Manchester section of the Alpha club, so much so that at times the two clubs almost merged but always retained their separate identities.

Anxious to get my own transport I asked Brian Barlow and Hugh Banner to accompany me when I went to buy my first motor bike. We settled on a second-hand BSA 250 CC. it was a good price and had a three months guarantee. Brian persuaded me to take the bike to his home saying that he would check it over for me. I was eager to get out on my new machine and show it off to the rest of the lads but I agreed to do as he suggested. The following evening I went on the bus to Brian's house in Heaton Mersey expecting to pick up my new toy. To my dismay, on being shown through to the back shed by Brian's mother, I was shocked to see a motor-bike frame with two wheels but without an engine. There were parts spread out everywhere. Brian said, "Don't worry I'll have it back together in no time. Come on let's go for a pint." The next night I arrived at Brian's again at about 7.30, his mother said, "He's gone out, I'm sorry but he's not done your bike." The next night it still wasn't ready. I was beginning to feel despondent. I couldn't very well complain because after all Brian thought he was doing me a favour. Two weeks later the bike was back in one piece and I was king of the road. My first time out on the bike was to the Roaches. Keith Taylor rode pillion as he possessed a full licence and being a learner I was only supposed to have a qualified person on the bike with me; so we were legal and confident. When we reached the steep hill down through Upper Hulme, Keith said "take it slowly, change down a gear". I tried the complicated manoeuvre but only succeeded in putting it in neutral. The machine started to gather speed, Keith shouted in panic, "Brake, brake". The panic spread, I pulled the clutch instead of the brake and we hurtled faster down the hill towards the river bridge which was on a sharp bend. I leaned the bike over at a fantastic angle forgetting that there were no foot-rests for my passenger. On the wrong side of the road we crossed the bridge, Keith trying to straighten up to stay on board, me leaning it over to miss the parapet. There was a notice on the other side of the bridge which said "GO SLOWLY THROUGH THESE PREMISES". We took it out. It landed on top of us in the brook which fortunately for us was only shallow. The bike was a bit bent but was soon repaired with a peg hammer. We leaned what was left of the notice against the bridge, remounted the bike and roared off to the crag. I never really understood why Keith always refused lifts from me whenever I offered them in the future.

During the summer holidays, Paul and I went to the Pass for two whole weeks. We camped on the Grochan field where we met some climbers from Kent. Most of them were a little older than us, except for one who was about the same age as Paul. His name was Martin Boysen and he told us that he had first become interested in climbing after seeing pictures of High Rocks and Harrison's in some YHA magazines when he was about sixteen. He had gone to these crags the following weekend to have a look, and asked some climbers if he could tie on their rope. Finding that he had an aptitude for rock climbing he was hooked and from then on climbed almost every weekend. Martin proved himself to be a very good climber and I think this was his first visit to Wales and during that holiday, he seconded Joe Brown on the first ascent of Woubits Left-Hand on Cloggy. Joe used some aid on the top pitch and when Martin joined Joe at the top; he said he didn't think the aid was necessary. A couple of years later Martin joined the Alpha when he came to study botany at Manchester University. More about Martin later.

On Friday nights on the Grochan field Paul and I waited in great expectation for Ray Greenall to arrive for the weekend. Ray was a member of the Rock and Ice Club and I think he probably saw something of his younger self in us. He knew we were on a shoestring budget so in return for having a brew ready for his arrival he would bring sausages and bacon. Sitting listening to the hiss of the primus stove, the babbling of the river and telling him about climbs we had done that week, we waited our turn for a bacon butty.

One day on West Rib on Dinas Mot, we met two lads of similar age to us, Alan Clarke and Barry Ingle. Barry said that he was about to move to Manchester from Nottingham to work as an engineer in

Trafford Park. We told him he could get in touch with us at our Wednesday night meeting place, Richard's house.

Barry Ingle and Pete Crew, another good climber, were both members of the Peak Climbing Club but not yet regular climbing partners. They had done some good new routes together at Shining Clough in Longdendale, namely Electra, Oedipus and Nagger's Delight, but their big partnership was yet to come.

Pete had been introduced to climbing by his Geography teacher while at grammar school. They used to go out on field courses to the Lakes and Wales and this involved a lot of walking and Pete found that he really enjoyed being in the hills and gradually started to go regularly. Eventually he met up with members of the Peak Climbing Club and started to climb with an older man called Albert Shutt, who took him on his first visit to Stanage, where like many before him, his first climb was Flying Buttress.

Finding that he had a natural aptitude for climbing, from then onwards he started to go out walking and climbing with two school friends, becoming young members of The Peak Climbing Club.

That summer of 1959, all these promising young climbers were camping in Llanberis Pass. Pete Crew was climbing with his mentor from the Peak Climbing Club who was pushing him on routes which at that time were above his limit. It was rumoured that Pete was once heard at night, whilst asleep, shouting out for a top rope.

Baz Ingle joined the Alpha when he eventually moved to Manchester followed some time later by Pete Crew. This pair struck up a climbing partnership which was to rival the legendary Brown /Whillans team in their exploration and production of new climbs in north Wales.

The weather was good for the whole two weeks that we were in Wales. Paul and I did most of the older routes on Cloggy, climbs like Longland's Route, Pigott's Climb and Curving Crack etc. We also did some of the easier Brown/Whillans climbs like East Gully Groove plus a good number of classic routes in the pass.

We watched Hugh Banner and Rodney Wilson on the first ascent of Troach; again Banner was pushing the grades higher.

One night in the pub we met a group of climbers from Sheffield, Ted Howard, Barry Pedlar, Tanky Stokes and a 15 year-old lad called Clive Rowland. Paul had already met Clive at a Peak CC. dinner in Derbyshire and they had climbed together in the pass, doing such climbs as Brant and Unicorn.

All these four later became members of the club and good friends to the rest of us. Pedlar incidentally had at least two claims to fame. (1) There are four climbs on Stanage which bear his name and another two with corruptions of it and yet he only did the first ascent of one of them. (2) He served in the Coldstream Guards and was a sentry at Buckingham Palace and had a medal for being the smartest Guardsman in his detachment. Ted was the most experienced climber of the four having done a fair amount of new climbs on gritstone as well as some of the hardest climbs of the day. That year he had done Cenotaph Corner, bivvying with Jim Wright at the foot of the climb to ensure he got the ninth ascent! He first visited the Alps in 1959, again with Jim Wright, hoping to do the first British ascent of the NE Face of the Piz Badile but their plans were dashed when Jim broke his leg crossing the glacier.

Clive was their apprentice and had done the Girdle Traverse of the west buttress on Cloggy with Ted when only 15 years old. When Clive was older he became a top alpinist and a very steady and capable mountaineer. Bryan (Tanky) Stokes had been in the Tank Regiment and was probably in his early thirties when we met him. He was built like a Tank and had a big laugh to match. He was good company being quite mischievous and although he hadn't been climbing much at the top grades, he was very keen. Tanky once made an anonymous phone call to Mrs Thomas, where he disguised his voice and said," Your eggs are slimy and your chips are greasy," then laughed. Mrs Thomas screeched down the phone, "Tanky, I know it's you, you're banned." So for weeks Tanky wasn't allowed in her café.

At the end of the holiday, we went back to Derbyshire for a weekend on grit. Going straight to Stanage, we were on good form and polished off a few outstanding ambitions. Paul at last led the Right Unconquerable and I did the first ascent of Billiard Buttress. We both soloed Wall End Slab Direct. So feeling invincible we went along the Edge ticking off many routes that had previously repulsed us.

That day we were introduced to Eric Byne by a mutual friend and chatted to him about possible new lines. That was the one and only time we met him, as he tragically died from cancer quite soon after that.

In September 1959, Paul, Bob, Roy Fryer and I did the first crossing of the Lower Tier Girdle Traverse at the Roaches. Roy had to leave early so abseiled off when we arrived at the stance on Valkyrie. The others and I crossed the Mincer Wall to complete the route.

One weekend at Stanage, Rodney Wilson and I did the first ascent of The Scoop- HVS 5A, then I led Easter Rib E1 5B which in those days didn't have any protection and was regarded as a very hard lead! Rodney had just returned from Wales where he had seconded Banner on White Slab at Cloggy; he was very impressed by it and described the route to me as follows. "There are two long pitches of 150ft with no protection and not a hold wider than a quarter of an inch; it took Banner 11 hours to lead it!" (This was probably the third ascent.)

It is no wonder that everyone had been scared off doing The Rock and Ice routes when these sort of myths were being perpetuated.

Paul was itching to lead Cenotaph Corner and with Bob Brayshaw went back down to Wales and led what was an early ascent at the age of sixteen. This was unheard of at that time and made the climbing world start to take notice of this very talented young climber.

In May of 1959 Hugh Banner had done the third ascent of Vember on Cloggy. This route had been unrepeated since Brown and Whillans had done it seven years earlier and Hugh's ascent was a milestone in Welsh climbing.

Paul, whose granny had bought him a brand new BSA 250 motor bike as a present for doing well in exams at school, decided to drive down to the pass with Bob for a weekend's climbing. It was late autumn and the weather wasn't good. They arrived at the Grochan field late on Friday night to find the Rock and Ice was there in force. Next morning it was very wet but they packed their climbing sacks and after telling Ray Greenall they would probably attempt Pigott's Route they set off for Cloggy. No one suspected what they really had in mind. It was almost dark when they arrived back at the tent soaked to the skin. Ray asked if they had managed to do Pigott's. "No," they replied. Ray remarked that the weather had been very wet and enquired if they had managed to do anything at all. "We did Vember,"said Bob. They had done the fourth ascent of one of Joe Brown's greatest climbs and in wet conditions at that! Bob had led the drainpipe crack and had frightened himself, only having one runner on the long wet first pitch. Paul led the rest of the climb and at the age of sixteen, this ascent elevated him to the forefront of young British climbers.

Another notable event in 1959 was Les Brown started his portfolio of Lake District new routes when he climbed Inertia on Gimmer Crag.

Over the next few years Les produced a number of outstanding routes of great quality on a wide range of crags and anyone looking in first ascent lists can't fail to notice that many of his climbs have become classics. Les has done many first ascents in Wales and Scotland but it was mainly his Lakeland ascents that he became known for; routes such as Armageddon, Centaur and Nazgul on Scafell, Praying Mantis in Borrowdale, Gormenghast on Heron Crag and Isengard on Dow; the list goes on and on.

By late 1959 I had begun to climb a lot with Platty who was working at the same place as me as a contract electrician. My dad and I took the same train to Guidebridge station each morning, and then went our separate ways to our places of work. On Fridays, Brian would be waiting at the station exit with the Road Rocket ready to pick me up and instead of going to work; we would sneak off to Wales or Derbyshire for the weekend. My dad would have strongly disapproved if he had known.

On gritstone the exploration at Stanage continued. I led a team up Nightmare Slab, Brian Platt and I did The Blurter (a rather silly name but one we liked at the time), Count's Wall, Typhoon, Birthday Buttress and Counts Buttress Direct.

We had heard about Counts Buttress and understood that the route went straight up the middle of the wall. The story went that both Brown and Whillans had failed on the right arête but had done the Direct; so that was the way we went. Later we learned that the opposite was true and that they had done the arête after failing to top rope the Direct; reportedly Eric Byne had done the direct in 1932 although doubt has been cast on the accuracy of this. Paul and Bob had top roped Count's Buttress Direct with a view to leading it and I also had my eye on it.

It was my 20th birthday 17th October 1959 when Brian and I parked his Road Rocket at the plantation below Stanage and walked up to the crag. It was a bright day but there was a cold breeze blowing; the rock was very dry. At the cave under Counts Buttress we had a smoke then donned our PAs and roped up. The moves out of the cave on to the wall above seemed reasonably easy. I felt that I was going well. Moving up to the scoop in the centre of the wall I came to a full stop on a sloping foothold where a green streak leads up to a wide crack above a horizontal ledge. Using a downward pressure hold for my left hand I stretched for the finishing ledge but couldn't quite reach it. Pushing up with my foot, which left the hold in a sort of half-hearted semi-dyno move (in those days, this was called jumping for a hold and was regarded as not quite ethical) I just managed to reach the ledge but couldn't hold on. I thought this is it, I'm off and no runners. But good fortune smiled on me that day and I slid back down on to the sloping foothold and to my amazement came to a stop. This gave me confidence to have another try. Brian said, "Don't do that again, you almost gave me a heart attack." He asked if I could approach it in a more controlled manner, i.e. without the Dyno. I looked down and weighed up the consequences of a fall. It was about 40ft to a bad landing at the base of the crag and then a roll down the hill. If I was lucky I might not get hurt! Standing there, working out how to do it, I suddenly thought I can do this. I decided to go for it. Pushing down on the pressure hold and bringing my right foot up on to friction, I stretched out my right arm as far as I could. My arm seemed to be growing inch by inch my face was pressed up against the rock and I couldn't see my feet. Blessed relief, I felt my fingers curl round a hold on the ledge above and my feet stayed on! It was in the bag! Brian came up but as he was short he found it very hard.

Whilst doing this climb we had noticed a crack on the left which we knew hadn't been done; we climbed it next and called it Count's Wall. We then went to the Blurter buttress and did Typhoon and Birthday Buttress both new routes.

That evening when Paul and Bob arrived at Mrs Thomas's café, they asked what we had done. We told them Count's Buttress Direct and three new routes. Paul seemed pleased but Bob was a bit down in the mouth. A few weeks later Whillans came up to me in the pub and said. "Are you the lad that's done Count's Buttress Direct? I said, "Yes." He nodded but didn't say anything else.

It was a long time after that; we discovered that we had probably done the first ascent. Today, this route is graded E3 6A and along with Traversity graded E1 6A (done August 1959) these two routes were the first of this technical grade on Stanage. At that time these grades didn't exist and we just graded them Extreme and HVS respectively. The following year Bob Brayshaw went one better, when he led me up Daydreamer 6B, which despite what the guidebook says, didn't have a pebble to stand on, as this had broken off during an earlier attempt by Gray West. Another bit of mis-information in the Stanage guidebook that I would like to correct, and I don't know how it got there, is that Brian Platt and I used aid on the first ascent of Count's Wall. We didn't use aid, but we did have a nut runner. At the time, nuts were only just coming into use, and were engineering nuts with the thread drilled out and had a rope sling threaded through them. Some at the time thought these nuts unethical and regarded them as artificial aids. Perhaps that is where the story started.

That same October on Kinder North Edge, Lobster Crack VS 5A and Crab Crack HVS 5B were done by Richard McHardy and Roy Friar along with the classic Jester Cracks VS 4C. The first two were originally named Suspension and Gremlin Groove respectively but the names were changed on August 3rd 1961 when Malc Baxter thought he had done the first ascents. Richard said that Gremlin Groove (Crab Crack) was very hard and Baxter reiterated this on his ascent. All three climbs plus Parliamentary Climb VS, were originally done by McHardy and Fryer on the tenth October 1959.

On the same day Bamfield and Ellison did a number of climbs; Grotto Groove VS. Election Crack V Diff and Socialist Variation 60ft VS.

Every Wednesday evening all the lads who could make it used to meet up at Richard's parents' house in Droylesden. There would sometimes be ten or more of us in the front room. Richard was usually eating a giant potato pie with a crust on it, from a large enamel bowl, gradually loosening his belt the more he filled his stomach. The rest of us had to be content to sit like stray dogs waiting for any scraps that might be thrown in our direction. The pie was always big enough for there to be something left to share out among any who wanted some.

Richard's cousin Margaret often came over to do Richard's mother's hair on Wednesday nights so she was roped in to brew up for us. Margaret was an attractive girl of about sixteen. She was friendly and got on well with the lads. Stan Goodwin introduced us to a lad from work who he had talked to about climbing whose name was Jim Smith. Jim who was eighteen at the time had first been out climbing with Stan to Laurencefield quarry in Derbyshire. He was shown how to tie on using a bowline and soon found himself half way up his first climb; this was Gingerbread HVS. At the top of the crag he met Richard for the first time who greeted him with an "'ow do." Jim recalls that he found the whole experience so enjoyable and the lads so friendly that he felt like he had found a new family. Jim became a regular at Richard's on Wednesday evenings and over the following months; he and Margaret took a liking to each other and eventually started to go out together. They have now been married for many years so Jim was right, he did find a new family.

Jim Smith fitted in well with the Alpha, he climbed mainly with Stan and young Al and Andy Garvey and as young Al and Jim were the newest members they finished up as climbing partners. I remember Jim soloing a direct start to Campion Wall on Curbar which none of us could get up at first. We didn't believe he had done it so he did it three more times to prove it! His first climb in Wales was to second me on Brant Direct.

Chapter 5
A Club Dinner.

The biggest social event every year was the club dinner. Almost all clubs held them and invited friends from other clubs that were known to them. There were always a number of gate-crashers as well if a good night was expected.

Over the winter months there would be a club dinner somewhere on most weekends and depending on how many people you knew it was possible to have a full and eventful social season.

Alpha Club dinners became legendary and attracted large numbers. Each year they were held at different places, usually because of bans being imposed at the previous year's venue due to over enthusiasm on the part of some group or individual. Sometimes, if it had been a particularly good venue and a ban had been put on for any future dinners, it was possible to get round it by changing the name of the club when booking the date!

A memorable Alpha dinner was held at the Wasdale Head hotel when Wilson Pharaoh was the landlord. He was used to hard drinking rowdy events having been the host to many a club dinner held by the Langdale lads, so the venue was ideal. There was a barn next door for when things started to get wild and a bunkhouse to lie down in when Pharaoh decided that enough was enough! As he was an ex-champion Cumberland wrestler his decisions were respected and obeyed even if they were sometimes clouded with alcohol.

We walked over to Wasdale from Seathwaite, arriving at the pub as night fell. It was November and dark by about 4pm so as there isn't much else to do in Wasdale after dark, we settled into the bar for a quiet drink before dinner at 7o'clock.

People started to arrive, word had got around, and among expected guests were the Langdale lads, Mick Burke, Pete Turnbull, Muscroft, and Pete Shotton etc. There was a large group of climbers from Keswick, Carlisle and the north-east, Frank Carrol, Geoff Arkless, Geoff Oliver, Paul Ross and many more. There was also a contingent from the Rock and Ice.

Unexpected, were the Manchester Gritstone Club who came in force. Prominent amongst these were Graham West, Malc Baxter, Barry Roberts and a young Paul (Tut) Braithwaite; but the biggest name there, from the Gritstone Club, was Barry Kershaw.

Kershaw was noted for being a hard man, not so much for his climbing, although he had done some good first ascents, but for his reputation as a fighter who would take on anyone who looked at him the wrong way and any number of others who might join in. When drunk, he was unpredictable and it was not unknown for him to turn on his friends. He was a big man, wild looking and his nick name "The Big Dobber" says it all!

Pete Turnbull (Turds as he was known) also a big lad, had once thrown a drunken trouble maker out of his parents' pub, The Royal Oak in Ambleside, only to find out later and with much concern, that the troublemaker was non other than Kershaw.

Pete an amiable chap was a good person to stand next to when Kershaw was around!

The hotel filled up, and the Alpha and invited guests went in to dinner.

After the meal the room was cleared of tables and the usual gymnastic tricks, feats of strength and party pieces were performed: who could do the most press-ups or place a beer bottle furthest away without moving his feet and get back to a standing position. And all the time the beer was flowing. By 11.30 the pub seemed to be shaking, there was no room anywhere, the place was jumping. Suddenly Les shouted that a rugby match had started in the barn, and then quickly left the room to re-appear minutes later with a black eye.

In the barn, the rugby match was between the Gritstone Club who made up one team and their opponents who were the cream of all the others put together. There was only one rule, get the ball to the opposing side's end. Paul Ross was referee because he had a whistle. He stood to one side and blew it if he thought things were getting out of hand; sometimes he was taken notice of. Spectators lined the sides of the barn, sitting on bales of hay 15feet above the action. I sat on a beam with Richard, Mick Burke and some of the Langdale lads 20feet above the "pitch." Paul Nunn, Ted Howard and a selection of giants and lunatics were in the thick of it below, fighting for the ball.

At one point Paul had his shirt ripped from his back; someone else crashed into some farm machinery and started to bleed. The opposition seemed to be ganging up on Paul, probably because of his size. Little Mick said, "The next time they get Paul let's all go down to sort them out." We all agreed. Minutes later Paul was brought down again. "Right," shouted Mick, "let's go." I leapt off the beam into mid air, and as I looked back saw the rest of the lads still sitting there howling with laughter; gullible me. I landed amid a mass of fighting bodies and was immediately thrown to one side.

Then the whistle blew, we all looked up to see Wilson Pharaoh pointing to the door. Enough was definitely enough!

The next morning nursing sore heads and limbs on the walk back to Borrowdale, hangovers were blown away by the cold November air and reminiscences of the previous night caused much merriment.

Barry Johnson above Langdale 1956

Cae Gwegi 1956

Ralph Harris, Wales 1956

Les Brown on "Brant" 1956

At Stanage late fifties (L to R) P Nunn, D Upton, D Kirk, A McHardy, Bob Brayshaw, A Parker

Les Brown on Hangover, Llanberis Pass 1956

Mrs Thomas's café Hathersage (L ro R) P Nunn, A Parker, A McHardy

Anniversary Arete, Stanage, Al Parker, 1ˢᵗ Ascent 1959

Cosmic Crack, Stanage, A Parker 1959, 1ˢᵗ Ascent

See Saw, Stanage, A Parker 1960 1ˢᵗ Ascent.

Surprise, Stanage (L to R) B Platt, A McHardy, B Brayshaw. 1960

1ˢᵗ Acent "Cleft Wing Super Direct "Bob Brayshaw 1958

Paul Nunn, top roping "Count's Buttress Direct" 1959

Chapter 6
Swinging Sixties
Reminiscences of 1960 -61

Once at Christmas time, camping at Ashness Bridge in Borrowdale, the weather was bitterly cold. The stream had frozen almost solid, eggs which were left in the tents, burst their shells. Christmas morning whilst we were making breakfast and trying to keep warm by taking swigs from a whisky bottle, a Landrover pulled up at the gate to our camping field.

Out jumped a big man sporting tweeds, a ruddy face and a bushy moustache. Thinking he was the land owner we prepared ourselves for trouble by ignoring his existence. He peered at us over the wall and bellowed in a military fashion,

"I say, chaps, did you camp out last night?" "Yes," we replied cautiously. He looked at us admiringly and said, "Well done, chaps, last night there were 28 degrees of frost!" Then, shaking his head, he climbed back into his car and drove off up the road.

★ ★ ★

Brian and I sat in the cave of Oxford Street on Millstone Edge, belayed securely to an assortment of pegs. The ledge was just about wide enough for us to sit uncomfortably, with all our gear clipped to pegs. It was a November Saturday, 5pm, dark and cold.

Les Brown had laughed when we told him we were going to practise bivouacking. "You don't need to practise, wait until you're forced to do it" he had said. I was beginning to think that he was right!

Too late now though, all the lads had watched us climb up to the cave, then shouted a gleeful good night and tootled off to the pub. Doubtless they were now having a good laugh at our expense.

It was a clear starlit night, we sat in our sleeping bags and at first it didn't seem too bad. We had plenty of fags, a flask and Platty had prepared the food. "What have we got for tea, Brian?" "Brown sauce butties on white bread" he replied. "Not again," I moaned. "Sorry, that's all we've got."

It was going to be a long night; I vowed to take more notice of Les in future!

I was just warming up a bit and nodding off when Brian slid off the ledge and wakened us both. After tightening his belay, we just got settled when he decided that he wanted to pee. Contortions followed as he endeavoured to stand up in his bag to pee down the crag. He successfully avoided wetting his bag but I can't say the same for mine.

Morning at last, and the lads were there at the crack of dawn.

"How did it go?" they shouted up. "It was a doddle," we lied.

"I think we'll skip the top pitch, eh, Brian?" "Yeh, let's go to Mrs Thomas's for breakfast; Les was right, we don't need to practise anymore, we know how to bivouac!"

★ ★ ★

Another Saturday night, another winter with a lot of snow on the ground, Paul, Richard, Platty and I left the Millstone Inn at closing time and headed for Millstone Edge to find somewhere to kip. Richard and Paul shared a tent as did Brian and I. It was very cold and we could feel it striking through the ground sheet and our poor quality sleeping bags.

Richard, who had that week been given an air mattress as a present from his sister, was extolling the virtue of being well equipped.

Brian said, "We'll have that off him; you pretend to have a bad back". I started to moan and groan saying that my back was killing me. Brian shouted to Richard, saying that if he considered himself a friend he would let me have the airbed to ease my pain. Richard wasn't having any of this and said that he knew what we were up to.

I kept up the moaning, Brian kept up the pester power, going on and on keeping the two of them awake until at last Richard gave in and threw the mattress into our tent. We placed the airbed sideways across the tent so that we could both cushion our upper bodies. Such luxury, the night was made bearable convincing us that it would be a wise investment to buy one each at the earliest opportunity.

Next day to avoid ill feeling between us and our friends I had to keep up the pretence of having a bad back. The pair of us heaped thanks and praise on Richard for being so unselfish, though we did feel a certain amount of guilt.

★ ★ ★

By 1960 a lot of the lads had transport, Stan Goodwin had a BSA 250cc motorbike, Jim had a Lambretta scooter and Keith Taylor was the proud owner of a Hillman Minx car so as a club we were now quite mobile and able to go further affield at weekends.

At Easter 1960, the weather was brilliant, we were all camped on the Grochan field again, and Brian Barlow had his Vincent Black Shadow stripped down in the road, - trouble with the main bearings or something. Platty was acting as assistant mechanic. I had exchanged my BSA for a 500cc Velocette Venom and had decided to keep Barlow well away from this one!

In the Castle Hotel on Friday night there was a gang of climbers from Liverpool, friends of Bob Beasley. They all had motor bikes and according to them, they were fast. There was Big Clive with a Tiger 110 and Ralph Lloyd (Ace) with a Norton Dominator. They were the main men.

I had gone to the pub on the pillion of Brian Platt's Velocette Venom 500cc Single, leaving mine at the camp site. Paul was on his new BSA 650cc Gold Flash and Beasley had a Gold Star. There were also various less powerful bikes and some of the lads in vans.

Just before closing time, I went out to get some chips, leaving the lads comparing bikes and arguing as to which one was the fastest.

Returning from the chip shop, I found Brian sat astride the Velocette, revving it loudly and the Liverpool lads were doing likewise. Brian said, "Get on quick, we're having a race." I thought why did I leave my bike at the Grochan field? Climbing onto his pillion we set off with the others at great speed. My feet came off the footrests and I almost fell off backwards, grabbing hold I threw the chips away and clung on for dear life.

Down the straight to the Snowdon railway station, with Big Clive and Ace in front of us, I knew I was in for a fright! We were doing 80 by the time we got to the Victoria Hotel. On round the bends slowing only slightly, gear changes ringing loudly in my ears. On the next straight we passed Ace, Clive was still in front, living up to his reputation. Round a left-hander then a right, bikes hard over. Coming to the next straight, downhill to the head of the lake, I could see Clive braking hard, the red tail lights coming on brightly. There in front of us on the left hand curve was a van; and coming towards it we could see over the wall the lights of a car, the reason that Clive had slowed down. Brian, instead of braking, accelerated past Big Clive, overtook the van on the bend and shot through the narrowing gap. When I opened my eyes the car was gone, the road was clear ahead. Now we were really moving, pressing home our advantage. On through Nant Peris, and up the Pass, using the entire road, the Velocette seemed to stick as though on a mono-rail; Clive had missed his chance to overtake.

At the Grochan field, screeching to a stop we leaped off the bike, sat down on a rock and lit cigarettes, pretending we had been there for ages.

Clive was there a few seconds later, then after him came Ace, now re-christened ex-Ace. Both were going so fast they overshot the finish and had to go up to Ynnes Ettws to turn round. That night was talked about for a long time afterwards, becoming known as the night of the Llanberis Grand Prix.

Also that Easter of 1960, Les Brown and Geoff Oliver did the third crossing of the Girdle traverse of Dinas Cromlech. Geoff was one of the lads that Les had teamed up with when a friend from work at Windscale introduced them; he was a leading activist in a group of climbers from the northeast who frequented Keswick most weekends. Being interested in doing new routes and both climbing at the same standard, it was natural for Les and Geoff to climb together. The rest of us didn't know him at that time, but any friend of Les's was a friend of ours. Geoff later joined the Alpha.

★ ★ ★

Bob Brayshaw did Overlapping Wall on Carreg Wastad but failed to do Cenotaph Corner. Not very long after this he gave up climbing, got married and we never saw him again. The Alpha had lost one of its stars.

Pike who had become a steady VS climber and a popular member of the club met a girl and disappeared from the scene for a period of about four years. My old friend Ralph (Rastus) qualified as a radio operator joined the Merchant navy and set off to see the world.

Barry Ingle moved to Manchester with his work and started to come out regularly with the Alpha, so even though we had lost a few members we started to gain others.

Barry was a quiet, modest lad with a wiry physique, he and I climbed together on Grit and I was very impressed by how good he was. He didn't give the appearance of being strong but his technique was exceptional and he had great determination. I seconded him on Goliath on Burbage south, a route that he did by a combination of layback moves and wedging but he got his head stuck in the crack near the top which caused more than a little consternation!

One day arriving at Grindleford on my Velocette Venom with Ingle on the pillion, driving down the road to the Padley Mill café, we saw two girls walking towards us. Drawing level with them we could see that they were very good looking; as we passed by we turned our heads to look at them and they waved to us. We waved back, and then Barry turning to face forward noticed that I was still looking back. He shouted out in horror; I whipped my head round and was just in time to see that I had veered onto the grass verge and that I was heading for a lamp-post. I swerved, missed the lamp-post but the wet grass took the bike from under us. Picking ourselves up from the road, we could hear the two girls laughing hysterically. Luckily for us the only injury was to our pride. We re-mounted the bike and road off into the sunset.

★ ★ ★

Les Brown phoned Paul and asked if he fancied doing the girdle traverse of the East and West buttresses of Cloggy in one go. Paul, who was always game for adventure, agreed and setting off at 6am to avoid crossing other ropes, they did the Traverse of the east and west in a day.

★ ★ ★

Throughout 1960 everyone in the Alpha seemed to be doing new routes.

Pete Bamfield and Allan Ellison did ten new climbs on Kinder north edge, the best being Eureka, a really good VS and a Girdle Traverse of the Cabin Buttresses 510ft VS.

At Stanage, Alpha members continued with new route activity doing among many other climbs Seesaw, Countess Buttress, Marble Arete and the very hard Daydreamer.

On Scafell East Buttress, Les Brown climbing with Steve Read did Centaur and Geoff Oliver did Ichabod; on Cloggy Hugh Banner produced The Hand Traverse and Les Brown climbing with Trevor Jones did Steep Band.

On Dow Les Brown led Sidewalk and on Heron crag he found the fine route Gormenghast HVS.

Pat Fearnehough did the first ascent of Sentinel VS on Pikes Crag.

Barry Ingle and Pete Crew did Hiraeth on Dove crag in the Ullswater area; Pete was a very intense and driven type of climber and had wanted to join the Alpha after Baz became a member. That night Pete bought a crate of beer, to take to the hut. He slung it over his shoulder and all the bottles fell out, so we let him join the Alpha for proving he was human, and after all, it's the thought that counts!

★ ★ ★

Dave Sanders, even though he was a good climber; had been given the name Festy. This was because of his love of festering. In the early sixties Dave stopped coming out, so there was a vacancy for the post. I immediately applied and consequently inherited the name Festy.

This was mainly because of Platty and I having festering off to a fine art and only wanting to climb when the mood took us. It must be said though that there were lazier ones than us in the Alpha. Sometimes we would do next to nothing for a while and then suddenly go and do something quite hard; we did Deadbay Crack and Birthday Groove at Curbar during this period. Then we would fester, resting on our laurels until we deemed it time to perhaps do a good new route. It was all a big game and a bit silly really.

The idea of all this was to prove we could fester and still climb well and to astound the lads by our casualness; we also enjoyed festering!

In addition to doing new routes, we were all busy ticking off some of the Rock & Ice routes which until then we had thought to be beyond us, climbs such as the Dangler and Unprintable at Stanage, Peapod, at Curbar and Great Slab at Froggat.

Richard, Paul, Bob and myself all led these climbs at some time or other usually after one of us had shown the way, then a big team would second us.

There was always a good section of the lads doing VSs who were capable of seconding the harder routes, so no one was ever stuck for a climbing partner.

I remember Richard leading the Unprintable at Stanage with John Smith holding the rope. He had one runner on the large chockstone below the overhanging crack. He tried to jam all the way but came off. John, who hadn't been paying attention, almost let go the rope but managed to slow the fall. Richard came to rest on his back on the ground, luckily unhurt.

After a brief rest he went back up swung from jams into a layback and did the climb successfully.

★ ★ ★

One Friday evening in June 1960, Paul Nunn and I parked our motor bikes outside the quarry at Hobson Moor near Mottram in Longdendale.

At that time not much had been done there and the quarry was in a much nicer setting than it is today. Then, the quarry floor was covered in heather and the place was private property. There were some wooden chalets on the opposite side of the road, and whenever we went there to climb, an elderly woman would come out of her chalet to try to clear us off. She used to shout at us and when we took no notice, would then say in a loud voice, "Ernie, they're here again." Then again to us, "Clear off or Ernie will come and throw you off." We never saw the mysterious Ernie. He probably didn't exist.

I was keen to free a climb that I had done with Pete Bamfield using aid in 1957, and also if possible do some new routes.

There were two good lines in the far corner of the quarry. Paul led the first one, a corner which we called Epitaph Corner; it was a really pleasant climb of about VS standard but a bit unprotected. Then it was my turn to do the wall to its right, the one I had aided in 1957. There was still a peg in place at the overlap, one that we had been unable to remove. I did the climb using that peg as a runner (at that time the only runner on the whole route) and as I neared the top I pulled off a loose hold which hit Paul on the head but fortunately didn't injure him. A couple of moves later, we both heard a motorbike engine. Paul shouted up to me," Is that your bike Al?" "No," I replied, "I know the sound of my bike." We called the climb Parker's Eliminate because we thought it had similarities to Brown's Eliminate at Froggat. It's a climb that has become very popular over the years and is about HVS 5A.

Then it was Paul's turn again. He did the next line to the right, a hardish VS which we named Gideon, a superb climb with a variety of techniques.

It was nearly dark as we packed our sacks and headed for the road. On reaching our parking spot, there was Paul's Gold Flash but instead of my Velocette Venom there was a patch of oil in the road where it had stood. I couldn't believe it, my pride and joy, gone, stolen. Off we went to the police station to report the theft, then to my parent's house to sleep.

The bike was found undamaged on Sunday, unlike the culprit who was never found!

★ ★ ★

Over the summer, limestone became popular with the lads, particularly at Water-cum-Jolly. Paul and Dave Peck shared leads on St. Paul and quite a few new routes were done, and then it was decided to save this rock for the winter months and concentrate on doing some Lakeland climbs. Richard had been going to the Lake District a lot and had been doing some good stuff around the Langdale area. Once whilst doing Kipling Groove on Gimmer, seconded by Roy Friar and in front of an audience of the Langdale lads, on reaching the hand-traverse he was unsure of which way to go. Shouted advice from the lads seated in the gully below encouraged him to climb the green looking groove directly above. This he did accomplishing an unintentional first ascent of a very hard and uninviting groove.

★ ★ ★

Paul and I opted for the Keswick area, becoming obsessed with Castle Rock at Thirlmere. We did most of the hard routes there, Rigor Mortis, Thirlmere and Triermain Eliminates etc. Keswick made a good centre, the Borrowdale crags and Castle Rock were pretty much all weather crags and access to the higher crags of Scafell and Gable was good.

Rosthwaite dance was also an attraction as were the Saturday night sing-songs in the Keswick pubs with the Craig Lough lads.

Once while camping down below Castle Rock, a crowd of us decided to construct an aerial runway across the widest part of the river. A climbing rope was stretched over a deep pool from a tree high up the bank on one side, to one low down on the other. Richard volunteered to go first. He climbed up the high tree, sat in a sling, clipped on to the rope and pushed off down. Gathering speed he hurtled towards the opposite bank. What we hadn't allowed for in our calculations was how much nylon ropes can stretch. With a great splash he hit the water and disappeared from view but quickly resurfaced to tell us how good it was. I don't think anyone believed him as I can't remember any of the others having a go.

That summer Les went to the Dolomites again, this time with Trevor Jones. They did amongst other routes the Pilastro on the Tofana and the Comici route on the Cima Grande.

Richard and Stan went by train to Chamonix, where they met up with Andy. This was the first time in the Alps for all three of them. Stan did the Aiguille du Plan with Andy then the two of them did the Aiguille de l'M and then finished off their holiday with a walk up to the Couvercle hut. But as there was a lot of new snow, climbing was out of the question.

Richard in the meantime concentrated on some rock climbs, things like the north face of the Aiguille de l'M and the Pointe Albert.

The rest of us took our holidays in either the Lakes or Wales. Paul and I did the Girdle Traverse of Gimmer Crag plus classics like Gimmer Crack and Groove Super Direct. On Bowfell we did Sword of Damocles, Great Eastern on Scafell and Eagle Front on Eagle Crag, Buttermere.

It was during this period that we got to know Paul Ross. Ross was a well known climber on the Lakeland scene and had a laid back attitude to climbing. He was an amusing companion to be with, fun being the name of the game. He was also a very accomplished climber, one of the best of his day, with a long list of first ascents to his name, the first of which he did in 1955. Living in Keswick at his mother's house he was very much the local expert. I remember once at the top of Shepherds Crag, after a few of us had soloed Little Chamonix, walking toward the descent somewhere near Shepherd's Chimney, when Ross frightened us all by pretending to accidentally not see the top of a groove and stepped into space. It turned out that this was a party piece; he stepped off one side and grabbed good holds on the other, scaring any onlookers to death. He did this dangerous trick for a laugh and seemed to enjoy our panicky reaction.

When we first got to know him he suffered with a bad back which eventually put him in hospital for 12 months. We used to visit him at the small sanatorium on the slopes of Saddleback near Threlkeld and he would tell us of his latest efforts to relieve the boredom. One thing that he once did was to throw out some bread for a flock of seagulls. Tied to one particularly hard piece of bread was a length of string which in turn was attached to a toilet roll. Paul took great pleasure in watching this streamer following the gulls as they headed off towards St. John's in the Vale!

★ ★ ★

Another local expert was Ray McHaffie, who did many first ascents in Borrowdale and elsewhere. His party piece (it was rumoured) was to climb Little Chamonix on Shepherd's Crag in boxing gloves and roller skates. Ray came from Carlisle and worked at a timber yard on a circular saw and had a few fingers missing. He possessed a good sense of humour and one of his favourite tales was about him falling off a route in Langstrath and breaking a leg. When asked by his rescuers, "What happened?" he replied, "I was on these minute (minnit) holds and I fell off." The rescuer said, "Do you mean minute (mynute) holds?" "No," came the reply," I could only stay on them for a minute!" Mac incidentally wasn't an Alpha Club member.

★ ★ ★

Back in Llanberis Pass, a few of us were camping on the Grochan field during a very wet week. Looking out of our two-man waterlogged tents we were interested to see a large bell tent being erected by a group of very attractive young women.

It turned out that they were teenage French students on an exchange visit and they were accompanied by an English chaperone who spoke in an extremely posh voice.

We thought, "Great." We had been looking for somewhere dry and cheap where we could all congregate to brew up and play cards to while away the time until the weather cleared. This seemed to be ideal; it also had the added attraction of eight French girls who seemed to be very friendly. All we had to do now was separate them from their chaperone.

Ingratiating ourselves with the snooty English woman, who by the way wasn't much older than us, we gained access to the tent.

Sitting in a circle round the perimeter of this giant tepee with a primus stove singing away in the centre, we began to feel that things were looking up!

Brews were passed around until all the water was finished. Anxious to get well in with the snooty one, I offered to brave the elements to dash to the river to replenish the kettle.

On returning, I witnessed the arrival of a large motorbike and sidecar. The driver turned out to be Don Whillans with Audrey his wife, in the side car. I asked them if they would like a brew and invited them to the tepee.

Sitting cross-legged in the circle, Don produced a packet of cigarettes. He took out one for himself and offered an already part smoked one to Audrey. When she complained, he said, "I'm thinking about your health." No one else was offered one.

When the kettle had boiled Whillans held out his cup whilst the snooty one prepared to fill it with boiling water. Don demanded that she should hold the cup whilst pouring, but the chaperone insisted in a haughty manner that she would pour and Don should hold the cup. Whillans looked at her through squinty eyes and said, "Pour that on me bloody hand and I'll smash you int't ground." The poor girl looked shocked, and while we all looked on in silence she poured out his brew without spilling a drop.

When they had finished their teas, Don turned to Audrey and said, "Come on, we'll put the tent up, you can have the motor-cycle jacket, and I'll have the pacamac cos it's more waterproof."

They left the tepee. The snooty one said to us, "I'm not very keen on your bad mannered friend. I think we will be leaving tomorrow."

We thought thanks, Don, let's hope the weather improves.

★ ★ ★

The previous episode reminds me of another time back in 1958. We had been climbing on Froggat on Saturday afternoon. Whillans was there and I recall that he soloed Broken Crack, a fairly strenuous VS. Nothing really special about this you may think, excepting the style in which he did it. It was Whillans at his best, very fit, very strong and poetry in motion. The same day he did Cave Wall.

That night in the Chequers Inn below Froggat, Richard and I were playing darts against Platty and Whillans. Don was in a good mood. Brian and he got on well together, both being small, stocky and keen on motorbikes. They were also very happy because they beat us and we had to buy the drinks.

At closing time back at the camp site on the lawn, which was just that, the lawn of a bungalow further up the road, Brian and I lay in our tent, Richard and Rastus in theirs. We could hear music coming from Don and Audrey's radio. There were a couple of other tents on the lawn occupied by some guys from Cambridge University.

There was a lot of noise and swearing coming from these tents and we could hear that they were having a late night fry up. Don being with Audrey, or perhaps because he was being kept awake, took exception to the bad language and went across to issue a word of warning.

Brian and I lying there in the dark suddenly heard Whillans say in his flat Salford accent, " We all know you can swear, but if I hear you one more time I'll come across and ram that frying pan down your bloody throat."

Everything went quiet. Next morning when we awoke there was no sign of the miscreants or their tents. It seems they had decided to make an early start and had left without saying goodbye!

★ ★ ★

In November Paul and I decided to go to look at a new line on the limestone at Water-cum - Jolly. The day was cold but sunny, the road icy as we carefully negotiated the bends down to our destination on the overloaded motorcycle. Not fancying gritstone, Paul had suggested that swinging about in etriers, knocking in pitons would be a much warmer option; consequently we were carrying two large sacks full of ironmongery. As the log bridge had been swept away by the river we were forced to walk back to Litton Mills in order to cross via a narrow metal water pipe.

Arriving at the crag Paul pointed out to me the line of the proposed route. It looked impressive. The sacks were emptied to reveal enough gear for an ascent of the West Face of the Dru; most of it was homemade pegs and wooden wedges and about 30 Stubai steel karabiners.

Paul eagerly took the lead climbing with the absolute minimum of aid to what seemed to be a good resting place bridging the groove below a bulge. Here he placed what he thought to be his first solid peg. Clipping the ropes and an etrier, he took tension to move up the rungs and to gain maximum height leaned out to step up into the third and top rung.

He was just about to smash another peg into a superb crease above the bulge, when PING! The top peg came out and Paul, the etrier and another lower peg were travelling at 32ft/sec2. Smash. Landing on his feet he hit the ledge where I was belayed and immediately sat down rubbing both ankles. "Are they broken?" I asked. "I don't think so," he said, "let's go to the café".

I packed the sacks, and then somehow managed to get Paul and the gear across the river and back to the bike. A visit to the hospital showed that Paul had sustained two badly sprained ankles.

A month later, Paul returned with Barry Ingle and Brian Barlow for another attempt. This time it was cold and raining. Paul led the bottom pitch and Brian led the top pitch belayed by Paul. As time was getting short, Barry decided to abseil off into the gathering dusk. As Paul was de-pegging the top pitch by torchlight, a peg came out and spinning on the rope he was lowered to join Barry at the foot of the climb. Cold, wet and tired they went home satisfied in the knowledge that "Behemoth" had at last been done. But only Brian Barlow had done the route in its entirety.

Chapter 7
The Sheffield Connection 1961

Paul started at Sheffield University to study economics where he joined the SUMC. This meant some new members came on the scene, Oliver Woolcock (Wool), Mike Richardson and Brian Griffiths (Griff) all fellow students with Paul. Woolcock was originally from Workington and had done his first graded climb at the age of 15, a diff on Lower Kern Knotts. At 18 he went to Sheffield University where he joined the SUMC and met Paul Nunn, and through him, also met Richard.

Wool had already met and climbed with Martin Boysen in the Lakes before either of them joined the Alpha; he and Martin did things like Rigor Mortis together and other routes that Paul Ross pointed out to them. Over the next year or so all these climbers became Alpha members as did the climbers who we met in Llanberis in the summer of 59, Clive Rowland, Tanky Stokes, Ted Howard and Barry Pedlar. Others from the Sheffield climbing fraternity to join the Alpha were Pat Fearnehough and Al Wright.

Dave Peck joined Paul at Sheffield University the following year and Tony Riley, after dropping out of university, also went to live in Sheffield. Tony worked in the steel works as a labourer for a while, before taking up a career as a photographer; at which he became very successful.

Another ex-school friend of Paul's, John Moss, went to Leeds University; he was a good climber and a really nice bloke and had become an Alpha club member soon after Paul, as had Dave Sandall who disappeared from the scene at about the time that they all left school.

The club was now split into two sections, the original Manchester group and the newer Sheffield section. Because of dwindling numbers on the Manchester side some people began to think that the Alpha was a Sheffield club. But the Manchester contingent also began to take in new members and honour was restored.

One day Richard was boarding the Buxton bus in Manchester when he saw Martin Boysen getting off another bus carrying a suitcase.

Martin had just arrived to start at Manchester University and learning that Richard was going to the Roaches decided on the spot to join him, with suitcase in tow!

Martin didn't join the club until a year later but we used to see him out on gritstone and couldn't believe that anyone so laid back could be such a good climber. It must have been all that sandstone training that he'd had at High Rocks and Harrison's.

★ ★ ★

Early in the year, a few of the Alpha were again staying in Borrowdale. The weather was very cold with a lot of snow on the Fells.

At a lunchtime session in the Scafell Hotel drinking rum and blackcurrant with Wool and Paul, it was decided we should venture out on to the hill. We were joined by Clive Rowland and Pat Fearnehough

January afternoons aren't long enough for the route we had in mind but we set off anyway, heading for Great End Central Gully.

The walk up Grains Ghyll was hard as we were all full of rum and blackcurrant and it was very icy underfoot. At one point I went through the ice into a bog up to my knees. By the time we arrived at the foot of Great End my trousers were frozen and rattled like tin against my legs.

Setting off to climb the gully, all had axes but no crampons. The only sensible thing about the whole episode was that we had at least had the foresight to take a couple of ropes along. Everyone soloed the first half of the gully kicking steps in the hard snow until eventually we came to a full stop below a small rock face which was sheathed in ice. Various ones tried and it was eventually decided it would be safest to rope together with Pat in the lead.

After much strenuous effort Pat managed to climb the steep ice by cutting steps and handholds where needed. It was by this time getting quite dark and the realisation that we had bitten off a bit too much infused the situation with a sense of urgency. Luckily, the top half of the gully was quite easy and was overcome quickly. Pat, who had done such a magnificent lead on the ice, was now in a state of collapse probably brought on by the cold, the effort and the rum and blackcurrant!

Paul and Wool led the way in the dark off the top of Great End down to Grains Ghyll. Clive and I followed with Pat who needed some help off the mountain. It was a cold and epic descent in the dark and on the ice and we were all glad when we reached Seathwaite.

Some lessons were learned that day!

* * *

John Smith came out of the army in February and fitted back into the Alpha straight away. While in the army, he had been posted to Hong Kong where he had climbed on some cliffs above the city. This meant that he wasn't totally out of climbing practice and he was soon back on form.

Easter 1961 camping near the Cromlech boulders it was bad weather. Looking up from the road through the mist and rain, Pete Crew and Baz Ingle were just visible at the foot of Cenotaph Corner. We thought surely they're not going to do that today, but they did. Baz said later," We tossed up to see who should lead. I won, so Pete led."

Richard and I were fooling about round the tents throwing dixies of water about and one of us tripped over a tent guy line. The tent owner was extremely upset and whilst I was getting the Velocette started to go to Llanberis he came up to remonstrate with Richard. Suddenly without warning he dived at Richard, head butting him in the face. Richard fell to the ground, face covered in blood. Paul dashed forward and towering over this guy, fist clenched, asked if he would like to take him on also. The man declined.

Later we got to know the man's friend, Graham Evans, who told us that Richard's assailant was a paratrooper and was a nutcase who was always getting in fights. Graham was a married man and lived in Blackpool and was known to the Langdale lads. Over the next year or so he started to associate with different members of the Alpha. He was keen to climb well and in fact pushed his standard up enough to enable him to lead Cenotaph Corner.

On the way home that weekend my bike blew up going up the hill out of Ruthin. This was the result of driving at 80mph without oil because the oil tank return pipe had come loose. Richard and I had to leave the bike at a filling station and get lifts home.

The following week, a friend took me on his motorbike combination to pick up the Velocette. We tied a rope to his sidecar and the other end to the front forks of my bike, and set off for home. In Chester we were stopped by a policeman who said we were breaking the law. He asked to see my friend's licence and insurance and on seeing his address was in Holdsworth Square, Reddish, said, "My mother lives next door to you. Do you know her?" He did know her quite well, so the policeman said, "OK, on your way. Be careful how you drive. Give her my love and don't tell anyone else that I let you go." We got home without further incident and as my bike was badly damaged, I just covered it with a sheet intending to repair it when I could save enough cash.

★ ★ ★

Camping on the Grochan field, it was a lovely sunny morning. The plan was to go to Cloggy, me on the back of Brian Platt's bike and Dave Peck on the back of Paul's Gold Flash. Paul said we should leave the helmets behind to save having to carry them to the crag. Platty and I disagreed. We managed to convince Paul to wear his helmet and it was fortunate that we did. Riding very fast down the Pass through Nant Peris, Brian and I were startled by a loud roar as Paul and Dave overtook us on a slight bend.

Suddenly the bike slid from under them and they were bouncing down the road in front of us. Paul, who had been carrying a rope over his shoulder, was dragged along as the rope tangled in the bike's handle bars. Everything came to a stop when they hit the wall.

There was no Cloggy that day. Paul was pretty badly knocked about but nothing too serious; Dave had a broken ankle and other injuries so they both spent some time in hospital. That night it poured down. Brian and I slept out in the open and got soaked. Next day was another sunny day so this time, driving very carefully we went to Cloggy where we climbed Curving Crack and Pedestal Crack. That night after checking on Paul and Dave at the hospital we drove home.

★ ★ ★

Pete Crew with Jack Soper did the first ascents of Scorpio and the Pinnacle Girdle at Cloggy; this was the start of Crew's explorations on this great cliff! He followed this by sharing the lead with Ingle on Serth during October. This was just a foretaste of what they were going to do the next year.

★ ★ ★

Brian met a young woman from our home town and started dating her and although I still saw him sometimes during the weekdays he started to come out climbing less and less. Her name was Vera and she and Brian used occasionally to come down to Wales at weekends, mainly for the motorbike ride. They married the following year and I was his best man.

★ ★ ★

Les Brown was invited to join an expedition to the Everest area of Nepal and succeeded in doing the first ascent of Nuptse with Chris Bonington.

They travelled there overland and had many adventures, one of which nearly landed Les in trouble. The expedition members were staying at the British Consulate in Teheran, and one evening as guests of the Consul they were taken to a night club. They were sitting near the stage watching the show when a belly dancer reached down offering her hand to Les, obviously wanting him to go up on to the stage. Les grabbed the hand, pulling the girl down on to the table. Trevor Jones held on to her legs and a tug of war ensued. The matter was resolved when they both let go and the girl returned to her dancing unruffled!

Travelling back to the consulate at the end of the evening with the Consul and his wife, Dennis Davies apologised for the unruly behaviour. The wife of the British Consul turned to Dennis and said," Mr. Davies, you don't have to apologise to me. That was the best night out that I've had in years!"

On the mountain, Les also claimed the record for the highest fight of the year. This happened at 21,000ft when Les and Bonington were in a tent on a narrow ledge and facing the entrance of another tent on the same ledge. Les was of the opinion that the occupant of the other tent hadn't been doing his share of the load carrying. When Les remonstrated with him, the other climber who was older, said, "You cheeky young pup," and threw a punch at Les through the tent doorway. Les retaliated; and later said that each time they threw a punch they would collapse, take five breaths then throw another punch.

Bonington pointed out in a loud voice that if they didn't cease, all three of them would finish up falling down the mountain. This brought the bout to a close.

When Les returned to England, after a successful ascent, his home town of Stockport put on a civic reception for him at the town hall. He had to make a speech which he said was more daunting than the climb itself.

A few weeks later in Keswick he went in to a pub and met for the first time a young woman from Preston whose name was Margaret. They too were married the following year.

★ ★ ★

Meanwhile, climbing in the Lake District Paul, Wool, John and I did Deerbield Buttress which we all thought was very hard particularly as we were all hung over from the previous night.

On another occasion, Paul, John, Stan Goodwin and I were at the foot of Eagle Crag, Langstrath. Our objective was Post Mortem, a vicious crack climb first done by Paul Ross in 1956 and still awaiting a second ascent. Whillans had tried it but had fallen off; landing in a large bird's nest on the ledge. The day was sunny and warm. We sat watching a buzzard wheeling above the crag; Paul was the only one wanting to get moving and cajoled the rest of us into preparing for action.

John led up to the first ledge and Paul followed eagerly, impatient to get at the top pitch, the crux of the climb. I then led up the first pitch clipping the runners that Paul had left in place for me and joined the other two at the ledge. I belayed and shouted down for Stan to follow. Rummaging in his sack, Stan informed us that he had left his PAs in the van and so wouldn't be able to climb. John and I didn't believe him, thinking it was an excuse and wishing we had thought of it.

The crack above looked horrendous, a bit like a hard gritstone route, wide and overhanging with a roof at 20 feet then very steep up above.

Paul led up to the overhang, threaded a sling and after using this for aid, laybacked and jammed the upper crack, announcing that it was very hard. As we knew how good a climber he was this did nothing for our enthusiasm.

Sitting on a comfortable ledge in the remains of a large bird's nest, the one that legend had it Whillans had fallen into on an early attempt, neither of us wanted to move, let alone second the top pitch. There was a possible escape for one of us though. Somebody would have to abseil off to retrieve the runners from the first pitch. We decided to toss for it, John won and elected to abseil off. After all they were his runners that were left swinging there in the breeze.

I tied on to Paul's rope and started up the crack. On reaching the aid sling at the lip of the overhang I found it really hard to step out of the sling and unthread it while in a strenuous lay back position, even with a tight rope, as there was a paucity of footholds. It was a relief to find that things got easier above. Paul and I descended to join the other two at the foot of the crag and decided that we had done enough for one day!

★ ★ ★

John Smith, Clive, Tanky and I left the pub in Keswick one Saturday night to drive to Ashness Bridge in Borrowdale where we were camping. A local girl that we knew asked us for a lift as she was staying at her friend's house in Rosthwaite. On reaching Rosthwaite, we all sat talking in the car. It was pitch dark. I was sitting next to the girl in the back seat when I was pleasantly surprised to feel her get hold of my hand.

After some affectionate squeezing, she opened the car door and bade us all good night. The car door slammed shut and Tanky said with a laugh, "You can let go of my hand now, Festy." It was his hand that I had been holding in the dark. I thought at the time her hand was big and gnarled for a young woman but never suspected the truth! This gave us all a good laugh although the joke was on me. To this day whenever I see Tanky, which isn't very frequently, he often reminds me of the night he held my hand.

A few weeks later, John Smith fell off whilst leading the top pitch of Route 1 on Upper Falcon Crag and broke his ankle. He spent the next couple of months in plaster although this didn't stop him from coming out at weekends.

★ ★ ★

Summer holidays came and Paul and Richard went to the Dolomites in Bev Clarke's van along with a couple of Langdale lads, Ackers and Handsome Harry.

They climbed at the Tre Cima and had a very successful time. Richard with Paul did the Yellow Edge, the Preuss route and the Cassin route on the Piccolissima. They then did the really big one, the Comici route on the north face of the Cima Grande. Paul was still not satisfied and teamed up with another brilliant young climber of that period, Phil Gordon.

Together they did the Cassin route on the north face of the Cima Ovest in the fantastic time of four hours!

★ ★ ★

Before going away, Paul had lent me his Goldflash because my bike was still out of action.

Clive and I decided to go up to Fort William and hoping to climb on the Ben we camped in Glen Nevis next to the river. The weather was terrible and we lived in constant fear of being washed away during the nights when the sound of the rushing torrent was at its loudest. The highlight of the holiday was when we were feeding the seagulls on Loch Linnhe and the greediest one picked up a fag end that Clive had thrown away. It flew off with the still lighted dimp in its beak; this was a source of great amusement to us at the time and can only be explained away by the depth of our boredom. We camped for almost a week and it never stopped raining. One morning after a particularly wet night, we decided to retreat to the Lakes. On the way back the bike broke down during a hailstorm while crossing Rannoch Moor. We messed about cleaning the plugs and points etc then decided to push on with only one cylinder firing. South of Glasgow at a place called Lesmahagow we pulled into a biker's café for a meal and a brew. Outside the café was a line of very impressive motorbikes. When we eventually re-emerged from the café, the Goldflash was surrounded by admirers who asked what sort of speed it could do. We told them," Well over the ton," hoping that they would all go away. Remounting the bike, I started the engine and chugged off down the road to great applause from the gathered throng. We drove on one cylinder all the way to Cumbria where we eventually got it repaired. Arriving at Lower Falcon Crag in Borrowdale we set up camp. Paul and Richard were there having returned from the Alps. Listening to their tales of big routes and sunny days, we determined to go there ourselves the following year.

* * *

Pete Crew and Al Wright went to the Dolomites where they did the second ascent of what was then the hardest rock-climb in the Alps; the Phillip-Flam on the Civetta and in the Bregaglia the first British ascent of the SW Ridge of the Sciora di Fuori. They then moved on to Chamonix to do the Bonatti Pillar.

Pete, who was at Oxford University at the time, decided to drop out and with Pete Hutchinson set up a climbing shop in Manchester, which they called Mountain Equipment. The shop wasn't successful, probably due to their habit of closing up and shooting off to Wales every time they sold a pair of boots.

Crew finished up moving to Wales and Pete Hutchinson started to produce sleeping bags and Duvet jackets under the now famous name of Mountain Equipment.

During the autumn and early winter of 1961 we had many good times climbing on grit and meeting up on Saturday nights at the Miner's Arms at Eyam. This pub was popular owing to the fact that it had a jukebox and that the landlord's daughter was beautiful, or so she seemed to us after we had consumed large quantities of beer.

After the pub closed one cold, clear, moonlight night, ten of us rode on three motorbikes from Eyam to Grindleford. The first two bikes carried three each and the last bike in the line Brian Barlow's Vincent, took four.

Passing through Grindleford, an old man waiting to cross the road did a double take and it must have crossed his mind that the beers he had imbibed that night were stronger than he had at first thought.

During this period we either slept out in the open up at Lawrencefield or on the coke in the cellar of the Padley Mill café. The advantage of the cellar was that it was waterproof and we were on the spot for breakfast. The downside was that we arrived at the breakfast table looking somewhat black! The choice was either frost at Lawrencefield, or coal dust.

Another good place was a barn near the Plough Inn at Hathersage. This was a favourite because it was full of hay in the loft which was very comfortable to sleep on. Cattle were sometimes kept in the room below the loft and generated warmth as well as methane gas. To get up into the loft was something of an epic, there not being a ladder. The usual route to bed was to layback up a post which supported the roof, placing ones feet against some bales of hay.

One Saturday night Stewart Fulton and I got a lift to the Bradwell dance with Fred the Ted (Brian Fuller) and his wife Jo. Stewart was one of the many lodgers at Pat Walsh's house in Manchester and was a member of the Creagh Dhu.

He was a fit, lean, hard looking character and like other members of that club had also been an amateur champion wrestler; he was a really good guy to be with and good company. Arriving at Bradwell, I leapt over a wall looking for a place to pee and landed with a splash up to my thighs in the river. Stewart not to be outdone followed me. As it was a cold frosty night we didn't stay in there for long. We were both wearing jeans which we noticed on arriving at the dance were now a light blue from the waist down to the thigh, but changed to a dark wet look lower down. The men on the door at the village hall took one look at us and refused to let us enter. We couldn't understand why and argued our case. Just as we thought that we were near to persuading them to let us in, Fred the Ted leapt in through the doorway like a madman and yelled, "Let's rock it up." They were playing a waltz at the time. That was it. We were sent packing. Stewart tried to claim his money back but had it pointed out to him that he hadn't paid anyway.

Fred and Jo dropped us off at the Plough and we made our way to the barn. Stewart lay-backed up to the loft to join some of the lads who had arrived there earlier, I passed the sacks up to him and commenced climbing myself. As I neared the top, Clive appeared holding above his head a bale of hay. I tried to make it to the top but to no avail, he dropped the bale which swept me to the ground. Luckily I was unhurt but I lay there, still, feigning death hoping to frighten Clive into thinking that he had killed me. After a minute or so it dawned on me that my wet jeans were getting wetter. I got up quickly to find that I was covered in wet cow muck. Climbing to the loft, I was banished to the opposite side by my so-called friends. I undressed, hung the offending jeans over a beam to dry out got in my sleeping bag and fell asleep.

The next morning my jeans were frozen solid, I managed to straighten them out and struggled into them. While we were having breakfast at Mrs Thomas's café next to the fire, an agricultural smelling steam rose to the ceiling; I wasn't very popular. That day at Froggatt we saw Martin and his new girlfriend and I remember getting some strange looks!

★ ★ ★

Paul and I left the bike near Honister quarry and set off along the path which skirts the NW side of Grey Knotts. It was a cold December day and excepting a chocolate bar each, we foolishly didn't have any food with us. At Black Sail Hostel, which was closed, we stopped for a quick rest and a look up at our objective, Pillar Rock. Arriving at the crag we decided to attempt the North West Climb, a Mild VS first done by F.W. Botterill and party in 1906. Although our chosen climb wasn't technically very hard the verglassed rock tested us to our limit and by the time we reached the summit of the Low Man it was late in the afternoon. Descending the Old West Route as quickly and as safely as possible, we at last reached our gear. Packing the sacks we set off down to the valley, racing against the gathering dusk. It was almost dark as we passed the hostel and started the uphill climb out of Ennerdale.

The path that we had come along that morning had been very indistinct so we were anxious to find it before darkness closed in on us. I'm sure we must have broken the record for the climb to the valley rim and when we reached the top we both collapsed gasping for breath. After a short rest, wishing that we had brought some food with us we set off across the fell. It was pitch dark and there were snow flakes in the air and a cold wind blowing. I said at one point, "My torch has packed in." Paul realised that I must have been close to exhaustion because he said that far from packing in, my torch was giving a good light. He slowed the pace and stayed with me. Soon we were back at the bike. Paul drove and I slumped on the pillion. We arrived in Keswick dreaming of steak and kidney pie and chips. When it was set in front of me I was too tired to eat it. The only thing I wanted was bed!

★ ★ ★

Christmas again found four of us in Tanky's Morris Traveller heading for Keswick; Tanky driving, Riley in the passenger seat, me and Clive in the back. South of Milnthorpe on the A6 on a very foggy and icy Christmas Eve, a pair of headlights were suddenly coming at us on our side of the road. Tanky shouted, "Hold tight," and swung the steering wheel to the left.

The car bounced down the embankment into a ditch coming to rest almost on its side. Cakes and jam tarts and all manner of luggage and lighted cigarettes flew everywhere and panic ensued. Luckily no one was hurt but we nearly froze waiting for a truck to pull us out. Eventually we were on our way again. By some miracle there was no damage to the car and Tanky's quick thinking had saved us from injury.

Looking back now; the amazing thing about all this was that we took it in our stride, and apart from it being too late to get to Keswick before the pubs closed we thought it was a good laugh.

★ ★ ★

I can't remember the date, but we did have a club dinner at the Red Lion in Grasmere. Don Whillans was invited as guest and after dinner speaker. After a satisfactory meal Don stood up to deliver his speech. He had barely got started when Tanky who was sitting at the back of the room shouted," Would you mind standing up please." (For anyone who doesn't know, Whillans was only 5ft 2ins.) Don waited for the laughter to die down, and then replied, "See you outside, Cassius." For once he was only kidding; perhaps he had seen the size of Tanky's chest and decided to take the remark as the joke it was meant to be.

★ ★ ★

Tanky was by this time doing a lot of leather work; repairing boots and making items such as belts and rucksacks. He did some work with a local cobbler in Sheffield and they started to resole PAs. After a while, Tanky set up on his own (with some help from Bob Brigham) and opened an outdoor equipment shop in the city centre. A young man that Tanky knew, Trevor Briggs, went to work at the shop and started to come out climbing with the lads. He very quickly became well-liked and consequently became an Alpha club member.

★ ★ ★

Ted Howard did The Boulder on Cloggy followed by an epic ascent of Llithrig in a snow storm and some years later with Pete Maddocks he did Vember and Dyglyph.

Ted and Pat Fearnehough were one of the best teams in the Alpha and during the sixties decided to repeat at night everything that they had done in Derbyshire in daylight.

For five winters every Wednesday night, they did just that - the Big Plum in Chee Dale, Mortuary Steps, Aurora and Medusa at Stoney Middleton. They did the routes at Willesley Castle and High Tor all in the dark and sometimes in the snow and were once escorted by the police off the top of High Tor because their lights on the face caused concern in the valley.

Ted and Pat, sometimes with Geoff Oliver, had some good outings on Ben Nevis ice, doing Zero and Green Gullies, Cresta Run, Tower, Gardyloo and Observatory etc.

This prepared them somewhat for an attempt by Ted and Pat on the Silverhorn Face of the Jungfrau with ice like they had never seen before. Hard green ice near the top was all Pat's, as he was the best. At dawn after a bivouac Pat was delirious with cold and fatigue and tried to throw away his boots when he couldn't get them on. They descended by the Guggi route.

Chapter 8
Eastern Alps 1962

At the beginning of 1962 Paul Nunn and I decided that we would go to the Alps together that summer. This would be my first season in the big mountains but Paul had already been to the Dolomites the previous year and had done some impressive routes. Outstanding among these was the Comici route on the north face of the Cima Grande with Richard and the Cassin on the Cima Ovest with Phil Gordon, both in very fast times. Having read Hermann Buhl's book, we had big plans for our trip. We started training by doing long walks with rock-climbs along the way and by doing hard routes in the Lakes and Wales. On one of our training walks, we left the Pass by climbing Crackstone Rib and then flogged uphill to Craig Nant Peris before dropping down through The Devil's Kitchen to Idwal Slabs. After doing Tennis Shoe and Lazarus, we descended, and walked over the Gribin to the foot of the Milestone Buttress. After we had climbed the Direct Route and then scrambled up the North ridge to the summit of Tryfan, tiredness began to set in. The weather was quite hot and carrying sacks and climbing in big boots was beginning to take its toll. Dropping down from Tryfan to Bwlch Tryfan and ascending Bristly Ridge to Glyder Fach, we eventually arrived at Dinas Cromlech. After down-climbing Flying Buttress we ran down the scree and were just in time to see our lift to Llanberis leaving Ynys Ettws. We shouted and waved to no avail. Andy had waited long enough. There was nothing for it but to walk and hope that we could get a lift.

Astra on Pavey Ark was a climb that captured the imagination of quite a few of the Alpha lads and there had already been a number of ascents by teams from our club. These accounted for most of its ascents to that date.

Done in 1960 by Allan Austin it was regarded as a test piece and a very good climb. I teamed up with Wool and along with John Smith and Clive set off to attempt yet another Alpha ascent of this famous climb.

While Wool was leading the long unprotected crux pitch, John, Clive and I were laughing and joking. Wool didn't seem to appreciate this and let us know in no uncertain terms. When it was my turn to climb, I understood why Wool had been so upset. It was hard climbing with little protection. Clive led the same pitch as Wool, and John and I both led the top pitch. I was really pleased with that climb and felt that I was ready for my first visit to the Alps.

John Smith was by this time the proud owner of a mini van and early in June he, Clive, Wool and Paul went up to Scotland. They took advantage of the good weather and climbed on Carn Dearg on Ben Nevis. Clive didn't climb as he was suffering from an infected elbow, but the others, over three days, did Centurion, Sassenach and The Bat. This was an outstanding achievement for that time and served to strengthen Paul's reputation as one of Britain's top young climbers.

At Stanage during 1962 Pete Crew did Orang-Outang and The Wobbler. Clive Rowland battled his way up The Vice and Paul Nunn discovered Incursion. The same year Pete Crew did The Arete at Tintwistle Knarr, a climb of outstanding quality and Martin Boysen and I shared the lead on Svelt at Millstone Edge.

In North Wales, Barry Ingle and Pete Crew were busy doing a host of new climbs on Cloggy. This team were as prolific as Brown and Whillans had been in earlier years, producing an impressive list of first ascents. They started on 27th April with The Shadow E2, then the next day Ingle teamed up with Boysen on Daurigol E3 and the following day Soper and Crew did Bow Right-Hand HVS.

During May, Ingle and Crew did Haemogoblin and at the end of the month Crew succeeded in doing Great Wall, a climb that Joe Brown had long wanted to do having previously retreated from the top of what is now the first pitch. This line had become known as Master's Wall because of Brown's interest in it; and it was generally accepted that he would eventually climb it. Pete and Baz set out to do this wall together. Crew led the whole route in one run out, but then it rained so Baz didn't follow. They called the route Great Wall as they did not wish to appear presumptuous. This ascent established Crew as one of the leading lights of Welsh climbing.

June that same year, Martin Boysen picked a plum by climbing Pinnacle Arete E2, despite just recovering from glandular fever and being in a weakened state of health. Also in June Ingle and Crew alternated leads on Naddyn Ddu E2 and West Buttress Eliminate E3. In the Pass they opened up Dinas Mot Western Wing with their very fine climb Plexus, followed by the pleasant Gardd ; at Tremadog, Baz Ingle found Scratch Arete.

In the Lakes Les Brown and Richard McHardy did Isengard E2 on Dow Crag and on Esk Pete Crew and M Owen did the Central Pillar E2.

I was working regular nights which meant I earned more money and had more time, working four twelve hour shifts Monday to Thursday but only from 5pm until 9pm on Fridays. This gave me long weekends for climbing but less sleep, the result being that I was usually not fit for work on the following Monday night! My plan was to work until the end of June then hand in my notice and spend as long as the money lasted in the Alps. Paul was at university in Sheffield so didn't have these complications. What he did have though, was a B.S.A. Goldflash 650 cc motor bike which was to take us on our grand tour of some of the best climbing areas in Europe.

The big day arrived and I left my job at the company where I had worked since leaving school seven years ago. This in itself was an adventure but something that I had looked forward to for so long.

We had booked a ferry crossing to Ostende for Saturday 30th of June. The night before our departure we were staying at Paul's parent's house in Macclesfield to enable us to make an early start the next morning. John Smith phoned to say he had discovered this fantastic pub that sold the best Worthington E in the world, two or three pints was enough to make anyone really happy. So Friday evening, off we all went in John's mini van to the Monsal Head. John was right, it was a very good pub, an ideal venue for a farewell do. There was a good group playing and he was right about the beer; we set out to prove him wrong about the two or three pints though. Come closing time we had all consumed <u>seven</u> pints each and were decidedly the worse for wear, except for John's friend Del, who was fairly sober. Del drove us back to Buxton and left us in the van outside John's house, and then went home. Leaving Paul asleep in the back of the van, I went into the house with John who was shaking uncontrollably, due, he said, to the malaria that he had contracted whilst in the army and no doubt aggravated by the Worthington E. After putting him to bed I crept out to the van trying not to wake his dad and stepmother but I succeeded in slamming the front door on my way out. Next morning I awoke to find Paul being sick out of the back door of the van. There were two young boys playing nearby and I heard one say to the other, "Do you think he's dying?" Back at Macclesfield, tired and incapacitated by the previous night's beer, it was decided to delay our departure by one day. Sunday morning, feeling much better, the bike panniers were loaded and with a very large and heavy rucksack on my back as I was pillion passenger, we set off. Paul drove with a small sack on the tank between his knees. At last we were on our way.

Arriving in Ostende late at night and driving to Brussels, we were almost lulled to sleep by the regular bump of the tyres on the joints of the concrete sets in the road, so decided to call it a day and dossed down in a lay-by. Next morning after a brew and a bite to eat we were off again. Through to the German border at Aachen on to Cologne then down the autobahn to Karlsruhe where we cooked a meal on a derelict site in the city centre, next to a Gypsy caravan which conveniently had a water tap nearby. On again battling the wind and rain, sharing the driving until somewhere near Stuttgart, we turned off. Bumping up a dirt road, looking for somewhere to sleep, we spied a shed obviously used by workmen. We stopped the bike and found to our delight that the door was unlocked. After a welcome brew and some chocolate we settled down in our sleeping bags amongst the picks and shovels and were soon asleep.

Left right, left right, the sound of marching feet then as one voice, soldiers breaking into a German marching song. Was it a dream or had we somehow gone back in time to the Second World War? Then the shed door opened and in stepped a workman. He looked down at us in our bags and beckoned us to the door. "This is it," we thought, but then he pointed outside and we saw the source of the singing. Our resting place of last night was right beside an army barracks and a company of German soldiers was marching out through the gates. The workman asked us in English if we would like coffee and where were we heading. After a pleasant chat about motor-bikes and a drink, we thanked him and were on our way again. After Munich, we left the autobahn and headed toward the mountains now visible on the horizon. The Karwendelgebirge rose up jagged from the plain and by the time we reached the Alpine village of Scharnitz we were impressed and excited. There was a lot of new snow high up, but undeterred we pitched our tent next to a rushing mountain stream on the outskirts of town then went shopping for supplies. High on the list were cigarettes. I smoked in those days but Paul didn't, yet he never objected to me buying them out of the kitty. We had pooled all our money and I think that I had possibly contributed the lion's share as I was a wage earner and he a student so I felt justified and anyway he always ate more than I did. In fact Paul had a huge appetite and was a very fast eater;

he always finished well before me. Knowing that I invariably left some food and had a smoke after my meal, he would sit there staring at my plate like a big friendly pet dog begging for scraps.

Wednesday morning dawned bright and sunny. Breakfasting by the river we planned our next moves. Our main reason for coming to this area was the Laliderer North wall, 3000ft of extreme climbing, and a climb that we had read about in Hermann Buhl's book. This was our objective. We discussed whether to do a training route first but discarded that idea in favour of going straight onto the Laliderer before the weather got any worse. After all it was sunny, warm and we were feeling fit and strong. The side valley above our campsite was the way to the Falken Hut, our take off point for the wall, a long walk over two passes. Following the path upwards through the pine forest weighed down by our heavy sacks, counting the Stations of the Cross that marked our progress, we were thankful to reach the shrine at the top where we took a well-earned rest. The track levelled out a bit now, leading gradually up to the col. The trees became sparse due to logging work that was in progress so the mountains on either side were now visible to us. The large amounts of snow concerned us slightly as did the looks the woodcutters gave us when on their enquiry as to what we had in mind we answered, "Laliderer North Wall." We walked on and on and on. The sound of cowbells was beginning to drive me mad, my shoulders were aching and I was starting to question the wisdom of going straight onto a difficult climb. Paul seemed tireless and forged ahead. Mid afternoon, coming to the top of another col we at last got our first view of the Laliderer. Our hearts sank, the view was magnificent but our mountain was plastered in snow and the north face appeared to be glistening with ice. Sitting there on a rock, we decided there and then to go to the Dolomites. Hurrying back down the way we had come we answered the woodcutter's questioning looks with "zu Dolomitten".

Thursday afternoon we arrived at Cortina in awful weather and drove up the steep winding track towards the Tre Cima. On the last bend below the Auronzo hut we fell off into a foot of snow. Abandoning the bike we shouldered our sacks and staggered through the deepening gloom of the snowstorm up the track to the Lavaredo hut, only to find that it was full to bursting point. There were people everywhere, on tables, under tables, all the bunks were taken, it was standing room only. We managed to get served with a bowl of spaghetti each and a litre of red wine. Eventually some of the throng began to move outside to their tents and we were able to get a table each to sleep on. Next morning was dazzling, the bright sun reflecting off the carpet of snow. This was not what we had expected of the Dolomites in July! After breakfast, leaving our sacks at the hut, we set off to retrieve our tent from the bike's panniers. The scene was beautiful, range after range of yellow mountains plastered with snow on every ledge and summit. After setting up camp near the Laverado hut it was decided to go on the bike to Cortina as I needed to buy a new pair of boots, my old ones having given up and fallen to pieces. I found just what I wanted at the shop of Lino Lacidelli, the famous Italian mountaineer. By mid-day the hot sun was beginning to melt the snow off some of the peaks so having bought everything we needed, we drove back up the hill. On arriving at the Auronzo hut, it was heartening to see that a lot of the snow had cleared and only the summits were left with white caps. Back at the tent a welcome brew put new life into us and we decided to go round to look at the North walls of the Cima Grande and the Cima Ovest. I was very impressed when Paul pointed out the lines of these routes which he had done the year before, almost 2000ft high and overhanging for the first 700ft. Paul said he would like to try the direct route on the Cima Grande north face but we would have to do something else first which would get us fit and also give the conditions time to improve. That night a couple of hundred Alpini (Alpine troops) arrived and made their camp near the hut.

Early the next morning Paul and I were on the East Ridge of the Cima Grande (Dibona route). We thought we were the only ones on it until we heard a shout from above and a shower of scree narrowly missed us. There were two German climbers well above us and whereas we were on the vertical lower section, they had reached the very loose upper ledges. Informing them of our presence in no uncertain terms and climbing faster so as to decrease the distance of descent of any future stonefall, we almost caught up with them. Two thousand feet and five hours later, we arrived at the summit not long after the two Germans whom we recognised from the hut the night before. Finding an ascent book in a rusty old tin box, we wrote in our names and searched the pages to see if any famous names were present. As the top ledges and summit were quite thickly covered with snow we decided we should get a move on and started to prepare for the descent. Just a short way down from the summit our way was blocked by the Alpini who were ascending the ordinary route with a cannon! After what seemed a long wait, they were past us shouting and laughing, hauling the big gun toward the summit. In spite of the hold-up, we found there were compensations to being on the same mountain as the Italian army. Stretching downwards for hundreds of feet, were very thick fixed hemp ropes. We slid down them through waterfalls and over melting ice and were quickly off the mountain.

That night the two German climbers asked what other routes we had done in the area. I told them I was new to the Dolomites but that Paul had visited last year and had done the two big North faces amongst others. They asked Paul how long he had taken on them, to which he replied, "Four hours on the Cassin route on the Cima Ovest." Then before he could say anything further, they laughed in disbelief and one of them pointing to himself, said sarcastically, "North face of the Eiger two hours." Paul just shrugged, as much as to say," Please yourself."

All that day on the Dibona route, my left boot had been uncomfortable. It had felt a bit tight in the shop but I had assumed that it was because my left foot is slightly bigger than my right and thought it was bound to stretch. On closer examination, I found that I had two different sizes. Next day we returned to the shop where the owner quickly put the matter right. Back at the hut we were told about two Scots lads who were bivvying under some boulders up at the col and that they were hoping to do the Brandler Hass direct on the Cima Grande. This news stirred us into action and we set off to find them. Approaching the col we spied a tough looking pair, one was crouched over a Primus stove and the other collecting melt water from the foot of a nearby snow-slope. They were holding a conversation across a distance of about 50feet and sounded decidedly foreign. They could see that we were weighing them up and suspiciously enquired, in what we now recognised as a broad Glaswegian accent, what we wanted. They offered us a brew and we learned that they were members of the Creagh Dhu. Their suspicions about us melted away when we told them that we knew John MacLean, Pat Walsh and Stewart Fulton.

They introduced themselves as Wee Davy Agnew and Con Higgins. We had heard of them. They asked our names and said they had heard of a young English climber known as Tall Paul. I said, "This is Tall Paul, "and pointed to my companion. Paul asked how they felt about doing the direct and making up a team of four. They said they would think about it. That night we all went to the hut for spaghetti. The place was full again. The Alpine soldiers were there fresh from carrying guns up the Cima Grande. A good night was had by all, everyone had imbibed too much wine and there was an unofficial singing competition between Italian marching songs, German drinking songs and Scottish rebel-cum-nationalist songs, all being sung at the same time! At the end of the night after haggling with the hut guardian about the enormous wine bill, we all fell out of the door into the sobering cold night air. One of the Scots, I don't know which, tried to climb the wall of the hut to where two Italian waitresses were hanging out of the window shouting all kinds of things in Italian which we didn't understand, but assumed to be encouraging and complimentary. After a while, deciding the ascent was too difficult he gave up and we shouted goodnight to the two girls. Paul and I, having torches, escorted the Scots up the hill to their cave as the terrain wasn't really conducive to drunken travel in the dark. After satisfying ourselves that they were safely back to their beds we descended the hill to our tent and were soon asleep.

Chapter 9
Western Alps 1962

Next day the weather had changed again for the worse. We visited the Scots lads and told them that we had decided to go to the western Alps to take our chances there.

Driving to Bolzano, we treated ourselves to a restaurant meal then camped for the night. The next day, somewhere along the way, we pulled over to ask an elderly woman directions. She took one look at the mountain of gear we were carrying and exclaimed "Mama mia!" We all laughed. Continuing on our way towards Sondrio, we were overtaken by three large motorbikes, Triumphs driven by Italian lads. They signalled for us to race with them but we declined the challenge, pointing to our luggage. At the end of a long straight, they stopped and waited for us, wanting to take a look at Paul's bike. Arriving at the village of Promontogno, in the Bregaglia area of Switzerland, we were immediately taken by the unspoilt beauty of the steep wooded side valley leading up to the jagged peaks of the Badile, Cengalo and Sciora. The main Val Bregaglia which leads to the Maloja Pass is home to the medieval villages of Bondo, Promontogno and Vicosoprano and is a special place even to the Swiss. Being mainly owned by farming families who have refused all efforts to get them to sell their land, it has remained picturesque and unspoilt, in contrast to the town of St Moritz 20 miles up the road beyond the Maloja where the rich and famous take their mountain vacations. Stopping the bike we looked up at the N.E. Face of the Piz Badile. We were disappointed to see that there was a lot of ice glistening on the north ridge in the late afternoon sun. This meant that our objective, the Cassin route on the NE face, was probably out of condition. Driving through the narrow streets of Bondo the noise of the exhaust reverberated off the walls as though announcing our arrival. On up the rough and winding forest track, passing through a couple of rough hewn tunnels, we eventually crossed a wooden bridge over the torrent which had its source several thousands of feet higher amongst the glaciers and snowfields. Driving slowly, trying to avoid hitting the largest rocks, we came to a small parking area at the end of the track. This was where the footpaths to the Sciora and Sass Fioura huts started. Not able to go any further on the bike, we parked it and crossed a wooden footbridge over the rushing glacier river to pitch our tent on the far bank. After our evening meal, lying in the tent discussing what to do the next day, Paul produced from his rucksack descriptions of routes in that area. These he had copied onto note paper from an Italian guidebook, all in Italian, guidebooks to this area being unavailable in English at that time. The usefulness of these descriptions was called into question when it was found that neither of us could read more than a dozen or so words.

In those days the Cassin Route on the N.E. Face of the Badile had a big reputation and although there had been a number of ascents by continental climbers there had been very few by British climbers.

We were hoping to make what we thought would be the third British ascent, but later learned that this had been done by Ted Howard and Barry Pedlar in 1960.

This face had first been climbed by the great Italian mountaineer Ricardo Cassin with friends Esposito and Ratti. They were joined by two other Italian climbers and achieved success in storm conditions taking three bivouacs but at the expense of the lives of two of his companions who died of exhaustion and hypothermia. The second ascent by the French guide Gaston Rebuffat and Bernard Pierre was also an epic, taking three whole days. The dramatic history of the climb and our lack of a detailed English description gave it an air of great seriousness. We were aware that Herman Buhl had climbed it solo in four and a half hours but he was in a class of his own!

Waking to a dull and cloudy day, we decided to pack our sacks with food and climbing gear and go up to the Sciora Hut, where we could decide what route to do when viewing the mountains from close quarters. With our heavy loads the steep walk up through the forest was very tiring and seemingly never ending. Taking our time and many rests, drinking in the majestic scenery, we eventually reached a bend on the path above the tree-line where a large slab of rock faced us. Knowing Oliver Woolcock, a good friend of ours, would be coming here to attempt the Cassin route in two weeks time, we decided to leave a message for him scratched on the slab, it read, "Tired, Youth?" We walked on, chuckling, hoping that he would see it just as he reached this most tiring section of the walk. Knowing that we had been there before him, he would realise who had written it and curse us all the way to the hut.

The mountains were cloaked in clouds. The Badile NE face in particular was hidden from our view from about half height. Arriving at the Sciora Hut, we found that there was plenty of room, a guide and his client being the only paying guests. Paul and I claimed a place each in the dormitory then returned to the eating area for a coffee and a bought meal. The hut guardian was an old lady who came up in the spring to spend all the summer there. Her grand-daughter, who was around 19 or 20, helped with the cooking and other chores. She was a typical dark-haired Italian girl, very attractive and from all accounts an experienced climber.

The guide asked us which climb we were planning to do; we told him the Cassin route on the Badile. He shook his head and said the face wasn't in condition. We said we would have a look anyway as we could always come back if we didn't like the look of it. After the meal we made our preparations for the following day then retired early to bed. As is usual for me before any big event, I didn't get much sleep and in the warmth of the hut I drifted in and out of consciousness. Too soon it was time to get up. Creeping downstairs we were surprised to find the young woman had risen before us and was busy making our breakfast. The time was 3am when we put on our boots, shouldered our sacks and stepped out into a dark, cold morning. Waving goodbye to the girl, we set off, our head torches lighting our way down the path towards the moraine. The going was very tiring. After crossing the river swollen with melt-water and negotiating some wet boiler-plate slabs, we arrived at the first of three steep dune-like and extremely loose moraines where large boulders supported by rock dust and rubble waited to pounce on the unwary. These were followed by a long narrow glacier leading up below the N.E. Face to the start of our route. Kicking steps and regretting only having brought one ice axe between us and no crampons, we made slow progress up the steep hard snow. At the foot of the face, we stopped for a snack and a quick brew which went down very well. At this point, I would like to describe our equipment, which was quite basic even by the standards of the day. We had two full-weight nylon ropes both 150 ft long and quite heavy, an assortment of pegs, two hammers, some slings and about 20 karabiners. Divided between our two sacks, we had a stove, food and water, a billy-can and warm clothing in case of bad weather or bivouac. This consisted of a duvet jacket each and in the absence of thermals, pyjama trousers. We climbed in boots, corduroy trousers, thick shirts, sweaters and gabardine smock-style anoraks.

It was just about light when we roped up. Above us a vast sweep of overlapping slabs rose up to meet a canopy of dark cloud halfway up the face from which large snowflakes were beginning to gently fall. What should we do? Our discussion went something like this: "He who always watches the weather gets nothing done but he who ignores the warnings courts disaster!" The decision was made to press on for a couple of hundred feet to see how the day would develop. A steep corner and a few diagonal pitches up slabs led to the site of the first Cassin bivouac. The face had steepened again and we had an impressive view down to the snowfield some hundreds of feet below. By that time the snow had stopped falling and the cloud appeared to be lifting so we decided to go for it. The view across to the north ridge of the Cengalo put these mountains in perspective and made us realise the size of our undertaking.

Leading through, making good progress, we soon arrived at the snow patch which used to be a permanent feature at approximately half height on this face. Stopping here for a bite to eat we were impressed by the wall above which reared up into the cloud. Time to move on. A steep crack led directly upward then out right. Paul tackled it confidently. It was bristling with pitons. Climbing swiftly, clipping the occasional peg, he was soon out of sight. A tug on the rope told me it was my turn. The rock was steep but superbly rough in texture. The exposure was impressive. I joined Paul at the foot of a steep corner capped by an overhang. I led 70 feet to the roof, which caused me to stop and ponder the best way round it. Turning it on the left, feeling grateful for the abundance of pitons in situ, I arrived at a stance. The angle eased off again and a few more pitches led to the foot of the long chimney system which leads towards the summit ridge. The climbing here got quite serious, the cracks being filled with snow and ice. At first, we were puzzled by the absence of pitons, then realised they were there, but unreachable under a thick covering of ice. We felt unprotected but fought our way upward, the strenuous climbing helping to keep us warm. At the top of the chimney, our progress was barred by a bulging icy wall. The obvious way was out to the left, and according to our description led to a long traverse to the central couloir. Because of our lack of crampons and our guess that the couloir would be iced up we decided to take a more direct line up delicate slabs. From the stance, Paul cautiously moved out on verglassed rock, round the left arête of the chimney, then climbed direct up slabs right of the couloir. Out of sight round the corner he was obviously experiencing some difficulty as the rope snaked out very slowly. I shouted up to let him know that he was nearly out of rope. "How much is there?" he asked. " About 20ft, " I replied. "There's a stance 40ft above me. Take the belay off, we'll have to move together." I did as he asked and climbed very carefully on the iced rock hoping that he had clipped some pegs on the way up. After what seemed an eternity, I was relieved to hear a peg going in. At the stance, we agreed that pitch must have been HVS. Paul had sunk the belay peg in up to the hilt. I led through towards the summit ridge. When Woolcock passed that way a couple of weeks later, suspecting it was our peg, he tried to remove it but soon gave up. He knew Paul didn't give away gear easily and that if it had been removable, it wouldn't have stayed there. At the ridge we turned left and climbed the last few feet to the summit. We had done one of the six classic north faces of the Alps, 3000ft, graded TD Superior.It had taken us eight hours. We had been the only ones on the face so were not held up at all, in fact we didn't see anyone else all day on the whole of the mountain.

At the summit ridge we were hit by a strong wind so deciding to forego the brew that we had promised ourselves we began to descend as quickly as possible by the North Ridge. Somehow, we got onto the SW face on very loose rock, enormous loose flakes but nothing solid enough to belay on. Deciding that it was too dangerous we retraced our steps to the summit and went down the Italian side, reaching the glacier at dusk. We could see the lights of the Gianetti Hut and following these arrived there after dark feeling very tired.

The guide and his client from the Sciora Hut the night before were there and seemed pleased to see us. He asked if we had climbed the Cassin Route and we told him we had. Both he and the hut guardian said," Bravo, bravo. Bad conditions, much ice. " We agreed about the ice, but thought conditions could have been worse. They asked us our ages, I told them,"22 for me, 19 for Paul."

"Ah, Bambino!" they said pointing to Paul. We all laughed and they poured us some red wine. As the night wore on they kept on pouring it. We thought, this is great, until at the end of the evening they gave us the bill. We had been convinced that they were so impressed by our ascent in what they had said were bad conditions, that they were treating us to free wine. No such luck! We paid up reluctantly and went to bed. A little later we were awakened by a group of around a dozen Italian youths shouting and wrestling on the dormitory floor.

Ignoring them at first we tried to get back to sleep. Suddenly there was a loud bellow, "Shut up or I'll flatten the lot of you." There in the middle of the floor stood Paul, fist clenched and raised. Silence descended.

Next morning after a little lie in, we returned to the Sciora Hut over the Passo Bondo, our legs aching from the previous day's exertions. Abseiling off the top of the pass down steep mixed ground we leaped across the Bergschrund on to the Bondo glacier. This was the first real glacier that either of us had been on and there were a lot of crevasses. Foolishly, through lack of experience, we didn't rope up and received some funny looks from a party of Swiss climbers coming up in the opposite direction. At the hut we were told by the guardian's grand-daughter that she had watched us through binoculars the previous day and seemed really pleased that we had done the NE face. Both she and the old lady appeared relieved to see us back safely. I think they had been worried about us. Saying goodbye to them, we set off for the valley. They continued waving to us until we reached the bend in the path where the hut disappears from view. At the tent we ate the remainder of our food and slept right through to the next morning when some German climbers arrived and pitched their tent near us. They told us they had come from Chamonix and that the weather was bad there. This news caused us to change our plans as the weather in the Bregaglia seemed to have taken a turn for the better. After a day sampling the delights of St Moritz and buying in fresh supplies we returned to our camp by the river. Whilst Paul fried steak and onions and chips, I collected wild strawberries in the woods. We had them smothered in cream for desert. What a feast! The evening was spent trying to read Italian route descriptions and planning for the next couple of days.

Back on the path to the Sciora we ruefully read the scratched message on the rock, "Tired, Youth?" The laugh was on us. At the hut were two English climbers, Trevor Jones and Jim Swallow, whom we knew slightly They had just arrived and were planning to do the Flat Iron Ridge, graded TD, and asked if we would like to make up a team of four. Knowing that they were experienced Alpinists who had also climbed in the Himalayas, we thought it would be a good chance for us to learn from their experience.

Six-o-clock next morning plodding unroped up the approach glacier, Paul and I were content to bring up the rear. Suddenly hearing a shout from above we were just in time to see Trevor disappear down a crevasse. Luckily it was quite a shallow cleft and we were able to reach down to pull him out unhurt. It was then that Paul and I made the unspoken decision to go into the lead! Leaving our sacks on a large ledge at the start of the rock climbing, we had a last drink of water and set off.

The climb was very pleasant, 1,000ft of slabs on perfect rock following a whale back ridge. Paul and I went first leading alternately; the climbing was mainly grade 4 with the occasional grade 5 pitch and well protected with in situ pegs. At the top where we waited for Trevor and Jim the view all round the cirque of peaks was tremendous and we were able to see clearly the route we had planned for tomorrow. The other two joined us and we prepared for the descent. Having four ropes between us, we decided to use two for abseiling on, and a rope between each pair for safety. Ten abseils later we arrived safely at the ledge where we had left our sacks. Then it was back to the hut for food and wine. It had been a good day. The hut was now full of climbers from the local area as it was Saturday night. One small group wore red sweaters with a white badge on one arm. The grand-daughter told us they from Lecco, members of the same club that Riccardo Cassin belonged to, "The Ragni."

At four the next morning the two of us were threading our way through the many boulders to the foot of the S.W. Ridge of the Fuori di Sciora. This ridge reared up 2,500 ft to the summit and was graded TD. The righthand side had a large scar from a rock-fall which had obliterated the original route. Our objective was fairly new and had only been climbed once by a British party (Pete Crew and Al Wright if my information is correct). It was reportedly very loose as a result of the rockfall. The morning was beautifully clear and starlit for a change, with no trace of the cloud experienced on the previous two climbs.

Starting on the left of the ridge we climbed until a 70ft artificial pitch with all the pegs in situ led round to the right hand side, across and then up a steep wall. Good rock so far. The climbing was around grade IV to V/ V+ and we moved quickly. Suddenly we came to the loose stuff, big tottering flakes etc. The sky began to darken and the sound of distant thunder quickened our pace as pitch followed pitch. Soon we were in a long chimney behind a massive flake about 400ft high which appeared to be just stuck on the steep sidewall. The chimney started at about 8ft in width and got narrower the higher we climbed. At first we scaled the back and side walls, then as it narrowed, we chimneyed, feeling very insecure, imagining that the whole thing could come off at any time. Then as it grew narrower still, we wedged, lay-backed and eventually hand-jammed. We were thankful for our gritstone training. Some years later the big flake detached itself from the rest of the mountain creating, so I'm told, what is now a very loose climb.

As we emerged out of the chimney at last, a series of easy angled grooves and corners led to the summit. Our summit brew was interrupted by a flash of lightning and a loud clap of thunder. We were on an exposed ridge and could feel the electricity all around; time to move. At times like this, the advice is to discard any ironmongery, but we needed it to get down so we took the chance. It started to snow heavily. Our descent route led down slabs. Abseiling we ended up in a steep couloir which was split by a rognon and fanned out lower down into several other couloirs. Crossing a deep Cresta Run-type snow chute, dodging the large rock toboggans that were whistling down at irregular intervals we reached the comparative safety of the rognon (a rock island dividing the snow -filled gully.) Soaked to the skin, with wet and heavy ropes and fingers cold from our wet gloves we descended carefully. It would be foolish to invite an accident by rushing things at this point. The snow was very wet and there were occasional avalanches. At least the lightning had stopped and that made us feel a bit better. Eventually, as we reached the nose of the rognon, a dodgy looking flake provided us with a last abseil to the easier snowfield below us. Belaying to a second dodgy flake, I paid out the rope for Paul who went first carrying the sack. We reasoned that if the flake held him, it would hold my lesser weight. He clipped a peg halfway down for my benefit then carried on to the bottom. I quickly joined him, then running down the last snowfield to rocky ground, we emerged into bright sunlight. Oh, how good it felt. We lay there on a rock, our clothes steaming. Looking back at our mountain we could see it was beginning to clear. Pretty soon the whole route was visible and we could see water pouring down it. Down we went to the hut where the only food that we had left was a bag of green beans, which we boiled in a large pan. Then, almost gagging, we forced down the most unappetising meal that I have ever eaten. Feeling stronger, we set off on the descent to our tent in the woods. The walk down was very hard going after such a long day but what made it worse was the knowledge that we were returning to a tent that was devoid of food. As we neared the wooden bridge which led across the river to our camp, we could hear voices behind us. Dropping our sacks at the tent, Paul said," I'm going to see if they have any food to sell us." As he went back across the bridge I shouted, "See if they've any fags."

I could hear them talking above the sound of the river and laughing loudly. Paul came back with all kinds of goodies to eat and six cigs for me. He told me it had been the lads from the Ragni club going home after the weekend. They had emptied their sacks and given us every scrap of food they had left.

Arriving in Chamonix a few days later, we were pleased to find perfect sunny weather. Setting up camp at the Biolay campsite we met up with Richard McHardy and Jim Teasdale who had arrived after a visit to Norway where they had experienced poor weather. They had moved on to the Kaisergebirge in Austria where Richard teamed up with another climber and did the Dulfer Route on the Fleischbank in stormy conditions. They then left for Chamonix and arrived a day or two before us. Also at the Biolay were a newly married Margaret and Les Brown along with Paul Ross and a crowd of other climbers that we knew, including some Rock and Ice members. It was great to be among a large group of friends and acquaintances again.

Chamonix is a very busy town on the north side of Mont Blanc and is a mecca for mountaineers and rock-climbers from all over the world. In winter it is a famous ski resort. Originally it must have been a beautiful alpine village but the quality of the climbing and skiing in this area has attracted a lot of development, some of which is out of character with the splendour of the surroundings. Being young, and not knowing the Chamonix of the golden age of alpinism, the commercialism didn't bother us; after all, the mountains were still there to climb and we weren't averse to a good night on the town when we were in the valley.

One morning as Pete Muscroft was emerging from his tent rubbing the sleep from his eyes, he was confronted by a Cambridge University climber who was looking for other English climbers to team up with. For some reason known only to himself he assumed that Muscroft was a Frenchman and proceeded to address him in broken French. He said, "Pardon, monsieur, parlez-vous anglais?" to which Pete replied, "I speak it like a native, old chap." This caused great laughter from the other lads and embarrassment to the Cambridge student.

Paul was keen to get back on the hill as soon as possible but I felt the need to rest up a bit. So Paul with Les, Richard and Blond Rodney went up to do the east face of The Capucin which was a big aid route overlooking the Vallee Blanche.

Paul Ross wasn't climbing as he was suffering with a bad back so he and I spent a lot of time at the Plage swimming and improving our tans. Paul had lived for a while in Chamonix and knew the place well. (In 1958 Paul, along with Don Whillans, Chris Bonington, Hamish MacInnes and two Austrians, Walter Philip and Richard Blach, had done the first British ascent of the Bonatti Pillar on the Dru.) He introduced me to various night clubs where we would go after late sessions at the Bar Nationale. There we would try to get to know some of the good looking girls who frequented them, usually without luck. After all, what self respecting Frenchwoman would want anything to do with English men who had spent the last few weeks living rough and whose command of the French language was limited to "Une grand biere, s'il vous plait."

The weather was fabulously hot, with sun every day and clear blue skies. We would rise when the sun got too hot to stay in the tent and go down to the trough near the entrance to the campsite for a wash. Afterwards, a visit to the little shop near the Montenvers railway station to buy bread for breakfast was always entertaining. It was owned by an ancient Frenchwoman who was heavily made up, she had bleached blonde hair and bright red lipstick, and acted as though she was 21. We christened her Madame Tussaud! After breakfast it was off to the Plage stopping only to check the weather forecast and the barometer at the Guides' office. The Plage was a large artificial lake cum swimming pool with lawned areas for sunbathing. There was the luxury of a refreshments shop and changing rooms and an exercise area in a clearing in the wooded surroundings. The whole of the Plage was surrounded by a six foot high fence and the entrance was through a turnstile for the sum of four francs. That is unless you were a British, American or German climber. For these the entrance was over the fence in the woods, then a stroll out into the open trying to look as innocent as possible. After an exhausting day looking up at the mountains from by the pool and exercising on the ropes, rings and parallel bars, it was time to go down to the Mont Blanc tunnel canteen for a slap-up meal. The tunnel wasn't yet complete and the workers ate their meals in the canteen at vastly subsidised prices, so did most of the climbers. They were really good meals and more importantly, cheap! Then after the walk back to town, it was table football at the Nationale Bar.

The owner of the bar was probably the only Frenchman in Chamonix who was liked by and got on with the English climbers. He got to know all the lads and was always welcoming. He never seemed to mind when things got a bit rowdy later on as the nights developed. Maurice had very poor eyesight but even so he had an eye for the ladies, if you will pardon the pun. There were always two women behind the bar, one was his wife and it was rumoured amongst the lads that the other was his mistress. My first night there, after quite a few grand bieres, I climbed the stairs intent on visiting the toilet on the first floor. At the landing I was undecided where it was located as all the doors were closed and there was no indication as to which was the right one. Opening the first door on the right, I was surprised to find, not the toilets but a man and a woman in bed together. Embarrassed I backed out of the door muttering what I thought to be apologies. My French wasn't very good, so instead of saying "Pardon, Monsieur," I said "Merci, monsieur!" From then on I got funny looks from Maurice whenever I went into his bar.

The lads came back from the Capucin having had a bit of an epic ascent experiencing some big rock falls. They were all in need of some rest days, so it was a bit more sunbathing time for me. When at last, we decided it was time to do another climb, Les and Paul Nunn said we should all go onto the west face of the Dru and asked Richard and me to make up a four, two ropes of two. Both Richard and I thought it was a bit too ambitious because although I was fit from the Bregaglia, it was my first time in Chamonix and Richard had only done the one route that season plus the route in the Kaisergebirge. We felt we needed to do another climb before embarking on something as serious as the West Face of the Dru.

Les, being the most experienced, tried to convince us we would be OK, but to no avail. We had made up our minds to do the north ridge of the Peigne with two lads from Sheffield University, Sid Clarke and Nev Crowther. We felt that this would be more in keeping with our experience or lack of it. At first, we had tried to persuade Les and Paul to do an easier route but they argued sensibly, that as the weather was exceptionally good we should take advantage of it and go for the West Face, whilst we had the chance.

Next day Paul and Les set off for the Dru; Richard, Sid, Nev and I went up on the telepherique to the Plan Des Aiguilles.

The weather was still fantastic so we were sleeping out in the open by the side of the small lake below the Aiguilles. We had our evening meal and prepared our sacks for the following day then turned in. Lying in our sleeping bags, looking at the marvellous view across the valley and listening to the rushing glacier streams and the distant sound of rock falls, we fell asleep.

All too soon it was time to get up. It was another bright dawn. Nev prepared breakfast while the rest of us lay in our sleeping bags trying to raise the energy to get out. Eventually we were ready to go, a sack and one axe between each pair, no bivvy gear as we expected to be up the route and back down sometime that afternoon.

Waiting at the start of the climb for Nev, who had developed a bad case of the runs, the rest of us didn't feel so good either. We put it down to the pilchard sandwiches that Nev had served up for breakfast.

The Aiguille de Peigne is at the right hand end of the chain of rock peaks overlooking Chamonix before reaching the Midi and Mont Blanc. The north ridge is a 2000ft rock-climb graded TD, the first half of which is quite easy. Broken rocks led to a couloir which was part rock and part ice. At one point I was crossing an icy bulge when I noticed a rucksack embedded a couple of feet under the ice. It was in too deep to recover but we suspected it belonged to Les Brown who had dropped his sack from the upper part of this route a couple of years before, losing his camera and photos in the process. It would have been nice to get it back for him but it would have taken far too much time, that's if it was at all possible. The couloir finished behind an enormous gendarme (rock tower) on the ridge below the start of the difficulties. The next 700ft or so followed a steep corner consisting of all kinds of crack and chimney climbing. Richard and I climbed together leading through. We went first, a few pitches ahead of Nev and Sid. At one point on my turn to lead I went round to a ledge on the left to a very exposed stance below a bulging wall up which the next pitch lay.

This was the only artificial section on the whole route and as we hadn't taken any etriers with us Richard had to do it on slings and free climb as much as he could.

We were making good time and were well in front of the other two lads. Arriving at the summit just after midday, we made ourselves comfortable on the slabby rocks. Lying there in the scorching sun looking at the magnificent scenery all around us, waiting for the others, we ate some food, drank some water and I smoked some cigarettes. Although Richard didn't normally smoke he tried a couple of mine. I think he was curious to see if it enhanced the enjoyment we were experiencing atop our lofty throne. Looking across at the Dru, wondering about Les and Paul and estimating whereabouts they would be on the west face, we heard shouts from below.

A little while later Nev and Sid appeared and joined us on our airy perch. Obviously the others wanted to spend time on the summit soaking up the scenery and the sun. Richard and I were in agreement that another hour wouldn't do any harm - after all, the guidebook said the descent was straightforward and gave an approximate time of three hours so we kept them company.

Roughly an hour and a half later, abseiling from the summit block down the south west side to a large ledge, I was quickly joined by the others. Consulting the guidebook which said, "Descend an icy couloir," we peered over the end of the ledge into an uninviting abyss. Richard said, "That can't be the way, let's abseil down in the same direction that we came from the summit." Everyone agreed this was the best idea. So down we went. Abseil followed abseil mixed with scrambling. At one point, whilst trying to retrieve the rope, it stuck on something and we couldn't budge it. All of us pulled together but it still wouldn't move. There was about 50ft already down on the ledge and the other end was 50ft above our heads. The wall was unclimbable but we had to get the rope back or we could be in a dangerous position. Without further ado Nev went hand over hand up the rope. If the snagged rope had come loose before he reached the end above our heads he could have fallen and been injured. It was a calculated risk and Nev took it while the rest of us stood and watched. He was half-way up before we could stop him, but the rope held and he continued up until he could loosen it, then abseiled back down to join us on the ledge. This time the rope ran smoothly down. We scrambled down easy rock into a large basin, crossed under a pinnacle on the right and into a couloir. It was getting late with light fading fast. After another abseil, Sid and I coiled the ropes while Richard and Nev set off down an easy-looking ramp. Following behind them we met Richard coming back up through the advancing dusk. He told us they had reached a point above the snow where Nev had judged it possible to jump down. Richard had disagreed and turned round to come back up to us. As it was now too dark to descend further we decided to spend the night where we were.

Nev shouted up that he was on the snow and in one piece and tried to persuade us to follow him but we declined.

It was going to be a long night. Sid and I had three cigarettes left between us, the only food was a jar of marmite and the only water was a trickle down the rock behind our heads. We put on all our spare clothing, sat on the ropes and sacks and cursed ourselves for spending too much time on the summit.

It was a clear cold night. We could see the lights twinkling down in Chamonix and imagined the lads enjoying a night in the National Bar. We thought about Nev in his sleeping bag by the tarn, eating and brewing up, then we thought of Les and Paul on the Dru in a similar position to us, and that made us feel better. What we didn't know was that Les had strained a muscle in his stomach a good way up the face and that he and

Paul had decided to retreat and at that moment were in the National wondering what had happened to us.

The Marmite was all gone, the fags were finished and the trickle of water had frozen. We dozed fitfully. I awoke at one point and my jaw was locked. I'd been sleeping with my head resting on the rock behind me with my mouth open, and it had kind of frozen in that position. After a few minutes of massage it began to work properly again. I looked beyond the Midi to Mont Blanc and it was so clear, I was certain that dawn was breaking. I woke the others saying, "Come on, let's get ready to move, it'll soon be light." Just at that moment the full moon appeared from behind the mountains at our backs. Sid said, "Get back to sleep, it's only midnight."

At first light we descended the remaining 300ft of the gully, which after all proved to be easy, but we couldn't have known that the night before, so convinced ourselves it had been the right decision to bivvy.

Approaching our little camp by the lake we could see Nev curled up in his sleeping bag. We thought, the lazy beggar, he could have had a brew ready for us. To our delight we discovered that he was kidding us and that he had porridge and a brew ready. He had heard us coming and pretended to be asleep

Chapter 10
Tragedy on the Yellow Edge 1962

Back in Chamonix, we were pleased to find that Tanky, Clive and Arthur had arrived from the Dolomites, but they were bearers of bad news. Graham Evans, who had driven out in the van with them from England, had died whilst climbing at the Tre Cima.

All four of them had set off to do their first route, the Yellow Edge on the Piccolissima. Graham knew of a variation done the year before by Pat Walsh and wished to do this.

Part way up the climb after a long traverse to a small and awkward stance, for some reason the lads had decided to abseil off. Graham said that Pat had descended from this same point to a ledge system and had found an easy way off.

Graham went first down the overhanging wall below the stance. He was supposed to swing in to another stance lower down but went a long way past it with nothing below him for 600ft. Graham panicked. Clive shouted down for him to wrap the rope round his leg to enable him to attach prussic loops. Still panicking he wrapped the rope around his waist but was too scared to attach the loops. He hung there pleading for help. The three above him, belayed to a peg with insufficient rope to go to his assistance, could do nothing but try to calm him. (Nowadays with harnesses and friction devices the situation would have been much easier.) This went on for some considerable time. Their predicament had not gone unnoticed down at the Laverado Hut, and a team of guides started out to assist them. The guides arrived at the small stance with hundreds of metres of rope. One guide set off for the summit with the three lads and the others fastened a rope to Graham's abseil rope and started to lower him.

When the lads arrived back at the hut they were shocked to discover that Graham was dead. It seems that every time a new rope was attached, the bounce when lowering had tightened the rope at Graham's waist and he had died of asphyxiation.

This was a tragic incident and serves to underline the risks that we run when attempting big and difficult climbs. The loss of a good friend in a mountain accident is very sad and should remind us that one small mistake or misjudgement can have dire consequences no matter how experienced the climber.

Clive and Tanky and Arthur had to try to put this behind them in the knowledge that they had done everything possible to help Graham.

Together they climbed the East face of the Grepon and Clive did the north ridge of the Peigne with Barry Ingle before deciding to go home.

Paul asked me if I wanted to do another route with him, possibly the Walker Spur. Les had done the Walker in 1959 so we asked him what he thought. He pointed out that the conditions were perfect and urged us to have a go at it. The next day after shopping for supplies, we were preparing to set off when a roll of thunder sounded over Mont Blanc and the sky was streaked with mares' tails. That was it, the weather had changed drastically, and the season was over. Next day, we dropped the tent, loaded up the bike and headed home.

Chapter 11
Mrs Tangye's Boys
(Late 1962—Early 63)

After a few days at my parents' house getting my washing done and enjoying some home cooking, it was time to move off again. Paul arrived on the bike and suggested we go to do a climb that he'd had in mind for some time. Leaving the bike at the Snake Inn, feeling fit from our alpine holiday, it only took us three quarters of an hour to walk up to Kinder north edge where Paul led the first ascent of his fine route Legacy. We then raced back down to the bike and drove to Keswick. There we met up with the rest of the lads, Richard, Clive, Wool, Jim Teasdale and Bill Bowker - Bivouac Bill as he was nicknamed because of his ability to sleep no matter where on alpine bivouacs. Bill came from Blackburn and had packed in a good job as a foreman to spend the summer in the Alps like the rest of us and had done some good routes. We all lived in a barn at Threlkeld along with some others who we knew and spent days either climbing or touring the cafes and pubs of Keswick depending on the weather. Paul Ross lived in Keswick so we spent time in Borrowdale with him, where he pointed out the test pieces for us to climb. Saturday nights in Keswick were always pub crawls with the George and the Lake Road Vaults being favourites, then it was off to the Threlkeld or Rosthwaite dance to try to do the Twist and get to know the local girls.

Martin Boysen and his girlfriend were in Keswick and it was about this time when he went back to Manchester that he started to climb with the Alpha.

After a week or two some of the lads drifted back home to work or to university, leaving Jim, Bill, Richard and me at the barn. By now we were running short of money and had no transport so all four of us decided to move in with my cousin Barry who lived in a very small two-birth caravan on the outskirts of Keswick. Barry worked at Threlkeld quarry as a fitter and seemed to enjoy his life in Keswick. This made us think that we too might find it a good place to live and work so we paid a visit to the local labour exchange. Richard and I got work on the Keswick by-pass and Bill started as a labourer on a building site at Rosthwaite in Borrowdale. Jim got a job with the council, driving a road roller.

Having run out of cash and having to work a week in hand we were in dire straits.

Then like a revelation, we remembered that the previous Christmas we had buried some left over cans of food in a wall near Ashness Bridge. With visions of a feast we hot footed it to Ashness, trying hard to remember where the treasure was buried. After a few abortive attempts to find it, we at last struck gold. There were quite a number of cans, more than we remembered, so we were delighted, the only snag being some of the cans were punctured and all of them had lost their labels!

For the next few days, meals were a lottery. Richard and I would open a couple of cans for breakfast. One might be peas the other strawberries and the same situation again at lunchtime.

Midway through that week one of the lads, I have forgotten who, saw an advert for four working men to be lodgers at a house on Main St. Richard, Bill, Jim and I went to the house that evening and knocked on the door. A small wiry woman answered our knock and asked what we wanted. We told her we had seen her advert and asked if she still had vacancies. She said she had. Introducing herself as Mrs Violet Tangye, she told us that she charged £4 a week full board, soap and towels provided. Whilst talking with her, we noticed that she never stopped rapidly blinking, almost talking with her eyes shut. At first I found this a bit unnerving but decided to overlook it when she suggested we all go there the following evening at 6.30 for a trial meal.

All we could think and talk about the next day at work was the coming evening.

At 6.30 on the dot, the four of us were seated at a large table in the front room. Another man from the bypass job (another Bill) was seated at the table. He was in his sixties and said he lodged there and that Mrs Tangye was a really good cook! Two other men from Carlisle who worked for the telephone company and who also lodged there agreed. We couldn't wait to get started.

The meal arrived, soup and bread to start. The main course was chicken, three veg and as many potatoes that we could eat. This was followed with apple pie and custard followed by coffee and cheese and biscuits. She was a good cook!!_We signed on the dotted line but wondered if she had just put on a show to get us hooked.

Mrs Tangye was a widow and was probably about 60 years old but it was difficult to know as she was very active. She had a cleaning job at the council offices every morning starting at about 6 o'clock, before coming back to cook breakfast for everyone.

During the next few days we found out that it hadn't been the show that we had at first thought. Breakfasts were three courses, cereal, porridge or juice. A full cooked main course was followed by toast and jam, tea or coffee. We had a packed lunch to take to work then a three course meal at night and if we got back from the pub early enough Mrs Tangye would make us some supper. We could have as many baths as we liked all soap and towels provided and we were made to feel at home.

Richard, Bill, Jim and I shared the large front bedroom, a single bed in each corner. Old Bill had a room next to ours and we could hear him shouting out in his sleep. "OK, Sandy, I'll move that barrow now, then I'll do some pointing". (Sandy was the general foreman on the bypass.) Poor old guy, he must have been worrying about work. He was a single man and his home was wherever he lodged. The two men from Carlisle lodged four nights a week then went home for weekend.

Richard was a joiner by trade so he worked in the shuttering gang. I was labouring and worked with all the navvies shovelling concrete and anything else that was heavy. A few of the men lived on the site in their cars or vans and used to spend all their wages on drink. The road we were building had to cross over the River Derwent which meant a bridge had to be built on a steel framework which could be dangerous in the wet with the river in spate. One slip and we could end up in Bassenthwaite Lake. Each night Richard and I would compare notes as to who'd had the hardest day. At the end of the second week my right wrist had swelled up and was very painful. I couldn't even strike a match to light a cigarette. I went to the doctor who gave me a note and said, "Take a week off."

When I took the note to the foreman, he kindly told me. "Come into work and I'll put you on a light job so that you won't lose money."

I told Richard this when I saw him that evening and he said. "He'll probably put you in the stores." The next day, I was put to work with Richard as joiner's mate. I rubbed it in about being put on a light job!

Every morning about 8. o'clock, a lorry pulled up outside our lodgings. On the back was a gang of men who worked with us. This was our lift to work. They all stood there on the truck muffled up against the weather and looked down through the window gesticulating for us to hurry. Richard and I were usually finishing off our breakfast and had to either rush out bread in hand to get the lift, or walk the mile or so from the digs along the riverside to arrive late at the site. If the morning was bright and sunny, I usually chose the latter, drinking in the scenery and wishing I was going to the hills instead of to work. We worked a six-day week and it was hard work at that. Sunday morning we could lie in a bit as Mrs Tangye cooked breakfast a bit later.

As it was winter, the weather wasn't very good for climbing and after six days on the bypass, neither were we! The winter Sundays were short and all too soon, we were back to work. We did a bit of climbing but not as much as we had imagined we would. Instead, we took things easy on Sunday mornings, with perhaps a walk in the afternoon or a visit to the pubs and cafes if the weather was bad.

One evening whilst we were drinking at the Lake Road Vaults, in walked an American climber whom we had met in Chamonix during the summer. His name was Garry Hemming and we knew him to be a very good mountaineer. Garry was a bit bohemian with long hair on his head and his chin. He was a friendly type in a quiet way and as he had nowhere to stay, we invited him to stay with us. When we went back to the house that night, Mrs Tangye had gone to bed. Creeping up the stairs to our room, Garry settled down on the floor between our beds.

At the breakfast table next morning Garry was sitting with us waiting for the food to arrive. When Mrs Tangye carried it in, she did a double take and demanded to know why a King Neptune look-alike was sitting at her table. She softened her attitude when Garry stood up and in his quiet way offered to leave. He was told to sit down again and that he could have breakfast but as there wasn't enough room at the house, he couldn't stay.

One Saturday night my cousin Barry and I were walking from the George Hotel to the Keswick Pavilion dance accompanied by two girls that we knew.

Half way to the dance, we literally bumped into two lads coming in the opposite direction. Barry said to them, "Hey, mate, look where you're going," where upon one of them punched Barry and knocked him to the ground. Barry leaped up and adopted a boxing stance and was instantly knocked down again, only to bounce back up to be floored yet again. During all this, which happened at lightning speed, the other lad and I stood and looked on in amazement as did the two girls. Then without warning the victor turned round and punched me in the face. I dropped as though hit by a train. The next thing I remember was Paul Ross standing over me, grinning and saying," I warned you never to mess with Podgy Peel." Then I passed out again. When I came round, I could hear women screaming. The two girls had taken me into a nearby café and were bathing my face in the ladies' room. There was no dance for me that night!

When I woke up next morning Richard said, "Shall we go and look for him?" I replied," You must be joking, I've had enough. Forget it."

A week or so later, I went into the pub and looking round saw two navvies from work sitting with another guy whom I didn't know. I bought a pint and sat down with them.

After a while the one I didn't know leaned towards me and said, "I'm sorry for that night in the street, if I'd known you were a friend of Paul Ross, I wouldn't have hit you." I looked at him and recognition dawned on me. It was Podgy Peel, the amateur champion boxer of Cumberland. "Don't worry about it, it was nothing," I lied. He gave me a long look and my blood ran cold. He stood up and said, "What are you drinking?"

Richard and I were laid off from the by-pass and were looking for work again. Richard got a job at Honister quarry and used to come home at night covered in dust and dirt. Mrs Tangye always insisted he take his boots off at the door. One evening for a joke, Bill (who had also been laid off) and I watched for Richard coming home from the quarry. When we saw him approaching we leaned out of the bedroom window and shouted, "Quick, Richard, look at this up here." Wondering what was going on, he dashed up the stairs in his dirty boots. Boy was he in trouble! It took him ages to get round Mrs Tangye.

The winter was cold and the lake froze over. We had some good evenings down near the boat landings making long slides on the ice. Some people even walked right across Derwentwater! It made a change from spending time and money at the pub but we were beginning to get bored. The weeks went by and Richard and I decided it was time to go home. We were both out of work again and felt that we were getting nowhere with our climbing. Bill and the others had already gone. A climber we knew who lived in Carlisle was selling his motor bike., Richard had managed to save some money so decided to buy it. The plan was for him to own it and for me to drive it as I possessed a full licence. We said goodbye to Mrs Tangye who had been like a mother to us and promised to return to see her.

Picking up the bike, an AJS 350CC, in Carlisle we set off for home. At Carnforth our new machine broke down. Taking it to a local garage, we were informed that it was the main bearings that had worn out and that we would have to leave it with them. The following Saturday after taking the bus from Manchester, we were back in Carnforth to collect the bike. On the road again we got as far as Staveley, when we noticed that the dynamo had come loose and was hanging by the wires.

The only tools we possessed were a peg hammer and a pen-knife. Searching round below some trees we found some thick twigs which we carved into wedges.

Hammering the wedges between the bike frame and the dynamo, an improvised repair was accomplished. This enabled us to get to Keswick in time for the pub that night. Next day the weather wasn't very good so we decided to drive down to climb in Langdale as this was on the way home. The day was showery. We ambled up to White Ghyll, did a route on the slabs then did Inferno just managing to finish as the rain started in earnest.

It was going to be a miserable ride back to Manchester. Donning our cagoules and overtrousers we set off. I drove; Richard was on the pillion with a big sack on his back. At Garstang on the A6 there was a transport café where we always broke our journeys to and from the Lakes. It was called the Mayfield and was always very busy. The café was on the northbound side of the road. I halted the bike in the centre of the road to allow oncoming traffic to go by. Richard had his arm stuck out, signalling to turn right, when a lorry pulled up behind us, also signalling to turn right. Suddenly there was a loud crash and we felt ourselves being carried along on the bonnet of a car. The car stopped, Richard was flung over my head and luckily for him was saved by landing on his back on the large rucksack. I fell to the road with bike, putting out my right arm to try to save me. Standing up, I turned to see the car that had hit us. It was side on across the road. The driver had overtaken the stationary lorry behind us, cut in sharply and ploughed into us. My right shoulder was very painful and I was walking like the Hunchback of Notre Dame. I went over to the car and swore at the driver. He looked shocked; in the dark and the rain he hadn't seen us.

Fortunately for us a police car had been parked on the forecourt of the café and the cops had seen it all so we had good witnesses. Richard came with me in the ambulance to Preston Royal Infirmary where I was told I had a dislocated shoulder.

The shoulder was put back in place and we were allowed to go to my aunt and uncle's house in Preston to stay the night.

Next day we took the bus back home. The bike was a write-off; twice it had taken us south from the Lakes but it had never made it home.

Back home in Manchester, I had my shoulder examined by a specialist who declared the injury to be of the non-recurrent type and said that I should be alright to carry on climbing[1]. I was awarded the princely sum of £75 by the courts for pain & suffering and Richard got the price of the bike.

At Christmas some of the lads decided to go up to Keswick. About ten of us had arranged an evening Christmas dinner at Mrs Tangye's.

It had become a tradition that we all go up on to Great Gable at Christmas and that year was no exception. The day was very cold and clear and when the sunset arrived the rocks looked like burning coals. We had all done Needle Ridge and started to head back to Styhead Tarn to wait for any stragglers. Richard and little Malcolm were late coming down but assuming they would be OK, the rest of us decided to press on as it was getting dark. The descent to Seathwaite was awful. The path was iced over and without crampons was treacherous in the dark. It was a relief to get down without breaking something.

Sitting at the dinner table ready to tuck in we heard a knock at the door. It was a policeman who said they had received a message from a Richard McHardy who was stranded at Seathwaite and needed a lift to

---

[1] Approximately a year later in 1964, whilst trying a very strenuous problem at Stanage, I heard a loud crack and fell to the ground. My shoulder had dislocated again. Martin Boysen and John Smith immediately took hold of my arm, and probably more with good luck than good management, manipulated it back into place.
This time the Specialist said that my dislocated shoulder was recurrent. It took brains to work that out!
The result of all this, was that I would need an operation to fix it but that would have to be sometime in the future as there was a long waiting list. In the meantime I would have to be very careful about leading and then only pick well protected climbs.
This gradually eroded my confidence and I started to lead less and less

Keswick to enable both him and his friend to get their Christmas dinner! Andy set off to pick them up.

When they arrived, over dinner Richard explained what had happened. They had finished the climb and were descending just as darkness fell. The scree was welded together with the frost and was difficult to descend. Richard and Little Malcolm moved cautiously and kept close together; Richard said, "Suddenly I slipped and instinctively reached out and grabbed little Malcolm and holding on to him, used him like you would an ice-axe brake." This apparently worked as their plunge downward came to an abrupt halt. Malcolm said, "No wonder it's called Great Hell Gate screes!"

Chapter 12
Back Home 1963

In the New Year, some of the club started work on improving an old quarry building at Millstone Edge above Hathersage. We had occasionally used this building to sleep in and thought it would make a good club hut. It was a concrete construction, about 15 feet square with a flat roof and had the look of a nuclear fallout shelter. John Smith had been in touch with the quarry owner and had been given permission to use it for a small rent.

Ted Howard and mainly the Sheffield section set about improving the security. They fitted a steel door complete with lock and steel shutters on the one and only window.

A few primitive bunk beds were constructed out of wood and there was an already-existing brick fireplace in the middle of the floor for heating, with a brick chimney to the outside through the concrete roof. At last, somewhere to stay instead of under the railway bridge!

The winter of 1963 was very cold with lots of snow. One Saturday night about six of us were staying at the hut when it started to snow heavily. This was the weekend of what became known nationally as Siberian Sunday. When we awoke on the Sunday morning we found that we couldn't open the door. The lads, in their wisdom, in order to make more space inside the hut, hung the door to open outwards. The snow had drifted against the outside to a depth of around six feet. We pushed and pushed but could only manage to open a gap of about nine inches. Barry Ingle who was the smallest present was elected to get through this narrow opening and dig the rest of us out. Good old Barry - he saved us from starvation! Then came the difficult bit. To get the vehicles out, we had to dig along 200 yards of quarry track which was covered in three feet of drifted snow. It took us until the afternoon in a raging blizzard to reach the road. That Sunday I got a lift home with one of the Langdale lads, Pete Muscroft, in his van. The driving side window was missing, the empty space having been filled with cardboard. At every junction, to look to his right, Muscroft had to remove the cardboard then get it back as quickly as possible before the van filled with snow. That was an epic journey back via Peak Forest to Stockport.

The following weekend there was still a lot of snow. Great cornices over hung the tops of the crags. Martin Boysen and I did a winter ascent of a route that we had done the first ascent of the previous summer. This was Svelt at Millstone Edge. On the first ascent Martin had led the first pitch to the foot of a steep corner. I then led the next pitch up a shallow groove but on our winter ascent Martin led from the bottom of the crag to the top of the steep corner in one pitch. He belayed on a snowy ledge where I joined him before leading through to the top of the crag.

Another winter ascent that year was Ingle and Boysen's three day ascent of the iced-up Black Cleft on Cloggy. This was a major event and was achieved by step cutting, which was the usual technique at that time before the advent of front pointing and curved picks. This ascent set a new standard for winter climbing in North Wales.

Since coming back home from living at Mrs Tangye's I had started a new job at an ICI factory in my home town. I was working three shifts, weeks about, as a colour striker for leather cloth materials. The work involved mixing varnishes with colours which were then spread by machine on the cloth. The fumes that were given off during this process really upset my stomach and I suffered a lot of pain. Also the shift work meant that I was eating meals at very irregular times. It was a period of high unemployment in engineering so I didn't have much choice but to stick at it until something better might come along.

I visited the doctor about my stomach pains and he advised me to stick to a low fat, low spice diet and to stop smoking and cut down on alcohol and look for another job - in other words stop abusing my body. He gave me a diet sheet for a peptic ulcer saying that I was in danger of developing one if I didn't take more care of myself. After reading about the diet and what it involved, I decided to ignore it and threw it in the rubbish bin, something I was to regret later on.

Martin's girlfriend, a fellow student of his at Manchester University, regularly accompanied him to the crags at weekends. Her name was Margaret Muir (Maggie). She and Martin owned a Ford Thames van which Maggie drove, Martin not being a driver at that time. Maggie was from Calder Vale in north Lancashire. She was an attractive blonde with a lively and friendly personality. Maggie soon became a good friend to us all fitting in like a sister.

I climbed a lot with Martin at this time and remember us doing the Rasp on Higgar Tor. I set off to lead it but retreated, wary of the weakness in my right arm due to my recently dislocated shoulder, the memory of which was fresh in my mind. I was also aware that the best young climber in Britain was holding my rope and itching to have a go himself. Martin took over the lead. I belayed him whilst Maggie took pictures. Just below the top, almost where the traverse to the right begins, a hold broke off. Martin's nearest runner was approximately 15ft below him, so he fell 30ft before coming on to it.

As Martin hurtled down, I shot upwards. We both came to a stop, and as I was lighter than him, I finished hanging higher up the crag, with the weight of us both on the same runner.

As I started to pay out the rope, Martin went downwards and I stayed hanging there until his feet touched the ground, then I started to go downwards. Maggie in the meantime got some good shots of the action. We untied and decided to leave the ropes hanging there while we retreated to Mrs.Thomas's café for a brew. A couple of hours later, Martin re-climbed to his top runner and finished the route; I followed, stripping the gear. The runner that had held him was particularly difficult to remove!

The Manchester section now met every Wednesday evening at the house of Stan Goodwin and his brother Young Al who lived in a terraced house with their mother near Belle Vue. Stan's mother made us welcome but I think was only too pleased to use these occasions to go out and leave us to our own devices. It was about this time that Pete Maddocks, a talented young climber from the Levenshulme area, started to come to our weekly meetings. Pete's girlfriend Edna lived fairly close to where Stan lived in Gorton and naturally came along also. Pete was a tall, quiet and unassuming lad and had a style of climbing reminiscent of Martin Boysen. He eventually became a member of the Alpha and was a good addition to the club.

I remember once when Pete was with us at Stanage, Richard started off to solo Goliath's Groove. I soloed behind him and this set everybody off, John Smith, Pete Maddocks and others. Pretty soon we were all strung out up the groove. Someone took a photo which years later featured in High Magazine.

A young Sheffielder who was keen to join the Alpha was a lad called Howard Rainer, nicknamed Garth because of his strength and size. One day at Lawrencefield, Clive said," Garth carry me to the hut on your shoulders and you can join the Alpha." When they arrived at the hut, after carrying Clive what must have been nearly half a mile, Garth asked to become a member. Clive said "I was only kidding." Poor Garth, he was a gentle giant with not an ounce of malice in him, luckily for Clive.

There was a large stone at the side of the hut which no one could lift, except for perhaps Richard although I can't recall him having done so. Garth was told that this was the Alpha stone and that anyone who could lift it above their heads automatically became a member. He tried and tried without success. It's a wonder he didn't give himself a hernia!

That winter there were enormous snow drifts on Stanage up to within about 10ft from the top of the Right Unconquerable. One day a few of us jumped off the top and slid down the drift below. We decided to tell Garth when the snow had gone that jumping off the Right Unconquerable was a condition for anyone wishing to join the Alpha Club. Luckily he didn't try it. Eventually he gave up on trying to become a member and decided to take up boxing at which he became quite good, even making an appearance on television.

Another young Sheffield lad was introduced to the club by Pat Fearnehough. The lad's name was Gerry Rogan (nicknamed Grogan). He was about 19 years old and Pat was his mentor.

Gerry had been climbing since he was 16 and had climbed mainly with the Peak Climbing Club. He had done the Corner with Eddie Birch of the Black and Tans when only 17 years old.

Gerry was a plumber and like many of that trade, he was strong. He went on to do a lot of new routes in the Canadian Rockies but that was a decade later. The first time that I met Gerry he was with Fearnehough and Ben Wilson, a friend of Pat's; we were all in the Yorkshire Bridge, a pub near Ladybower dam. Pat and Ben were having a heavy drinking session and Gerry very much the apprentice was trying to keep up with them. He had two pints on the table in front of him and a half full pint in his hand. He was trailing behind. Pat came back from the bar to their table with three more pints. Putting one on the table for Grogan, he and Ben downed theirs in one. Pat turned to Gerry and said," Your round, youth." Gerry went green at the gills and rushed to the toilets. Later back at the hut we could hear him throwing up for most of the night. I think he realised then that in future it wouldn't be a good idea to try to out-drink the likes of Ben Wilson and Pat Fearnehough!

That year Pat teamed up with Geoff Oliver and Jack Hesmondhalgh to produce Intern HVS on Gimmer Crag in Langdale.

At spring bank holiday I had arranged to meet Wool in the Pass. We were planning to do White Slab on Cloggy. When I arrived, Wool, who had been there for a few days, had already done it with Al Clarke of the Peak CC. They were going really well and did White Slab, Carpet Slab and Longlands in the same day. He and I did Diagonal together leading alternately and were both climbing very confidently. Over the next few days we did various routes of which I particularly remember Brant and Unicorn Direct and I remember Martin and Paul doing the first ascent of Nexus. Other Alpha new routes in Wales during 1963 were done mainly by the team of Barry Ingle and Pete Crew, who were proving to be a challenge to the supremacy of the Brown/ Whillans era. Barry Ingle with Rodney Wilson did Crucible at Cwm Silyn. On Cloggy, Crew and Ingle climbed The Boldest, Pete placing a controversial expansion bolt for protection and back in the Pass Ingle and Crew found Great Buttress on Cyrn Las.

About this time Paul and I went to Cloggy hoping to do Red Slab. This route was first climbed in 1952 by John Streetly who did the climb of 300ft in one run out as no one present could second him. In 1963 it was still considered a test piece.

Paul and I ascended the Western Terrace to the foot of the climb. There was a cold wind blowing which seemed to penetrate our very bones. I said that it was too cold and that we should do something else but Paul wanted to try it and couldn't be persuaded otherwise. We were both wearing duvet jackets but hadn't brought gloves.

Paul set off on the first pitch which proved to be extremely difficult especially in such cold conditions. I sat at my belay watching his every move getting colder and colder. The pitch was lacking in protection and Paul still wearing his duvet was wisely taking his time, climbing very safely as usual.

The pitch took what must have been, or at least seemed to be, three or four hours. I whiled away the time composing a limerick-style poem about climbing in the cold.

When at last it was my turn to climb, I found that I was so cold my limbs wouldn't function properly. Halfway up the pitch I decided that I'd had enough and told Paul I was going back down. I felt really bad about this because of Paul's tremendous effort in doing this pitch but I didn't think that we would have time to do the rest of the route anyway, especially as there was still 200ft of similar climbing yet to come. Paul abseiled off and we went back to the Pass. I knew that Paul was very disappointed but he didn't show me any resentment; in fact on the way back I recited my poem to him and we both had a good laugh.

Second's Thoughts

A second has a miserable life sitting on ledges where cold is rife,
He sits there thoughtful at his belay waiting his turn to join in the fray,
He says let's do something warm and easy not this climb so desperate and
    freezy,
The leader says don't despair, ten more feet and I'll be there.
Then he climbs up fast and furious, makes the second rather curious,
Surely the leader is extremely bold to climb up there in this awful cold.
His turn to climb, his knees are shaking, eh you up there this rope quick
    take in,
He starts to traverse bit by bit, the rope goes slack, he thinks, this is it!
He's climbing now on a prayer and a wing, if he comes off he won't half
    swing.
Then he climbs up very fast thinking each move will be his last,
One more move he's at the ledge sits there with his nerves on edge.
He says, let's not linger, let's not stop I want to fester at the top.
At the top of the crag, a desperate time he's had, back at the bottom, well
    not so bad,
At halfway house, I didn't fall, back in the Pass not hard at all.
There is a moral to this story, climb for pleasure not for glory,
Cos if you climb in constant fear, I have two words for your ear,
GIVE UP!

Llanberis Pass 1960. (Lto R) Back; A Parker, Tanky, Clive Rowland, P Nunn
Front, Jim Smith, Alan Ellison, Pete Bamfield

How not to cross a river. Richard

Aerial Runway, near Castle Rock, Thirlmere.

Splash!

*Camp at Castle Rock (L to R) A McHardy, A Parker, Andy Garvey, Al Goodwin,
Jim Smith, Stan Goodwin, Alan Ellison, Mick Burke*

Tanky and John Smith "Training"

Alpha Hut, Millstone Edge. Maggie and Martin Boysen

Martin Boysen on "The Rasp" 1963

(L to R) Al Parker, Tony Brooder, Jud Jordon

Llanberis Pass, John Smith

(L to R) Clive Rowland, Paul Nunn, John Smith (three wise Monkeys)

The Sloth at Roaches. John Smith

Chapter 13
The English Abroad. 1963

Richard and I and Dave Peck and Ian Hartle (nicknamed Willy Hurtle) decided to go to the Alps in Ian's mini van. Four blokes and all the gear: it was going to be a tight squeeze.

Clive Rowland, Oliver Woolcock and Gerry Rogan were going out in Dave Gregory's van; and we planned to meet up with them in the Bregaglia.

Because Woolly and I had done the Badile N.E. face the year before there were loose plans for him and me to do the N. ridge of the Cengalo while Richard and Clive, with the others, would attempt the Badile N.E. face.

Martin and Maggie were going to the Dolomites, taking Paul with them in their van and I think it was that year that Pete Crew and Baz Ingle were invited to go to the Ecole Nationale in Chamonix.

Richard and I decided that we needed some new gear so we paid a visit to Bob Brigham's shop on Cathedral St. in Manchester. Bob said that if we were sure that we wouldn't get killed we could have it on tick. We assured him that we had no intention of dying prematurely and entered our two new ropes and other purchases in his book, promising to pay when we returned home from the Alps.

I packed the <u>mini </u>van: four big sacks plus four climbing sacks, two tents, and four sleeping bags. There was also climbing equipment - four ropes, four ice axes, boots clothes and bivvy gear. On top of all this we had stoves, pans and food. How did we fit it all in? It was a wonder that the 1000cc mini could even move let alone go over Alpine passes! I quite justifiably, became known as "Packer Parker." All that stuff and four men and believe it or not we were quite comfortable, although Willy Hurtle wasn't too happy about having his van so overloaded!

After a late afternoon crossing to Calais and driving on through France until darkness fell, we pulled off the road and followed a narrow track into some woods. At a widening we parked the van and made our way by torch light to a small clearing where we set up some candles on tree stumps and rocks and set about cooking a meal. Richard started to change a gas cylinder on the stove but being too close to a candle, succeeded in setting fire to the canister which went up with a tremendous whoosh! Dropping the potential bomb he took off to the woods at great speed with the rest of us in pursuit. From behind an embankment of earth we watched as this giant flare lit up the trees. All our gear was over near the flare, but none of us dared to rescue it. Preferring to let the blaze die out and hoping it wouldn't start a forest fire we crouched behind our protective earth mound until it was deemed safe to approach the stove. After very cautiously renewing the canister, a meal and a brew were soon disposed of and we settled down in our sleeping bags for a well earned night's sleep.

Next day, driving on through France, we eventually crossed the border into Switzerland at Basel and continued to Lucerne where we stopped for something to eat then kipped in a lay-by for the night.

The next morning after a swim in Lake Lucerne we continued our journey to the Bregaglia arriving there that evening. The weather was good in the valley and conditions on the mountains looked favourable. At noon the following day, leaving the van near where Paul and I had camped the year before, we set off for the Sciora Hut loaded down with food and equipment. The cramped days in the van had taken their toll and we were all finding it hard work. We rested frequently, drinking in the beauty of our surroundings. I pointed out to the others the climbs that I had done with Paul. I also showed them the inscription "Tired, Youth?" where we had scratched it on the boulder on our first visit to this area and which was now almost covered over with moss. It was good to see these familiar things and felt almost like I was returning home.

At the hut, the same young woman was still the guardian but now shared the job with her new husband who, like her, was a climber. She recognised me from the year before and told me that her grandmother due to advancing age had retired and now stayed down in the valley all summer.

Underneath the main hut there was a large room with mattresses which was used as an emergency winter refuge; we decided to stay in this room as it offered more privacy and would be quieter at night thus enabling us to get a good night's sleep.

Leaving early the following morning, the four of us made our way across the moraine to the small glacier that leads to the Flatiron Ridge of the Piz Gemelli.

I had climbed this route the year before with Paul and had suggested to the others that it would be a good one to warm up on being short (1000ft) but technically quite hard. They agreed and were keen to do this beautiful-looking ridge. Leaving our sacks on the large ledge at the foot of the climb, we roped up in pairs, Richard and I going first followed by Dave and Willy. It was a lovely sunny day, the rock warm to the touch, making every move a pleasure. At the top of the difficulties all four sat in the sun and wished that we had not left our sacks and axes at the big ledge. This would have enabled us to do the continuation ridge, a further 1000ft to the summit of the Gemelli and then down the Bondo glacier to the hut. Too late now though! Setting up the first abseil and using a rope between each pair for safety we started our descent. Richard and I went first and took a stance below, where Dave soon joined us. It was then that Willy Hurtle informed us that he had never abseiled before and didn't know how! There followed a hurried lesson in the art of abseiling, shouted up 150ft to Willy by all three voices on our ledge. Willy managed to get the gist of what we were saying and descended safely to join us. After doing a further eight abseils he became quite accomplished at it proving that experience is the best way to learn, especially when one doesn't have a choice! It didn't take long to get safely back to our sacks where we had a drink and a snack before returning to the Sciora hut.

Back at the hut we were pleased to see that Clive, Wool, Gerry Rogan and Dave Gregory had arrived. Comparing notes about individual ambitions it was decided that Wool and I climb together to try the North ridge of the Cengalo. Richard and Clive wanted to do the NE face of the Badile as did Gerry and Dave Gregory while Dave Peck and Willy would attempt the North Ridge of the Badile.

The next morning, the weather was warm and sunny with a clear blue sky. We spent the time until early afternoon lazing in the sun and preparing our gear for the climbs planned for the following day. Wool and I had decided to spend the night at the hut and go for the Cengalo at dawn. The rest of the lads were going off together to bivvy below the Badile to give them an early start the next day. We waved them off and watched their progress as they picked their way through the moraine towards the rognon that divides the Badile and Cengalo glaciers. When they eventually disappeared from view we went inside to make our evening meal. Later that evening after a glass of vino rosso in the hut we returned to our beds in the winter refuge. A breeze had got up and clouds were scudding past the moon. It looked as though the weather was changing for the worse. Crash! We both wakened up with a start as our room was lit up by a flash of lightning then another clap of thunder seemed to shake the hut. Lightning flashes and rolls of thunder were followed by the sound of heavy rain. We were glad that we had decided not to accompany the others and feeling smug pulled our sleeping bag hoods over our heads and went back to sleep.

We were awakened early by the return of our friends. They were cold and wet and noisy having spent an uncomfortable night under the rognon. I looked outside and saw thick cloud swirling around below the hut. The storm had passed but the rain had set in with a vengeance and the mountains were nowhere to be seen. The hut guardian told us that the forecast wasn't good for the foreseeable future so after a good breakfast and many brews we reluctantly decided to retreat to the valley.

On the walk down we had occasional glimpses through the clouds of new snow plastering the rocky peaks. It was time to leave the area in search of better weather.

The four in Dave Gregory's van decided to go to the Dolomites possibly to meet up with Martin, Maggie and Paul who had gone out to the Civetta. Our team plumped for going to Chamonix hoping that this bad weather wasn't all across the Alps.

Chapter 14
The Scotch Club Affair

Arriving in Chamonix we were dismayed to see that the weather was worse than it had been in the Bregaglia.

The Biolay campsite was running with rivulets from the woods; this wasn't good because that's where everyone went to the toilet and there was a definite health hazard in camping there! Baz Ingle and Pete Crew were camped near to us and were fed up with the weather. They had been up to attempt the Central Pillar of Freney but the weather had turned against them and they were ready to go home.

It rained solidly for two weeks and almost every day there was new snow reaching down into the trees below Montenvers. Nobody was climbing; the only thing at a high level was a feeling of disappointment and frustration.

Every morning we would crawl out of the tents, try to make breakfast in the sodden surroundings then head off down into the town for coffee. Most of the day was spent playing table football or liar dice in the Bar Nationale until it was time to go to the tunnel canteen for our evening meal. Each night after a few grandes bieres, enough to help us forget the wetness of our sleeping bags, we staggered back to our tents hoping the weather would improve the following day. It never did! Just as we were beginning to think about going home, Dave Gregory arrived with the rest of the lads followed soon after by Martin and Maggie but without Paul who, they told us, had flown home to get medical treatment after an accident in the Dolomites.

When the lads left us after the bad weather in the Bregaglia, they had gone to the Civetta and had met up with Paul, Martin and Maggie.

Clive and Wool did the N. Face of the Torre Valgrande and the Andrich Fae on the Punta Civetta.

At the same time, Martin and Paul wanted to do the Philip Flam which at that time was reckoned to be the hardest rock climb in the Alps. Pete Crew and Al Wright had done the first British ascent but it hadn't yet been done in a day.

Setting off early on the climb, they soloed for quite a way before deciding to rope up. Two of the top German climbers of that era had set out the previous day and were bivouacked somewhere above. Martin and Paul overtook this pair before they emerged from their bivouac and climbing quickly and confidently past them were soon well in the lead. Six hundred feet from the top whilst leading up a loose section of rock, Martin accidentally dislodged a block which struck Paul on the leg, breaking it below the knee. Martin climbed quickly back down to Paul and fashioned a makeshift splint from a ripped up shirt. Then with Martin in the lead and Paul held on a tight rope and using aid slings, they succeeded in completing the climb that same day!

The following morning after an uncomfortable night near the summit they continued the descent to the hut from where they were assisted by the rest of the lads down to the valley. Paul was loaded into the van and driven to hospital and kept in. The next day the lads went back to see him, only to find that the hospital would not put a cast on his leg because of the injury.

Paul was keen to get medical attention in England as he didn't have medical insurance so he was smuggled out of the hospital by the lads and taken to Venice airport and with Clive pushing the wheelchair and Wool holding Paul's leg out straight He was put on a plane for home. This decided the rest of the lads to pack up and leave for Chamonix.

Down the street from the National bar was the Hotel de Paris which had a nightclub on its premises called the Scotch Club. One night after drinking at the National bar, Maggie, Martin, Wool and I decided to visit the Scotch Club to see what it was like. We were accompanied by a lad from Sheffield, Brian Shirley.

On entering the hotel, we found the club through some glass doors to our left, halfway down the hallway. Through the doors was a darkened room with low wooden tables and stools and a well stocked bar. At the far end of this bar there was a back room with tables in alcoves, encircling a small dance floor. After getting drinks, we settled down at a table in one of the alcoves and listened to the loud music which was very much to our taste, being mainly Beatles and Rolling Stones records.

Suddenly a drunken Frenchman appeared in the doorway and addressing us in a loud and threatening voice said, "You will not get out of here alive tonight," then turning on his heel, he went back through to the bar.

Not knowing what to make of this we left without further trouble and decided that it must have been the drink talking.

The following night, (Maggie's 21st birthday) we decided to pay the Scotch Club another visit. This time some of us went straight through to the dance floor in the back room and started dancing. Richard, Clive and Brian Shirley stood outside in the street discussing whether to come in or go back to the campsite. Brian decided to go in and left the other two still talking at the door.

On his way through the bar, Brian came face to face with the French climber who had drunkenly threatened us all the night before. Suddenly and without reason, the Frenchman attacked Brian, knocking him across a table. Two men who were sitting at this table jumped up and, grabbing Brian by the arms, held him while the attacker hit him with a broken bottle, cutting him badly in the face. Breaking loose and turning round, Brian dashed outside to Richard and Clive. The barmaid locked the doors behind him to prevent anyone else coming in.

The first we heard of all this was when Richard smashed his way in through the doors and confronted the Frenchman who was by this time cowering in a corner defended by three others who stood in front of him brandishing bottles. This was the scene that met our eyes when we came back through into the bar from the back room. Richard was saying to the culprit," Right, Frog, you've had three on to one, lets have one on to one outside." The barman was trying to calm the situation when one of the Frenchmen picked up a heavy wooden stool and aimed it at Richard's head. One of our lads stuck out an arm and deflected the stool but got hurt in the process. Richard's response was to pick up the heavy table and throw it into the corner, flattening all three Frenchmen.

Then all hell broke loose. Every Frenchman in the place set about trying to tear to pieces anyone who was English. It was obviously assumed by ones who hadn't witnessed the beginning of this affray that we must be the cause of it all as it had only started since we had entered the club. The barmaid had again bolted the doors cutting off our escape; we were fighting them off with our backs to the door, bottles, tables and chairs were flying everywhere. I saw one stool sail over the bar and sweep all the optics off the wall. It was like something from the Wild West! Suddenly and mercifully the doors gave way and we all fell out into the hallway. Most of the lads went to the right out of the main door, but Brian and I by mistake turned left into the hotel. Realising our error, we did a quick about turn and headed for the door to the street. Retracing our steps down the hallway until level with the broken doors of the Scotch Club, we thought we had made it, when a stocky tough-looking character who seconds before had been fighting with Clive and me dashed out of the doorway and smashed a large bottle over Brian's head. I grabbed Brian by the arm and dragged him, looking dazed, outside to join the others in the street.

Turning to face the angry mob that now stood in the hotel doorway, shouting and gesticulating and throwing missiles at us, we felt greatly outnumbered and decided to retreat, some with Brian to the hospital, some to the Gendarmerie to report this vicious and unprovoked attack.

The police station was in darkness, but after ringing the doorbell with persistence, eventually a gendarme appeared. After reporting what had happened, the gendarmes promised to go to the Scotch Club to question the culprits. We were allowed to return to the campsite. On the way back we met Don and Audrey and told them about the fight. Whillans reckoned that the French climbers in the Scotch Club probably didn't like us encroaching on their territory.

The next morning, when everyone was getting up a gendarme appeared at our tents. He asked to see our passports and when we naively handed them over he pocketed them and headed off towards the town, beckoning for us to follow.

It must have looked quite comical to any onlookers, a gendarme followed by a motley procession of sleepy-looking climbers.

We thought, good, something is being done and assumed that we were on our way to the gendarmerie to identify our attackers of the night before. On arriving at the police station, Dave Peck who spoke French quite well was ushered into the police chief's office. The rest of us waited in the hallway, some leaning against the wall, some sitting on the floor. Suddenly the chief gendarme, a short stocky man with crew cut hair, strode out of his office waving a stick and ordered everyone to stand up straight with backs to the wall. He was followed by a shocked looking Dave who said that the chief had told him that our passports would be returned to us when we had paid a large fine and recompensed the Scotch Club for the damage caused during the fight. We were then to leave Chamonix and told that we would be banned from France in the future. When Dave asked about the French climbers who had started the whole affair, he was told that they had left for Paris the night before and their identities were unknown.

When pressed for the fine we refused, saying that we didn't have enough money and that without passports it wasn't possible to cash traveller's cheques.

Back at the campsite, it was decided to sit it out for a day or two to see how things would develop. We were being watched. Gendarmes peeped out at us from behind trees. Some of the lads waved to them cheekily and we had a laugh when they ducked out of sight. The American climber Garry Hemming phoned the British Consulate to say that as an independent observer he thought we were getting the blame for something that wasn't really our fault.

Being a resident of Chamonix, Garry knew the French climbers involved saying that they were some of the top climbers in France and frequently acted as mountaineering instructors for the Gendarmerie, so the gendarmes and the alpinists all knew one another. At least three of these French climbers were internationally famous and one it was rumoured was a High Court judge. The British Consul said it was a matter for the local police and left us to our fate. Feeling that the odds were loaded against us we began to worry.

The cat and mouse game with the gendarmes went on for a few days with them piling on the pressure by taking into custody some of the English climbers from the campsite. Even though these were totally innocent and hadn't even been to the Scotch Club they were thrown into cells for a few hours and then released without charge.

The whole situation was resolved when Don Whillans phoned a reporter he knew on the Daily Express in London. The story was reported in the paper and the Express got in touch with the Chamonix police.

The first we knew of this was when we were told to report to the Gendarmerie where we were given back our passports and ordered to leave Chamonix immediately. We didn't argue!

Back in England and two months later we received summonses to appear in court at Bonneville (near Chamonix) charged with causing a nocturnal disturbance. After clubbing together to send a statement via a solicitor to the court, to our relief the case was thrown out by the judge. This was probably something to do with the fact that the French climbers involved had high connections with the judiciary and did not wish to appear in court themselves.

That was the last that we heard of this episode leaving us free to visit France in the future.

Chapter 15
Accidents and Adventures 1963/64

Richard, Grogan and I were travelling down Borrowdale in the back of Maggie's van. Martin was driving for the first time ever. Maggie had decided it was time that he learned and she was instructing. As we entered Keswick, things were going well. Maggie said, "Park up behind the Oasis café." Martin drove confidently onto the large car park where there was only one other car parked. "Park next to that," Maggie instructed. Martin swung the van round in a great arc and instead of pulling up at the side of the parked car, he ran into the back of it. Maggie wasn't happy and let Martin know this in no uncertain terms - the air was blue. Martin responded in like manner. Richard and I were collapsed in fits of laughter. Gerry sat quietly wondering what to do, not wanting to antagonise Maggie or Martin. The result of this episode was that Martin didn't get any more driving lessons for quite a while after that!

About this time out of the blue, our old friend Malcolm Cundy turned up again. Richard and I were on a climb at Burbage south, when this youth in a black leather jacket showed up and shouted to us; it was Pike. We were really pleased to see him and he said he would like to start climbing again but he was courting and would have to check with his girlfriend.

Some weeks, later a few of us were on Froggatt one day when Pike appeared with his girlfriend, an attractive girl called Diana. They walked back to Grindleford with us and I remember that Diana was embarrassed because she had torn the back of her jeans and Maggie lent her a sweater to tie round her waist to preserve her modesty.

Pike was working as a joiner and he and Di had been saving up to get married.

But after this reunion, Pike decided that he wanted to take up climbing again and Diana agreed to it. They spent their savings on a dormobile and climbing gear and became regular members of the Alpha and the connected social scene.

Since Paul and Dave Peck had started at Sheffield University it had become custom for all the lads to attend the annual Beatnik Ball which was always a good night, plenty of drink and Rock and Roll. In 1963 it was no different except that all the groups now played Beatles tunes as they were the new "in" group.

We had all spent the early evening in the pub before moving on to the University Ball. At the dance the group was playing "Twist and Shout", and a circle of five or six lads and girls were dancing about passing round a bottle of whisky that Woolcock had produced. He said he'd found it under a table. We all kept taking a swig in turn.

Needless to say, none of us were fit for much by the end of the night.

Around 3am the following morning, Maggie, Martin and I arrived at the Alpha hut on Millstone Edge. Not wanting to drive home from the Beatnik Ball we had decided to sleep at the hut. Next morning we set off for home as I had to be at work by two o'clock that afternoon. I was still working a three-shift system and had taken the previous night off to go to the dance.

The following Sunday after days of stomach pains I was again out in Derbyshire. A group of us had gone to Chatsworth Edge and were trying Sentinel Crack. I was feeling particularly weak and had pains in my back and stomach.

The Beatles were due to appear on TV that evening on the Royal Command Performance. Richard and I had a lift back with Maggie and Martin and on reaching my parent's house I invited them in to watch the Beatles.

On came the Fab Four and broke into their song" Twist and Shout". I had a sharper than usual pain in my gut which seemed to be getting worse by the minute. Getting out of my chair, I went into the kitchen and drank a glass of milk. The pain continued to get worse. I went upstairs with difficulty to the bathroom where I started to vomit bile and blood. My dad came up and helped me to my bed. As we didn't have a phone, Maggie went in the van with my mother to get the doctor.

By the time the doctor arrived I was writhing in agony. It felt as though I had a fire inside me; I went into shock and the muscles from my abdomen to my chest went into spasm, restricting my breathing. The doctor took one look and said that I had a perforated duodenal ulcer and left immediately to call an ambulance. As I was carried from the house, I noticed the serious expressions on the faces of my parents and friends. I thought, that's it I must look bad, I'm going to die!

At the hospital, as it was late on a Sunday night, they had to send out for a radiologist to X-ray me. I was then prepared for theatre and the next thing I knew, I woke up on the ward with no pain. I thought am I dead and in heaven, I saw all the tubes etc. connected to me, and then I remembered.

The surgeon came to see me. I thanked him and asked how many ulcers there had been. He said "Only one. How many did you want?" Then more seriously he told me I must have been living a bit too wildly to have developed an ulcer at so young an age and advised me to be more moderate in future. He said that I could have died and that the ulcer couldn't be removed during last night's operation and had only been repaired and could return if I didn't change my ways. This scared me! I've never been keen on the Beatles "Twist and Shout" ever since that night!

I was in hospital for a week or so, and then I was allowed home. The lads visited me; Paul and Wool arrived on the motorbike looking strong and fit, while I felt like an old man, shuffling round, hunched forward clutching the wound in my stomach.

I felt sorry for myself. I had been advised not to smoke or drink, I was on a strict diet of milk and light foods and I had been told that it would be three months before I could climb again.

After a week or two I was asked by ICI to go in to be examined by the works doctor. The outcome of this was that as my job entailed shift work, my employment would be terminated when it was deemed that I was again fit for work elsewhere. I was informed that I would get full pay in the meantime and severance pay when I finished. Wow! I cheered up straight away, no work for three months after which time I would be able to afford a van and start climbing again.

In February 1964, I started a new job, back in my own trade in a small engineering factory in Hyde; the money was good and I had enough from ICI to buy a Morris 1000cc van. I managed to get one that was in good condition. While I had been off work I had taken some driving lessons and had passed my test. Morris 1000 vans were favoured because of there reliability and by that time several of the lads owned them

Back on the rock again after my long convalescence, I was climbing quite confidently. I remember (how could I forget) a few of us at Stanage trying a hard problem near Count's Buttress without anyone succeeding. I was having another try; it involved a very strenuous mantelshelf on my right arm, and as I pushed up I heard a loud crack and I fell to the ground. My shoulder had dislocated. John Smith supported me in my armpit whilst Richard pulled steadily on my arm. Martin was feeling at my shoulder to see which way the ball had come out of the socket, when suddenly it all relocated!

I think that possibly the muscles around my shoulder joint had become weak due to my four month layoff from climbing whilst recovering from the ulcer operation.

The outcome of this was another appointment with a specialist who told me it would be recurrent and the only cure was an operation. I was put on his waiting list which at that time was 18 months. This meant no more leading, unless I wanted to kill myself, only seconding from then on being careful at that.

About this time Ingle and Boysen started to talk about this Crag X which was supposed to have no routes on it but hundreds of possibilities. They shared their secret with the lads, but swore us to secrecy. Crag X turned out to be Gogarth on Anglesey. Barry Ingle and Martin Boysen did the first two climbs on the crag, Gogarth E1 and Shag Rock HVS thus opening up what was destined to become one of the most popular crags in Wales; Pete Crew and Barry Ingle did Gauntlet, Bezel, Emulator, Simulator and Pentathol. Arthur Williams did Pantin VS; and Martin Boysen with Clive Rowland Amphitheatre Wall HVS. The secret was kept for a while, and when any of the lads went there, false trails were laid and lies were told, anything to keep the secret from other activists. Eventually all the subterfuge and cover was blown and the word was out. The Alpha Club pioneered many routes at Gogarth over the years with Pete Crew spearheading the exploration accompanied quite often by the master, Baron Brown.

Others from the Alpha to leave their mark on Gogarth were Richard McHardy and Gerry Rogan.

Before Easter, Richard started work at Plas-y Brenin (The National Mountain Centre at Capel Curig) as an instructor and also did some joinery work there; Bill Bowker was there at the same time.

Easter arrived and most of the lads went down to the Pass and were camped on the field at Ynys Ettws next to the Climbers Club hut. On Good Friday it was a beautiful sunny morning. Richard and Bill were climbing on the Wastad with some pupils from the Brenin. Richard was with a lad who had performed really well all week so had decided to take him up something a bit harder than usual.

Some of the Alpha had set off to climb and some of us were enjoying a leisurely breakfast in the sun outside the tents. Looking up to Carreg Wastad we could see Bill on Crackstone Rib and down to his left Richard was leading Rackstone Crib, a route fist done by Hugh Banner in 1958 and graded HVS. This climb takes the steep arête directly below Crackstone Rib. Richard was approximately 80ft up. We lay there in the sun with our brews watching his progress. Suddenly to our horror he parted company with the rock and his only runner came off as the flake it was on broke. He plunged about 80ft and hit the scree with a terrific crash; the flake followed him down and struck him where he lay.

We all leapt up, some set off to notify the mountain rescue at the Pen-y-Gwryd while the rest of us dashed up the hillside. Arriving at the foot of the crag we found Richard lying unconscious with very serious injuries to his head and face. Bill came down off his climb and we did what we could until the rescue party from the Gwryd, led by Chris Briggs, arrived with a stretcher. Mountain Rescue teams in those days were usually made up of anyone who happened to be there at the crag or its vicinity. Apart from the RAF there were few trained teams.

Richard had a hole in the back of his head and his cheekbone had been smashed; some of the rescue people were of the opinion that he wouldn't live and that there was no point in rushing. We disagreed!

An ambulance had arrived on the road below and we hurried down with the stretcher to get him to it as quickly as possible. As the ambulance sped away a few of us followed in various vans. After going through Llanberis the ambulance suddenly stopped while the paramedics did some work on Richard. Standing there not knowing what was happening gave his friends some anxious moments. Then it was off again at full speed to Bangor hospital.

I don't remember much of what was done that Easter apart from Martin climbing on Anglesey on Easter Sunday and Maggie and I visiting Richard in hospital.

Richard remained unconscious for four days and had surgery to repair his skull and had his cheekbone wired. Over the next three weeks he made a remarkable recovery and was keen to be discharged; he even tried to persuade various ones to smuggle in his clothes and a rope to enable him to exit through the window. It is a good thing that no one gave in to these requests.

Three weeks after his accident, he was discharged and returned to Plas-y Brenin. That week I had booked the channel crossing for my van which was to take Martin and Maggie and Clive and me to Chamonix in the summer. The following weekend I went in my van down to the pass, taking Jim and young Al with me; Martin and Maggie were there and we all stayed on Ynys field.

I remember on Saturday morning Pete Crew came speeding onto the field in his Morris 1000 van travelling fast towards his own tent, hoping to scare the lads who were sitting around talking nearby. At the last minute he braked hard but hadn't allowed for the wet grass; the van skidded and flattened Pete's tent. The place was in uproar, laughter from the gathered assembly and bad language from a very sheepish Crewy. It's fortunate that no one was in the tent at the time.

On Saturday afternoon Maggie and I went in my van to see Richard at Plas-y-Brenin, after which Maggie said to me," You know, Al, you're going to have a bad accident one day, you're driving far too fast for your experience." To which I replied," What do you mean? I'm in complete control of this vehicle!" Richard, who had decided to go home to Manchester after the weekend, asked me if I would take him in my van.

Sunday evening at Ynys, Maggie and Martin set off for home. Ten minutes later with Richard in the passenger seat and Jim and young Al in the back, we set off in my van. Suddenly Richard announced in a panicky voice that he'd left his donkey jacket in Maggie's van and it had 10 quid in the pocket. Could I catch up with them?

Through the Bettws bends at top speed, then along the straights on the A5 to join the B5105 at Cerrigydrudion we were making good time despite the wet road. Just after entering the forest section we came up behind two motorbikes that were going slowly (sensibly on the wet surface) and taking up most of the road. I could see a right-hand bend coming up with nothing approaching us. Pulling out and accelerating I started to overtake the two bikes. As we sped into the bend, we hit a greasy patch of road. The van slid sideways causing a front tyre blow out and we started to spin down the road still going at high speed. Before I could do anything to correct our trajectory we shot off the road and came to rest roof down in the ditch facing back the way we had come. The passenger side door was jammed against the steep bank and the driver's door was up against a dry stone wall or at least what was left of it. Luckily for us the rear double doors had sprung open For a few seconds we sat there upside down, watching the upside down windscreen wipers still working. I turned off the ignition. Then there was a smell of petrol and panic set in. Richard and I made a dash for the back doors treading on Jim and young Al in our haste to get out, leaving dirty footprints on the van ceiling. Once outside we remembered the other two and returned guiltily to drag them clear. It was a miracle that no one was hurt, not even bruised. Richard obviously thinking about his recently wired up face and skull pointed upwards and said, "Someone up there likes me." Standing at the side of the road looking down to the van we watched the front wheels still spinning as all the petrol drained from the tank. A car pulled up; it was Pat Walsh and some of the Langdale lads. They offered me a lift to Ruthin where I went into the café where Martin and Maggie were seated at a table. I walked up to them and said to her, "You remember what you said about me driving too fast? Well, you were right!"

After organising to get the van towed into Ruthin garage, Richard and Jim left for home with Maggie and Martin whilst young Al and I slept in the back of my beat up van on the garage forecourt. Next morning, the garage personnel filled up the empty petrol tank and replaced the lost oil; then with both sides of the van squeezed in and the back doors hanging off, we drove home.

At my local garage I was told that the van needed a complete new back end and a respray and as this would take some weeks to complete and we did not know exactly how long it would take, we decided to cancel going to the Alps in my van and re-booked to go in Maggie's Ford Thames van instead.

One weekend in May camping at Ynys, Wool arrived and introduced us to his new girlfriend, a slim attractive girl with long dark hair whose name was Anne Fowler. Anne was a student at Liverpool Art College and came from Workington in Cumbria which was also Wool's home town. That weekend in Wales besides climbing, we all visited Black Rock sands near Portmadoc where we had a game of football. Anne threw herself into this game with great enthusiasm even though it was a trifle rough. At one point I trod on Anne's foot, tearing the strap off her shoe and causing it and her to part company. Despite this, we became good friends, a friendship which has lasted 45 years, proving that she doesn't bear a grudge, although occasionally she has reminded me of the event. Personally I don't accept any blame for this incident, reasoning that if you go by the name of Fowler you must either not play football or expect to be targeted by the opposition. That day was 3rd May 1964, Anne's 21st birthday.

Six weeks after leaving hospital Richard led Bill up The Grasper at Tremadog then later did Red Slab and Pigott's Climb on Cloggy. This was followed the next day with Chimney Route and The Boulder, thus announcing his return to fitness.

Richard with Martin repeated Crew's Central Pillar on Esk Buttress and Martin with Chris Bonington did the first ascent of The Medlar E3 on Raven Crag, Thirlmere.

Parking Maggie's van at the end of Llyn Cwellyn; Martin, Maggie, Clive and I walked along the old quarry track towards Castell Cidwm. The morning was warm and sunny, enough to put a spring in anyone's step, but after a boozy night at the Dolbadarn hotel in Llanberis the night before we were all feeling a bit jaded.

Before reaching the crag we came to what appeared to be an old mineshaft filled with water which gave a clear blue pool which looked ideal for swimming except that the sides were very steep, if not vertical, and the water was six feet below the top. Looking down into it we could see that it was very deep.

Leaving Maggie and me sunbathing by the pool, Martin and Clive went off to do the Central Wall E3. The day was hot and after a while I decided I would like a swim.

Stripping to my underpants I dived off the edge into the depths. As I hit the water I felt my shoulder dislocate again. I surfaced and treading water shouted to Maggie for help; she at first thought that I was kidding then realised that I was serious. Somehow, probably through sheer desperation, I managed to climb out. Maggie ran up to the crag to get the other two, returning with them quite quickly.

Martin tried to repeat his Stanage feat of putting my shoulder back in, but to no avail. There was nothing for it but to go to hospital. A very uncomfortable and painful journey followed to Bangor hospital where I had my joint reset under general anaesthetic.

(Before reaching Bangor though we saw a sign for a hospital and turned into the grounds only to be told that if I wasn't pregnant there was nothing they could do; it was a maternity hospital.)

The company I worked for at that time weren't as sympathetic as ICI had been and they told me that they would have to terminate my employment. This did have some advantage insomuch as it saved me from having to resign some weeks later when we were ready to go to the Alps.

Chapter 16
Alpine Action- Calanques Recuperation 1964

Clive was nearly ready when Martin, Maggie and I arrived at his mother's house in Sheffield to collect him. A few brews later with Clive's gear packed in the van we were ready to go. Our first port of call was Martin's home in Tunbridge in Kent, where we were made very welcome by Martin's mother and father. After our evening meal, leaving Martin and Maggie talking to Mr and Mrs Boysen, Clive and I went off to the local pub with Martin's brother Bill. After a pleasant stay, next day we were on our way to France.

Bill Bowker and his girlfriend Irene went with Les and Margaret Brown and family in their dormobile to Cortina, taking five days to get there!

After pitching camp below the Tofana in poor weather they spent a day buying supplies and settling in.

Les suggested starting with an easy route on the Cinque Torre. After a shaky start in rain and mist they did the South face of the Torre Grande. Three days later a two and a half hour ascent of the classic Franceschi route convinced them they were on form.

Leaving the girls, Les and Bill hitched to the Lavaredo hut where they were pleased to see some friends from England who had just avoided a wet bivouac on the Piccola and so they all celebrated at the hut.

The next day nobody felt like climbing but Les and Stan Bradshaw decided to bestir themselves and did the south wall of the Punta di Frida. Bill with Johnny Hamer did the Cassin on the Piccolissima.

The following day Les and Bill started the north face of the Cima Ovest, the Cassin route. They were slightly concerned about the unsettled weather which turned to mist and rain; it didn't seem to affect them much, that is until they reached the waterfall pitch where they were soaked by a great deluge. Emerging from this pitch cold and wet they were confronted by some tricky climbing, made more difficult by having numbed fingers. There followed a long snow pitch to the top of the couloir and the summit. Les knew the descent and they were soon back at the hut to enjoy a stew and some beers with their friends.

After enjoying a break at the Adriatic coast and another route back in the Dolomites, the south face of the Torre Venezia, graded V superior, Les and family left for home and Bill and Irene hitch-hiked to the Kaisergebirge.

The next day Richard, Arthur Williams, Arthur's girlfriend Sandra and Tony Riley arrived; all were travelling in Tony's car. Bill did the Sudost on the Fleischbank with Richard and Arthur then moved on to Chamonix. Richard and team moved on to the Dolomites where they did a lot of hard climbing. They then went to the Bregaglia where the three lads did the north ridge of the Piz Badile and following this Richard and Arthur did the NE Face in six and a half hours. In total that season the pair of them did 26,000 ft of high standard climbing. (This was only three months after Richard's accident)

There is an amusing story about Arthur's girlfriend. Sandra, who had no experience of climbing or camping for that matter, noticed that Riley had a cup exactly like hers. Obviously worried about the chance that she might get Tony's cup, she asked Tony how they would tell the difference. Tony asked her to pass her cup to him, whereupon he broke off the handle and said, "There you are, that's yours."

After the Badile, this team also moved on to Chamonix.

Meanwhile, Pike and Diana, Paul Nunn, Woolcock and Mike Richardson in Pike's dormobile set off for the Alps. Wool drove; they wouldn't allow Pike to drive as no one considered him safe. They arrived in the Kaisergebirge at the Stripsenjoch Hut; this was the first time in the Alps for Mike and Pike and they did a route on the Fleischbank. Paul and Wool did the Fleischbank SE Face and the SE Verschneidung. Later, Paul and Wool set off to do the Predigstuhl west face and found themselves behind a German team of three who looked to be heading for the same climb. The Germans were scrambling up well above when one of them fell and went about 300ft, cart wheeling and bouncing before a free fall to land on small, fine scree; which probably saved his life. Wool was the first to reach him and said he was trying to get up despite many injuries. The lads helped get the injured man into a rescue helicopter, and then they went down, put off climbing for the day. A year later someone saw this same German on his first trip back climbing. Paul and Wool then went round to do the Mauk West Wall. There was a hut close by but it was closed so they slept out near the route but couldn't find any water. Next morning they set off without a drink. By midday, in the full sun it was very hot. They were reduced to licking damp patches of rock wherever they could find them. Finishing the route and heading down to the valley they saw some cows drinking from a trough; chasing the cows away they drank and drank, then continued their descent. They then went via the Salbitchschen in central Switzerland and did the Zwillingsturm and Pike and Mike did the South Ridge. Arriving in Chamonix, Paul had arranged to meet Pat Fearnehough so Wool spent that time climbing with Rod Brown (SUMC) and they headed off to Courmayeur on the Italian side of Mont Blanc where they did the second ascent of the North Face of Mont Gruetta. Paul and Pat with two others had an attempt at the Bonatti Pillar but had to bale out 800ft above the couloir due to a bad storm.

Trevor Briggs and Willis Ward, also going to the Alps for their first visit, left Sheffield and hitched to the A1 hoping to get lifts to Dover. While standing at the roundabout a van pulled up. It was Dave Gregory and his climbing partner on their way to the Dolomites; they took the lads all the way to Chamonix. That must rank as one of the best lifts ever!

Al Wright and Gerry Rogan travelled by train to Chamonix. This was Gerry's first time but Al had done a number of good routes on previous visits.

Tanky had made an enormous sack for Gerry which was a good job because besides all the climbing and camping gear Gerry had packed 30 tins of corned beef and 30 packets of Knorr soups. These he had been hoarding under his bed all winter thinking this would keep expenses down on their coming trip to the Alps. I wonder if they ate them all.

I'm not sure what other climbs they did, but they did manage an ascent of the West Face of the Dru.

There was now a large contingent of the Alpha Club in the Mont Blanc area along with an assortment of other English climbers and some Americans, namely John Harlin, Mick Burke and colleagues from the International school at Leysin.

Joe Brown and Tom Patey were camped there and told us that they had done a new route on the Pic Sans Nom, a peak between the Aguille Verte and the Dru. Joe had also set off to attempt the first ascent of the

South Face of the Fou with Whillans but found that they had been pipped at the post by a strong American team who were accompanied by a Scottish friend of ours, Stewart Fulton of the Creagh Dhu. Don and Joe got fed up of wrestling with a ridiculously heavy rucksack and decided to retreat after climbing 600ft. (See "The Hard Years", by Joe Brown.)

After settling in at the Biolay campsite, Clive and Martin teamed up with Mick Burke and Bivouac Bill to climb the east ridge of the Crocodile. The four lads toiled up to spend the night near the Envers hut. As they prepared their evening meal and bivouac site, the famous French Guide Lionel Terray arrived at the hut with a female client. Starting very early next day they were surprised to find Terray and his client ahead of them on the first couloir. Terray pronounced the couloir dangerous and was proved right when an avalanche swept down hitting Mick head on. Bill had managed to shout a warning and had held Mick on a tight rope enabling him to make a sideways leap to emerge white and grinning.

Catching up with Martin and Clive as they were crossing the second couloir to the ridge proper, Mick was leading, 70 ft away with no runners, when a loud rumble announced a rock fall which narrowly missed him. After this second incident Mick was elected chief avalanche tester!

Terray lost the route (it was 20 years since he had last climbed this ridge) but after some exploration the lads found the correct line and went into the lead. Some chimneys followed which involved some sack hauling then an A2 pitch and sections of grade IV to the summit. The lads left some slings and etriers for Terray at his request and as the impending storm broke they raced down to the Requin hut with ice axes buzzing. They continued down the Mer de Glace, now slippery smooth, all the glacier grit having been washed away by the torrential rain. It took a while to find the exit ladders in the dark as only Clive's torch was working. At this point Martin announced that he needed the toilet and borrowing their only torch moved away to one side. He switched off the torch and put it down on the ice. When he had finished, he couldn't find it and shouted to the others to help look for it. Clive replied, "If you think I'm going to crawl about the ice in the dark when you've just been there you've got to be joking."

It was midnight when they reached the campsite where we welcomed them back with brews and a stew.

The next day Lionel Terray came to the camp to return the gear that the lads had left on the route for him. He thanked them for their help and told us that he and his client had bivouacked in the storm.

One day Mick came back from Chamonix with a big grin on his face. The young woman teller at the bank had given him £10 in francs in exchange for a ten shilling note. He was now visiting all the English tents, asking if anyone had two ten bob notes in exchange for a pound.

I was getting a bit restless, not being able to climb because of my dodgy shoulder, so I asked Maggie if she would like to accompany me on a walk up to the Requin hut and back. Martin had no objections to this, so packing our sacks we set off up the path to Montenvers.

It was a beautiful clear, sunny day and soon we were descending the ladders to the Mer de Glace. By the time we reached the hut it was early evening so finding a good spot to bivvy we cooked our evening meal and drank in the magnificent scenery.

Looking back and across the glacier we could see the Dru and the Aiguille du Moine and in the opposite direction the Grandes Jorasses and the Geant icefall.

I no sooner closed my eyes than it was morning. It was another crystal clear day and after a small breakfast and a brew, Maggie and I set off back the way we had come. Descending the path from Montenvers seemed endless and in the heat of the day we were very thirsty. Passing a chalet café half way down, I noticed a big bottle of lemonade on a table with no apparent owner.

Leaping over the small fence I grabbed the bottle and we both ran off down the track. When we considered it safe we took long drinks and continued on our way back to camp.

On arriving back at the Biolay we found the lads planning to leave for the S.W. Pillar of the Dru. There was a good weather forecast for the next three days which in the event proved to be correct. They departed for the Dru and that night on the rognon, Martin, Clive, Bill and Mick cooked and ate a big meal, leaving them with marginal three-day rations. At 5am the two ropes set off up the couloir; climbing its true left bank. The climbing was easy and one pitch across the snow would have taken them to the West Face. This was their alternative plan if the couloir above proved too dangerous. However as nothing had fallen during the night, Mick led up into the bottleneck of the couloir down which any debris must fall. There was plenty of snow and ice to contend with as they climbed up and up into the huge amphitheatre bounded by the Flammes de Pierres ridge. A threat of rockfalls from the poised blocks and loose ledges up above hurried them towards the foot of the Pillar itself which seemed to offer some shelter from the danger. Crossing to the upper subsidiary couloir, which they climbed in one long pitch, they reached the base of the Pillar and the start of the rock-climbing difficulties. About 1,200 ft had taken them almost six hours.

Bill Bowker recalls that after a short rest Martin and Clive took the lead on the Pillar. The initial series of V pitches provided magnificent jamming and bridging and led them to the first VI pitch, a Vee-groove with an awkward exit to the left. The standard was sustained on sound rock and the climbing was very enjoyable. A grade VI crack and a slanting gangway led to the first aid pitch which was followed by a strenuous VI chimney/crack. This landed them on a good ledge for a well-earned brew and a snack.

Off again up the steep red wall above to long cracks and strenuous climbing, until a move to the right brought them to the bivouac ledges below the A2 overhang.

There was just enough room for all four of them to sit comfortably, and it was there that they used the last of their water for a mixture of vegetable and tea-leaf soup, before settling down for the night. After a cold, dry breakfast the next morning they set off in fine weather taking the obvious line avoiding the A2 overhang, and instead swung immediately back on to the Pillar via an overhanging crack which led to a line of pegs up a crack fault in two pitches of A1 and A2. Splendid free climbing at grade V overlooking the West Face, followed by several short, awkward cracks brought them to the only easy ground on the whole route, and their first drinks of the day!

A hair-raising move over a loose peg where Martin, unusually for him, declined the lead was followed by a steep wall taking them to the foot of the final chimneys. One etrier move on the first pitch proved to be the crux, and soon they were hurrying along a quartz ledge to the descent.

Six abseils landed them on easy ground but an imminent storm decided them to take an early bivouac. Onion soup and tea were prepared just in time. The storm didn't last for long and the following morning they descended at their leisure.

Bill and Irene went back home and as Martin and Clive were planning to do the Walker Spur on the Grandes Jorasses and wished to keep more or less the same team. It meant that Mick needed to find a new climbing partner. Fortunately a Creagh Dhu member, Alec Fulton, Stewart's older brother, said that he would like to climb with Mick, so the team became four once again. The weather was very hot and appeared quite settled so as the lads prepared for the Walker, Maggie and I decided to have a go at the Grands Mulets route on Mont Blanc with four lads from the Black and Tans, Dave Little, Brian Sullivan, John Laine and Big Derek Farrington.

Sullivan was always joking and wisecracking and I remember one time when we nearly got thrown out of a café in Wales when he shouted, "Does anyone know where I can get a good meal?" and "How do you manage to cut bread this thin?"

Apart from Dave Little this was their first time in the Alps and they were keen to do something, so why not start with the highest mountain in Europe! Sullivan and Farrington were of the same type but Laine seemed a quieter and more responsible type. I had known Dave Little a long time and knew him to be a reliable and skilful climber.

We all went up on the telepherique to the Plan des Aiguilles and walked across to the old telepherique station where we intended to spend the night.

The old station was a cluster of disused concrete buildings reminiscent of World War 2 air-raid shelters and looked as though it could be home to rats and other undesirables; we fitted in perfectly. Finding a relatively clean and sound building we made our beds, cooked a meal and settled down for the night.

A late start the next day saw us making our way across the lower part of the Glacier des Pelerins where at one point we all stopped for a rest and a drink of water near some boulders. Sitting there chatting in a relaxed manner we heard a loud groaning noise from the glacier and felt sure that one of the boulders had moved; this was followed by the roar of a large avalanche in one of the couloirs on the Aiguille Du Midi. We felt it was time to move so with Maggie and I leading the way we crossed the rest of the glacier then followed a faint path across moraine to the edge of the Bossons Glacier.

The way ahead lay below some large threatening seracs so roped together in pairs we all hurried to pass through this dangerous area and were relieved to leave it behind.

From there on we only had large crevasses to contend with as we climbed the steepening glacier towards the Refuge des Grands Mulets where we planned to spend the night. At one point I was crossing a snow bridge over a wide crevasse with Maggie belaying me from below, when a Chamonix Guide who was descending with two German clients stopped on the opposite side waiting for us to cross. One of his clients suddenly staggered like a drunken man on to the same snow bridge as me but the Guide yanked him back with the rope and the small, fat German fell in an exhausted heap in the snow. The Guide said to me, "Pardon, monsieur," and after waiting for us to cross, he started to kick his exhausted client at the same time shouting, "Allez, allez." (go, go). The poor man got up and staggered across the snow bridge; he was obviously on his last legs but the Guide was determined to get him down. It's to be hoped that he had paid in advance!

It was late afternoon when we arrived at the hut. We were all tired and went inside to buy coffee, the price of which shocked us. On enquiring what the hut fee was for one night we were shocked again and decided to sleep in the old refuge further down the ridge of the rognon. The old refuge was a rickety wooden building perched on the edge of a precipice. The toilet was a hole in the floor of a small cubicle, on a platform which stuck out on wooden scaffolding overhanging the bergschrund on the glacier far below. Best not to walk under there!

Just as we were settling down for the night, the hut guardian came down to tell us we were not allowed to stay in the old hut. We argued with him saying that we couldn't afford the proper refuge. He started to jump around like Mohamed Ali with fists raised and said, "I box facile." At this we moved outside and said we would spend the night on the rocks. Then he told us that a grand tempest was forecast and that we wouldn't be safe outside and reluctantly said that if we stayed at the refuge we wouldn't have to pay; this was an offer we couldn't refuse and we willingly accepted the warmth of the new hut and its comfortable bunks.

Just after midnight we breakfasted on coffee and bread and jam, donned our boots, crampons and warm clothes and stepped outside into what was a very warm night for that altitude. The time was around 1am.

There were other parties in front of us, some of them guided. The going felt hard, mainly because we were tired from the day before and were above 10,000ft for the first time that summer. Plodding along in the light of our head torches, weaving between and crossing over big crevasses, we came to the Petit Plateau.

Around here we met the hut guardian, Mohamed Ali; he was out checking weather gauges. He again told us there was going to be a big storm and that it was too warm with water dripping off the seracs when it should have been frozen.

It was now almost light so we decided to press on a bit further to see how things would develop. A little higher up, looking back we could see cloud building up over the Aiguilles Rouges and on the upper part of Mont Blanc and the Dome du Gouter there was low cloud. High above us some were turning back. Maggie and I decided to do the same; the other four said they would go a bit higher.

Retracing our steps and having to make some big leaps from the upper lips of the bigger crevasses we were soon back at the hut. Collecting the gear that we had left there we set out to descend the Bossons glacier and looking back noticed that the others had also started to retreat.

The weather looked threatening as we hurried down to run the gauntlet of the dripping seracs. By midday back at the Plan des Aiguilles, sods law, the sun came out and the sky turned blue. That hut guardian and his weather forecast; he should get a job at the Met office.

Arriving back at the campsite we found that the lads had left for the Walker; that night they bivvied at the old ruined Lechaux hut. The next day the weather was bad but they decided to stay up there. The hut guardian's forecast had been right after all but one day late! The only trouble was they wouldn't have enough food. Clive volunteered to go back down to Chamonix to buy more rations. This he did and spent the night in our tent with me and a ginger kitten that had crawled in to escape the storm; then both he and the kitten left early next day, Clive back up to the Lechaux, as for the kitten it's anyone's guess!

The next day after Clive's return they started the climb in fine weather. The first 1000ft they found to be easy and decided to bivouac below the Fissure Rebuffat; but first, Martin climbed the crack to fix a rope for the next day and then abseiled back down to the bivouac ledge.

Next day they were away early and after 15 hours of climbing they bivvied at the top of the Red couloir. The following morning they reached the summit and descended to Entreves where they were pleased to see Anne Fowler and Dale Brown who looked after them and gave them a meal. Wool and Rod were away on the North Face of Mont Gruetta at the time.

The lads needed to get back to Chamonix but didn't have enough money for transport all the way back. So after a tiring walk up to the Torino hut, Clive suffering with bad blisters, they found they had enough for the telepherique from the Torino to Chamonix.

Maggie, Martin, Clive and I decided to head for the sun and set off for the Calanques. This is an area of limestone fiords to the east of Marseille and is noted for its splendid rock-climbs

Arriving at Marseille around midnight, we were immediately lost; I was driving and found myself on a dual carriageway going in the wrong direction. There wasn't much traffic about so I swung the van across the central reservation and we were back on route for the Callanques. An hour or so later, stopping at a wild rugged area down a rocky track, Clive and I dossed down in our sleeping bags on the ground leaving Maggie and Martin to sleep in the van.

The next morning, the weather was fantastic; hot sun and clear blue sky.

We drove slowly down to the end of the rocky track where it was found that we could park the van on a flat area at the cliff top overlooking the Calanques.

Looking down into the Calanque 500ft below us we saw a pebble beach and the clearest turquoise sea that I had ever seen outside a movie.

Leading down the cliffs to the beach was a footpath way-marked with red painted circles on the white limestone. A short way down the path and to one side was a ruined villa sitting on a stony terrace. At the seaward side of the villa was a small paved area with a wall to prevent any sleep-walkers from falling down the cliffs.

Exploring this villa, which had a good roof, we found that it was occupied by three German climbers who said they had no objections to us staying there as there was plenty of room for us all. After moving in some of our gear, we were told that there wasn't any water nearby and that it had to be carried in from the town of Cassis about seven miles away. We borrowed water off the German, promising to replace it when visiting Cassis that evening.

After some breakfast we followed the paint flashes down to the beach. The sea was lovely and warm and after our few weeks in the Alps it was good to relax in such a beautiful place enjoying the sun and the swimming.

Owing to the steepness and inaccessibility of the path there were very few people down there and the ones who were seemed to be mainly climbers.

That evening we drove to Cassis for a meal and groceries and after buying some containers, filled them with water to take back to the Villa.

Mick Burke, John Harlin and another American named Sandy arrived the next day just as the Germans were leaving, and judging by the amount of pegs that they had, it looked like they meant serious business.

Pike and Diana turned up, followed by Tony Riley with Arthur and Sandra. Richard had stayed behind in Chamonix with Mike Richardson, Wool and Rod Brown and the four of them went off to do the Roc -Grepon Traverse and were caught in a very bad storm. They completed the climb and got back safely but the storm claimed a lot of lives across the Mont Blanc range.

It was obvious that Arthur was getting a bit fed up with Sandra as he kept making cutting remarks about her but it was her own fault because she was always saying and doing silly things. Once when everyone except Sandra had been down to the beach we returned to the villa to find that all the water was gone; even the American's water had been used up. Upon asking Sandra what had happened to it she told us that she had washed her hair. The poor foolish girl was in the dog house from then on, particularly with Arthur, who had to drive with Riley the seven miles to Cassis to replenish our supplies.

It was an enjoyable week, climbing, sunbathing and swimming and there was a good deepwater problem traverse along the cliffs of the main fiord.

One day much to our amusement, Harlin, the tall muscular blonde god, walked down to the water's edge followed closely by Little Mick, scruffy, unshaven, bespectacled and looking typically English, in big baggy khaki shorts and flippers. He was carrying Harlin's scuba gear and a harpoon gun; we immediately christened him Commander Crab. He and Harlin donned their diving equipment and swam out to where there were some underwater caves. John dived to explore these while Mick trod water above in case John got in difficulties. I don't know what he could have done because Harlin had the only set of oxygen cylinders!

Another time on an evening out at Cassis, some of us were sat at a table on the edge of the quay enjoying a beer. Pike and Di came over to join us, Pike pulled out a chair and without looking was about to sit down with the back legs of the chair overhanging the edge of the harbour wall. I shouted a warning to him and averted what would have been a double somersaulting Pike and chair into the 20ft of water ten feet below us. Clive who had been watching the whole episode said, "Why did you warn him, Al, you've spoilt the fun!"

Our time in the South of France came to an end and we all went our separate ways;

Mick Burke and John Harlin back to Leysin in Switzerland and the rest of us headed home to England.

That was the last time that I saw John Harlin, who was killed during the winter of 1965/66 when a rope that he was jumaring on, snapped whilst attempting to climb the Eiger N. Face Direct which is now known as the Harlin Route.

Chapter 17
New Partnerships 1964-65

B ack home in England I was pleased to find that my van had been repaired and re-sprayed. I immediately set about looking for work and at first worked as a labourer on a big new housing estate on the outskirts of my home town. I eventually got a job as an airframe fitter at A.V.Roe's (British Aerospace) at Chadderton in Manchester; this was really good money but involved over an hour's travelling each day.

While at A.V. Roe's, I became friendly with an ex- MUMC member who worked in the Drawing Office. His name was Keith and he had been at Manchester University at the same time as Martin and Maggie.

Maggie had now started work as a teacher in Manchester but Martin and Richard were living in a caravan in the woods near Beddgelert working as woodcutters for the Forestry Commission. Another climber who lived at the caravan was Geoff Skitt, a friend of Arthur Williams. Most weeks Maggie, Arthur and I would go down together in my van to spend the weekend with the lads, but as winter approached Martin decided to go back to Manchester to become a teacher and Richard went to work as a joiner at the Pen-y- Gwryd. From then on our Wednesday evening meetings were held at Martin's and Maggie's flat in Chorlton.

Arthur had befriended a young climber whom he brought along with him to our meetings. The lad was very quiet and seemed quite shy. His name was Jim Perrin; others who came occasionally were some members of the Black and Tans climbing club, Eddie Birch, Dave Little Tony Brooder and Pete Cowie. All these climbers frequented the Manchester Sports Guild and it became a meeting place for us also, usually on a Monday, or a Friday night before going away for the weekend.

The Manchester Alpha and some of the Black &Tans became merged together almost like another club but remained independent of each other as far as membership of the original clubs was concerned.

On Thursday nights some of us would go to a nightclub in Longsight where there was a live Rhythm and Blues group and late drinking. The J&J club was run by students from Manchester University and it was there that, through Keith, we met the newest members of the MUMC, such as the Barley brothers, Robin and Tony who were from Harrogate in Yorkshire and were very good climbers, and some female members who were very good-looking.

One Sunday some of the other lads and I were climbing at Lawrencefield when who should arrive there but the MUMC. Among them were Robin and Tony Barley and a young woman called Sheila Jackson. Sheila told us that she came from Southport and that she was in her first year at Manchester University; we all chatted and climbed together and they mentioned that they were going to Wales the next weekend.

The following Saturday was very cold with a lot of snow on the mountains. Arthur Williams and I had winter gear with us and planned to do a route on Snowdon on Sunday.

On Saturday night Arthur and I went to the dance at the Swallow Falls Hotel where we were pleased to see some MUMC members. Sheila was there and told us that she and three other women were hoping to do the Snowdon Horseshoe. When we asked if they had ice axes, they said that they hadn't, so we warned them that it could be dangerous without proper gear, particularly along the Crib Goch ridge.

On Sunday morning Arthur and I walked up the Miner's Track as far as Glaslyn. The day was overcast and very cold and the lake was frozen hard. Leaving the track, we made our way round to the top end of the lake to where a long snow slope led up to the cliffs below the Snowdon summit. Kicking steps in the hard snow I was thankful for my axe but wished that like Arthur I had brought crampons along. At the foot of the cliffs an easy-angled buttress of broken rock and ice looked to be the obvious way to reach the chimneys and gullies of the upper crag. Soloing carefully, Arthur going first with crampons and one axe, with me close behind him with my old Aschenbrenner and Vibrams soled boots. After about 100ft, we came to a steep little ice wall about 20ft in height. Arthur climbed it slowly, cutting steps and handholds until he arrived at a good ledge where he stopped to watch my progress. When I was about 8ft below the ledge, I paused to cut an extra step. Suddenly I heard a whirring noise and glancing upwards, I saw a large rock turning end over end hurtling straight for me. I pulled my sack up to protect my head and probably prayed. The rock smashed into the ice at about my shoulder level, spraying ice particles everywhere. I moved up quickly to the ledge. Arthur said later that he heard the rock hit the ice and looked away, and when he looked back again I was stood beside him. It's surprising how a falling rock can spur you to action!

The rest of the climb we did roped together and reached the top without further incident.

Back down at the Pen-y-Pass we heard that a woman had been killed on Crib Goch; we worried that it might be one of the MUMC women.

The next evening I drove down Manchester to where I knew Sheila Jackson lived, rang the doorbell and was relieved when Sheila answered the door and assured me that they had all got back safely, having decided to take our advice.

I asked Sheila if she would like to go climbing with me in Derbyshire the following Sunday.

She agreed and this was the start of a long friendship and sometimes climbing partnership.

Over the following months Sheila and I climbed more and more with each other. It was good for me to be leading easier climbs rather than seconding hard ones and I began gradually to regain my confidence, but still had to be careful with my shoulder, particularly on mantelshelf moves.

There were now quite a lot of women attached to the Alpha. Paul and Hilary got married and Paul started work as a lecturer in history at Sheffield Hallam University. Wool and Anne also married around this time as did Mike and Judy Richardson and Pete Maddocks and Edna. Clive and Steph started going out together and Maggie and Martin got married in Maggie's home village of Calder Vale near Garstang. Some of us went to the wedding in Tony Riley's car but the exhaust fell off on the A6 and we arrived there late, just as they came out of church. The car sounded like a Lancaster bomber and we got some funny looks from the other wedding guests. We went to a pub down the road and waited there for Martin and Maggie to turn up. After waving goodbye to their guests at the reception, supposedly to go off on honeymoon, they met us at the pub and then we all went off to the Lakes together.

At Pike and Di's wedding, I was best man, and as we came out of the church everyone was kissing the bride except Tanky who grabbed Pike and made everybody laugh by giving him a big kiss. At the reception there was a bit of wild behaviour with some dancing on the tables; I don't know what Di's relatives thought of it.

Barry Ingle started to go out with Pat Braithwaite and Pete Crew always seemed to have a girlfriend with him. Les and Margaret had been married three years and were living in Scotland.

Stan Goodwin got married and so did Andy Garvey; it seemed that everyone was getting paired up, which meant ordering twice as many meals at club dinners.

Easter 1965 Pike and Di and Sheila and I went skiing at Aviemore. I had managed to borrow four lots of skis and sticks from Bob Brigham who generously wouldn't accept any payment for them; although thinking about it, I probably never even offered to pay. He did say though that we would have to pay for any loss or breakages.

Tanky, Trevor, Clive, Don Morrison and some others from Sheffield were there in Aviemore and most of them were accomplished skiers

Our team of four were complete novices so Tanky took us under his wing, showing us how to walk up hill in skis and how to turn.

At the top of the White Lady ski run on the nursery slopes in a small corrie we gained some confidence, enough to make Pike and me think we were ready to tackle something steep. Tanky had told us that when descending steep slopes, it was best to traverse back and forth across the slope.

Pike and I forgot about this and decided to have a race. Straight down! I don't know what speed we attained but it was fast and we were heading for a cliff or steepening lower down the slope.

Suddenly when all seemed lost, help arrived in the shape of Tanky. Skiing like James Bond, he overtook us on our left, cut in front of us and turning to face us so that he was skiing backwards he shouted to us to stop. "How do we do that?" we yelled. "Fall over," came the reply. Down we went in a jumble of skis, sticks and arms and legs. I was lucky to not dislocate my shoulder; the only casualty was a broken stick.

The day after, Pike and I walked up Cairngorm on a beautiful sunny blue day. That is what I remember most about that weekend, that and Bob Brigham letting us off for the ski-stick.

After the Easter weekend Sheila stopped coming out so that she could revise for her exams. We kept in touch and she often came to the Wednesday meetings at Boysen's flat.

Paul and Wool started working on the new Borrowdale guide which meant that between 1965 and 1967 they discovered a lot of new routes; among these were Plagiarism E2 on Lower Falcon and Eyrie HVS on Gillercombe. On Eagle Crag Langstrath, Paul Nunn and Paul Ross did Daedalus E2, The Sprogg HVS and Icarus HVS and were sometimes joined in their exploration by other Alpha members from the Sheffield section, i.e. Brian Griffiths and Mike Richardson. On Goat Crag during 1965 Les Brown pioneered his classic route Praying Mantis HVS and Woolcock and Nunn found Deadly Nightshade HVS.

Paul Nunn also took part in the first televised climb on Kilnsey Overhang in Yorkshire, managing to fit it in between the Alps and guidebook work.

Paul Ross who was fully recovered from his illness of the early sixties was again a major contributor to the new guide. From 1962 onward, Ross had continued to produce climbs on the Borrowdale crags, adding to his already impressive list of first ascents which he initiated way back in 1954.

After one weekend in the Lakes Paul and Wool were returning home on Paul's bike and were stopped at some traffic lights. Wool was riding pillion and feeling a bit stiff, stood up still astride the bike. He was busy watching an attractive young woman walking along the pavement and didn't see the lights change. Paul set off and left Wool standing astride in the middle of the road; the girl almost collapsed laughing!

Meanwhile in Wales during 1965 Martin, climbing with Arthur Williams, led the first ascents of Sexus, Black Spring and The Blade on Dinas Mot; and with Dave Little, he did the Plexus Girdle. Richard seconded by Bob Beesley did the second ascent of Martin Boysen's route, Pinnacle Arete on Cloggy.

Eddie Birch and I struck up a climbing partnership. Eddie was a member of the Black & Tans climbing club; he was good company and a very good climber. This partnership suited me as I no longer wanted to lead hard pitches but could second them and cut the risk of dislocating my shoulder. The pair of us did routes such as Firstslip and Legslip at Tremadog, Plexus on Dinas Mot and many more good climbs. I also remember us doing White Slab on Cloggy at Whitsuntide.

Arthur Williams and Duncan Knowles (Nogs) were with us on a separate rope climbing behind us. At the foot of the main slab, I was belayed to an old peg. Eddie set off to lead the slab. Arthur and Nogs were belayed to the same peg as me and as there wasn't much room on the ledge, I had a long belay so as to be nearer to Eddie and still leave a space for the other two.

All was going well; everyone was relaxed watching Eddie progressing methodically up the slab. He had a couple of good runners on but was quite high above them. Cleaning some grass away he discovered a small flake, enough for a thin piece of line. Climbing on he came to where he should have gone left into Gecko Groove but got off route, climbing directly up almost to the Lasso pitch. Then his foot slipped off a greasy hold and he came off. I had been paying out the rope round my waist. I tried to take in some slack, and then Eddie's weight came on the line runner; he had fallen about 50ft. I thought, "How many times has this happened to me with other leaders?" Because of my long belay I was lifted off the ledge so both Eddie and I were hanging from the same thread of line. As I took off, Arthur grabbed my sweater which stretched about 10ft before I ceased my upward journey; Nogs grabbed Arthur's jacket collar with one hand and held in the peg with the other! It must have looked like something from a Charlie Chaplin film; all that was missing were the bowler hats. Luckily for all concerned, the line held and the peg stayed in and Eddie was OK.

He resumed the climb, going the right way this time. On reaching the top of the crag without further mishap, we all enthused about the beautiful climb that we had just done.

One Saturday night in the bar of the Padarn Hotel, Barry Ingle came up to me and asked if I would like to do Taurus on Cloggy with him the following day.

At that time Taurus had an awesome reputation. I told Barry that because the route was reputed to be very strenuous I was worried that my shoulder might not stand up to it. Barry was very persuasive and with the help of a few pints I at last agreed.

Next day saw the pair of us at Cloggy. We climbed The Corner then traversed the Green Gallery still roped together. Barry belayed at the foot of Taurus and as I was pulling up to the belay stance a large flake came away from under my feet. Barry held me on the rope and we both let out warning shouts as the flake disappeared over the top of the East Buttress. We heard it crash into the scree below and hoped that no one had been in the way. This unnerved us slightly but after a fag and changing over belays we were ready to proceed.

Barry inched his way up the groove of Taurus. Protection was sparse. At the overhang he managed to get a thin sling on a small spike but after a few attempts he was beginning to lose enthusiasm and to my relief announced that he was coming down saying that he didn't fancy it.

Leaving the small spike runner in place to protect his descent he reversed the groove to join me at the stance.

Trying to flick the sling and karabiner off the spike without success Barry decided to lead the first wall of Spillikin HVS, which went up diagonally to our right to a very exposed stance. He would then be level with the overhang on Taurus, but some distance away from it horizontally. The idea was to flick the runner loose from there. It didn't work. He got to the stance but the runner wouldn't come loose. It came off partially but not the whole way. I would have to climb up to Baz with the rope going from me to the overhang on Taurus, through the now dodgy runner below it. From there, the rope went across horizontally for about 60ft to Ingle; this didn't inspire me with confidence but it had to be done.

As I climbed diagonally rightwards Barry had to pay out the rope to avoid pulling me towards the runner which was up to my left.

The hardest bit of that pitch of Spillikin is the first 15 to 20ft. I worried that if I fell off, there was a good chance that the runner on Taurus would pull and that I would go in the same direction as that big loose flake - over the top of the East Buttress. My fears were unfounded; I climbed the wall carefully and soon joined Barry at the ledge. A couple of flicks, with us holding both ends of the rope and the runner came off. It's amazing the lengths we used to go to so as not to lose any gear! We finished the climb and agreed that although we hadn't done Taurus our day had not lacked excitement.

Some weeks later I left my job at A.V. Roe's and with Eddie Birch set off in my van to drive to Chamonix. Leaving Stockport at 5.30pm on Friday, we drove down to Dover, crossed to Ostende then down through Belgium and France, driving almost non-stop to arrive in Chamonix at mid-day on Sunday.

On our arrival at the Biolay campsite, all the old faces were there. Richard and Mo (Julian Antoine) had come from the Dolomites where they had done the Phillip Flam in very wet conditions. Richard said there were waterfalls down the route, and soaked through, they bivvied in a cave five pitches from the top. Next day on these upper pitches of the climb, it was snowing. Nevertheless they finished the route and climbed up to the summit of the Civetta; this ascent was the third one by Alpha club members.

Back in the valley they decided to split up and hitch-hike to Chamonix.

Paul and Wool had been out to the Wetterstein on Paul's heavily loaded Triumph Bonneville. Wool tried to catch some sleep on the pillion only to be wakened up by Paul beating him on the knees; apparently the bike had been swaying all over the place.

Somewhere near Frankfurt, on the autobahn, they got a flat tyre. Paul managed to slow down to around thirty before dropping the bike.

Rolling over and over in the road with a big truck getting closer and closer they finally stopped and fortunately, so did the truck.

The German AA arrived but couldn't help them as a new tyre was needed and all they had access to were European sizes. Finally a local biker stopped and got their story. An hour or so later he came back with a bunch from a local bike club; they had found a used tyre of the right size. They fitted it and wouldn't take anything for the tyre or their trouble.

After a long walk up to the Oberreintal hut they received a good welcome being amongst the first British parties to visit there.

The hut warden insisted they do a fairly easy climb just above the hut and even went along with them accompanied by another German climber.

The next day he suggested they do a harder climb, The Gelbe U. When they got back to the hut that night, he asked how they had found it. When they said it had been straightforward, he told them to do the N Face of the Oberreintalurm, (V1) which they did next day. On returning again to the hut that evening he said, "Now you can do any route you want."

They did the SE Face of the Schusselkarspitze because it was in Hermann Buhl's book, then headed off to the Dolomites, to the Marmolata, which they found was plastered with snow. Not wishing to hang about they ended up in Chamonix where they did a route on the Peigne. In between rainy, misty days they made an ascent of the Central Spur on the Aiguille du Midi.

Richard and Mo who were also in Chamonix, went off to climb the West Face of the Blaitiere the first ascent of which had been done in 1954 by Brown and Whillans.

Richard said that the Fissure Brown and the Fissure Whillans were typical of many of the harder cracks on gritstone at home.

The lads climbed the whole Face to the summit of the Blaitiere instead of traversing off at the Fontaine ledges as many parties do. They said there were some hard pitches on the upper section and enjoyed going to the summit; after all, why traverse off after the hardest section when there is good climbing above?

John Moss was at the campsite with Bill Barker and this pair teamed up with Richard and Mo, hoping to do the Bonatti Pillar on the Aiguille du Dru. They had all been down to the Callanques together to get away from the bad weather in the Alps, returning to Chamonix after a nice week in the sun.

The weather was still very unsettled and we all spent our time eating massive communal meals. Mo had some catering size tins of corned beef and one of these along with potatoes and other veg was put into a massive pan and stewed.

Waiting with great anticipation for this meal to be ready were about ten hungry climbers. At last it was time to eat; everyone had a large helping and there was still plenty left. Most of us declined second helpings but Richard, Mo, Paul and Wool carried on eating. It appeared to be some kind of contest each one trying to out eat the others, loosening their belts and belching periodically to make more room in their slowly swelling stomachs. Eventually the pan was empty and all four competitors collapsed in a bloated heap like a pride of lions after consuming a kill.

During an upturn in the weather Richard and Mo with John and Bill set off for the Dru where they bivvied at the foot of the face.

They were puzzled by the sound of what they thought to be cow-bells, thinking, what are cows doing up here?

Then they saw the source of this clanking noise. It was the Americans, John Harlin and Royal Robbins, descending from an attempt at the West Face Direct. They were carrying some large new type of pitons, called Bongs, invented by the Americans for use in wide cracks; it was these banging against each other that sounded like cow-bells.

Also at the foot of the route were two other climbers whom the lads knew from climbing in Wales, Al Hunt and Ron James, but these two were going on the West Face.

Setting off before dawn, the lads were dismayed to see the beams of seventeen head torches ahead of them in the couloir.

The Dru couloir is infamous for its rock falls and being at the back of so many climbers wasn't a good thing; in fact one climber, a German, was hit by a rock and had to retreat helped by his friends. By the time the lads got to the narrows in the couloir which acts as a funnel for anything falling from above everyone else had either gone on to the West Face route or had descended.

As Mo was crossing the couloir to its left side with Richard belaying him, some big rocks came down just missing him. Mo looked up to the sky, shook his fist and shouted irreverently, "You couldn't hit me if you tried." Richard closed his eyes and said, "Please God don't chop Mo while I'm with him."

Arriving at the foot of the Pillar they decided to bivouac and get a good start the next day. Mo apparently amused everyone by donning ladies' tights for the bivouac, and pranced about pretending to be Nureyev.

After an early start with Richard and Mo going first, Richard doing most of the leading, they had a long day's climbing enabling them to reach a bivouac just below the shoulder. Next day after finishing the climb they made a safe descent to the valley.

Eddie and I set about getting fit by walking up to the Couvercle hut where Eddie did a route on the Moine with Jo Fuller. I had on some new boots and finished up with badly blistered feet.

Back at the Biolay John Smith had arrived on his first visit to the Alps.

John and I along with Eddie and Dave Little decided to go up to do the East face of the Aiguille du Grepon.

John and I took the train up to Montenvers and sat in the sun enjoying a beer overlooking the Mer de Glace. The view from here, looking up the glacier to the Grandes Jorasses and across to the Dru, must be one of the best views in the world; it's a pity it has to be tainted by the commercialism of the surroundings in which we were now sitting enjoying our drink.

As there was as yet no sign of Eddie and Lix who had decided to leave Chamonix later than us, John and I shouldered our sacks and descended the iron ladders which led to the Mer de Glace.

The afternoon sun beat down on us from a blue sky streaked with mare's tails. I had voiced my doubts about these clouds that morning at the campsite but had been accused by the others of wanting to fester. To shut them up and to and prove that my weather forecasting was superior to theirs, I agreed to go, thus proving my stupidity for letting them talk me into it instead of standing by my forecast and thus avoiding what was about to overtake us. I had thought OK, I'll go, but don't blame me!

John hadn't been on a glacier before and as I had said we only needed one axe, he had left his at the campsite. We hadn't brought sleeping bags knowing that there were blankets at the Tour Rouge hut. Taking our time we ambled along the almost flat glacier. When we reached the point below the Grepon we stopped for a rest and a drink and planned our route up the steep little glacier leading to the East face.

It was hard going uphill in deep soft snow and on reaching the Bergschrund, I was surprised to find it to be quite wide and overhung with a huge cornice. Roping up for the first time, with John standing well back, I crossed a snow bridge and cut my way up the opposite side. After belaying on the rock I threw my axe down for John to use and he quickly joined me. As the rocks above appeared to be very easy we unroped and put the rope back in the sack. Resting there on the slope at the foot of the East face we could see two figures far below us on the Mer de Glace.

It was Eddie and Lix; they seemed to be messing about near a crevasse and didn't appear to be making any progress. After a while they started up towards us so we decided to push on to the hut which was on a wide ledge about three or four hundred feet above us. Soloing up the rocks with the occasional tricky bits at possibly grade 3, we suddenly became aware that it had clouded in and a flash of lightning followed by a loud clap of thunder preceded a heavy downpour. Spurred on by the prospect of shelter, the final 150ft to the hut were climbed hurriedly.

It was only later that I thought of the possible consequences of climbing wet rock, unroped with the added danger of a recurrence of my shoulder dislocating; luckily this didn't happen and we arrived at the hut safe but soaked.

Looking at our accommodation for the night to come, we were less than impressed. The hut was made of wooden boards and was approximately 12ft square. It sat on a ledge of approximately the same size and was held in place with steel cables over the roof from the cliff above to the front edge of the ledge. There were splits in the boards which the wind whistled through.

Shortly afterwards, the lads arrived stripped to the waist to avoid getting all their clothes wet. They told us that they had found a rucksack full of gear in a shallow crevasse on the Mer de Glace and had hidden it under some boulders. They said it looked as though it belonged to a woman because it contained a bra and other items of women's clothing.

So that was what they had been doing when we spied them on the way up.

There were two other teams already ensconced when we arrived - a man from my home town and his wife who looked pleased to see us, and a French pair who didn't.

Stripping out of our wet clothes to our underpants the four of us donned our duvet Jackets; three of us laughed at John who was wearing army issue big baggy drawers. Asking the other occupants where the blankets were kept, we found that they had commandeered them all. The English couple gave us one of theirs; it was a ragged, threadbare thing and was barely big enough to cover the four of us. The French never spoke to us and didn't offer any of their blankets.

By this time there was a big storm raging. We set about making a potato and vegetable stew. John reached outside the door to where water was cascading out of a hollow space between the cliff and the hut; he filled the pan from this. Later we made many brews from the same source.

It was now dark and we were quite cold. Huddling beneath our only blanket, we shivered violently, teeth chattering; every time there was a lightning flash we could see right down the Face through the cracks in the outer wall;

Someone said, "I wonder how strong those cables are." He was told to shut up.

At dawn I was woken up by one of the Frenchmen getting up to go to the door to pee down the crag. I was cold and lay there waiting for the rest of our team to stir. Nobody seemed to want to move. The Frenchman returned to his bed saying "Tres mal." I couldn't decide in my sleepy condition if he meant the weather was bad or whether his friend was called Mal; either way he got back in bed and started to snore.

I got up and looked out. The storm had passed but heavy grey cloud hung over all the summits and it was very still and cold. Looking round the back of the hut at the place where the water had cascaded from the night before, I discovered that it was the place that generations of previous climbers, had used as a toilet! So that's why the stew hadn't tasted so good. After telling the others this disturbing news we decided to forego a brew and, after a bite to eat, tied on the ropes and Dave Lix set off across the face outside our door.

He had only climbed about 70ft when there was a rumble of thunder which rolled round all the peaks; it then started to snow heavily.

Dave came back to the hut and after waiting a while we agreed to call it a day and retreat. Having four ropes between us we decided to use two for abseiling and have one for each pair for safety.

Throwing down the abseil ropes, John and I went first followed by Eddie and Dave. On the second abseil, probably as a result of the contaminated stew the night before, John was caught short and had to drop his trousers whilst half way down the ropes. Luckily for the rest of us he was on a small ledge which we were able to avoid, but he looked comical with his big knickers round his ankles in the middle of a snow storm. When John had completed his toilet break, we all continued to the upper lip of the Bergschrund where a scary leap of about 10ft horizontally and 20ft vertically landed us on the lower snow slope.

Hurrying down to the Mer de Glace, without crampons or axe, John was slipping and sliding all over the place and cursing me for saying that we only needed the one axe, Mine!

After retrieving the lady's sack from where the lads had stowed it, we continued down the glacier. By this time it was sleeting heavily and none of the mountains were visible.

It was a sorry looking soaking wet group that finally arrived at the train terminus at Montenvers. There was nowhere open for coffee but an early train had just arrived and disgorged numerous American tourists carrying cameras and binoculars. One of these tourists approached us and asked, "Say, buddy, which is Mont Blanc? I couldn't see any mountains let alone Mont Blanc, which if clear would have been hidden from view anyway, behind the Aiguilles. I just pointed at the clouds and said, "It's up there somewhere." He then asked if he could take our photographs standing in front of it. We said, "We can't wait that long. We have a train to catch," and bade him "Goodbye, buddy."

Back in the valley we reported finding the rucksack to the police but as there was no ID in it and it had not been reported lost we were told to keep it. There was nothing of real value in it except a quilted jacket so we divided the contents the best way we could and got rid of the stuff we didn't want.

Eddie, Dave and I decided that we'd had our fill of bad weather and thought that a visit to the south of France would do us good. Packing everything into my van we set off to seek the sun.

Richard later told me, that he and Mo with Mike Kosterlitz and John Moss set off to do the Frendo Spur on the Aiguille du Midi. They took the telepherique to the Plan des Aiguilles where they met up with Whillans and Dan Boon who were also planning to do the Frendo. For some unknown reason Mo and Kosterlitz wandered off and went back down to Chamonix; Richard and John Moss teamed up together. The climb went well with Whillans and Boon in front until the top buttress which was badly iced up.

Richard tried to find a way up a wide crack reminiscent of a Curbar extreme but ran out of rope. Whillans found another way round to the left and brought the other two up then dropped a rope for Richard.

That night they all slept in the telepherique station then took the first car down in the morning.

Richard then got a lift home to England with Dave Woods, a Member of the Rimmand club.

Arriving at the Calanques, Eddie, Lix and I settled in at the ruined villa on the cliff top. As expected the weather was superb and after a day festering on the beach it was time to do some climbing.

We spent a week climbing, sunbathing and swimming and all had good tans. Dave Lix, being fair skinned, got badly sunburnt on his legs.

One evening, as we were relaxing after our meal, the conversation turned to what each one would wish for to complete his day. The wishes were along the lines of food, beer, Brigitte Bardot or some other beautiful woman, perhaps a good mattress instead of the cold stone benches to sleep on; all that was for me and Eddie. Lix said that all he required to make him happy was a barrel of calamine lotion and a hoist to lift him into it.

The following morning we decided to head for home via San Tropez.

We were probably hoping that we would meet up with Bardot and that she would invite us to stay at her villa. Either that or we would meet some rich woman with a yacht who would pay us to lounge around for a while before flying us back home in her private jet.

Alas, it was not to be, we didn't see Brigitte but we did walk round the harbour looking at the rich on their yachts. We went to sunbathe at Tahiti beach but found out that it was private so we went in a beachside bar where we received dirty looks before being charged 10 francs each for a small beer. After that we gave up on the dream of meeting a rich woman and got back in the van and headed north.

The only memorable thing about the journey back was a tremendous thunderstorm on the autoroute when we thought we were in imminent danger of being struck by lightning or washed away in a flood; that and Lix in the back of the van, having a pee in my water bottle to avoid getting out on the flooded road.

Back in Dover, Eddie said he wouldn't mind going to Cornwall for a week before heading home to Manchester. Lix and I thought that anything that would put off going back to work would be good so off we went along the south coast all the way to Bosigran.

Arriving at the Count House (CC Hut) we were pleased to find no one there. How we got in I can't remember because none of us were members of the CC, but somehow we had a key for the hut.

The first morning some post came through the letterbox. It was addressed to John Neil, the President of the Climbers Club. PANIC!

What should we do? We weren't even members of an affiliated club, we didn't have a CC member with us and obviously the club president was coming to stay.

We decided to brazen it out and we gave ourselves names of other CC members who were known to us and who we thought hadn't been out for a while. Our reasoning was that John Nield probably wouldn't know them anyway, and he didn't know us, so we should be OK to stay as long as we paid our hut fees so we entered our fictitious names in the hut book.

"Oh what a tangled web we weave, when first we practice to deceive."

That evening when we returned from climbing John Nield was there with his wife and family. We introduced ourselves, giving our false names.

Over the next few days we got on well with our fellow guests although there was the odd embarrassing moment when one or other of us would forget and use someone's real name; we did this quite often and got some questioning looks but managed to smooth things over.

The time came for us to leave; we paid our fees, said our goodbyes and set off for home congratulating ourselves on our successful deception.

Some weeks later, I was walking down the main street in Llanberis when who should I see coming towards me but John Nield. I said, "Good morning, John," thinking I'd have to bluff it out, to which he replied, "Good morning, Al," then he laughed. He had known all along.

Llanberis Pass, Easter 1960. Brian Barlow and Brian Platt repairing the Vincent Black Shadow.

First breakfast in Yugoslavia 1966

The Calanque. 1964. (L to R) Arthur Williams, Tony Riley, Clive Rowland

The Sciora Hut, Bregaglia, 1963 (L to R) Ian Hartle, Clive, Wool, Dave Gregory

Boissons glacier, Mont Blanc, A Parker 1964.

Pike, Di and Sheila, Near Trieste, 1966

Glacier below Flat Iron Ridge (A Parker, Dave Peck, Ian Hartle.)

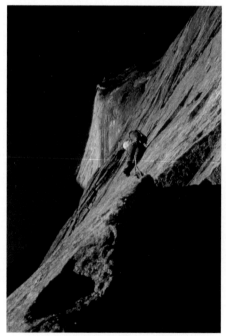

Piz Badile NE Face, Les Brown

Chapter 18
Back To Square One 1965/66

Late September, I got my old job back at A.V. Roe's in the same department and settled back to the old routine.

Richard was in Wales working at Plas y Brenin building an artificial ski slope on the hill at the back of the Centre.

I resumed climbing with Sheila and her friends from University and did some routes with the Barley brothers; we did Vertigo on Black Crag in Borrowdale together. I remember once on Stanage watching Robin trying Agony Crack, a route that I have always found OK but Robin wasn't having much success, probably being put off by having an audience of local experts. He was stuck at the overhang and couldn't see how to do it.

I offered a couple of suggestions but he still couldn't make any headway. Eventually he gave up and said, "Come on, Al, lead me up it." Tying on the sharp end, I climbed confidently up to the overhang and then came to a sudden full stop. I tried all ways to get over that little roof but tired myself out trying. I had to admit defeat and with tail between my legs climbed back down to the ground. I decided there and then to avoid offering advice in the future because nine times out of ten it backfires on you.

Down in Wales I led Sheila up some of the classic climbs, routes such as Tennis Shoe on Idwal Slabs and The Cracks and Crackstone Rib in Llanberis Pass. Eventually she started to do some leading herself and led Tennis Shoe. Then one Saturday in November we went climbing on Clogwyn y Wenallt, a beautiful little crag which overlooks the Afon Glaslyn before it flows into Llyn Gwynant a little further down the valley.

After doing Bovine HVS, I asked Sheila if she would like to lead a pitch of Oxo, a classic VS; she agreed, saying that it would be her first VS lead. I led the first two pitches belayed, and then she climbed up to join me. The top pitch is 90ft and a steep 4C. Sheila set off up it and after doing the steep initial crack started to find things a bit hard and was unsure as to which way to go. It was getting quite late and the light was fading fast. After placing a good runner she moved up slowly and steadily to the top of the crag in the twilight; I finished it in the dark.

That evening we called in to see Richard who was working for Joe Brown, helping him to prepare his Llanberis shop for opening. Richard was doing joinery work in one room and Joe was plastering in another.

Richard showed me a problem on the wall of the room saying that Joe had done it, but he himself had failed on it; he urged me to try it.

There were two iron bars each about a foot long sticking out of the wall at right-angles to it; they were about four feet apart and both about six feet off the floor. The problem was to get stood up on one of these metal bars without using anything other than both bars.

Reaching up for one of the bars, I pulled up and made a sort of strenuous mantelshelf move on to it and balanced upright; I then swung back down again.

Richard let out a shout, "Al's done your problem, Joe."

Joe came through from the other room and I asked him how he had done it. He said, "I did it this way," and proceeded to show us. Standing sideways on to the wall, he grasped the left-hand bar in his left hand, then kicked across to place his left foot on the right-hand bar. Pushing through with his left arm then leaving go, he let his momentum carry him into a standing position on the right-hand bar. It was all done in one fast movement and only a genius would have figured out how to do it that way.

Joe then asked me to show him how I had done it. I reached up for the bar and started to mantelshelf. Halfway through the move there was a loud crack and I fell to the floor; my shoulder had dislocated yet again.

So there I was lying on the floor of Joe's shop in agony instead of showing the Master how I had done his problem.

Dave Alcock and Sheila drove me to Bangor hospital where I had a general anaesthetic to put my shoulder back in place.

Hours later back at Joe's place we had something to eat and a brew then decided to drive home to Manchester. I had my right arm in a sling, so while I steered one-handed and worked the foot pedals; Sheila changed the gears when I told her to. After this episode I decided to teach Sheila how to drive.

At Christmas we all went to the Lakes as usual then in the New Year the Alpha had a club dinner at Grassington in Yorkshire. This was a typical rowdy affair with some of the Manchester Gritstone Club there, amongst them Stan Wroe whom I hadn't seen for many years. Stan was the lad who had fallen off Tower Face at Laddow Rocks and had burned my hands back in 1956; he and Richard were good mates, but whenever I saw him, he never spoke. Richard told me that Stan thought that I bore a grudge for the injury that he had caused me, whilst I thought Stan was not speaking because he was ashamed of what had happened. It was a misunderstanding all round. That night Stan and I became friends and it shows how wrong we can be if we don't make the effort to find out the cause of imagined grievances.

At Easter, Stan and I drove to Cornwall in his VW Beetle and camped at Sennen. Sheila was staying at the house of a friend from University who lived at Helston about 25 miles away.

Stan and I climbed at Sennen Cove, doing the classic climbs there and the following day I went in the VW to pick up Sheila and drove back with her to Bosigran. That day we did Black Slab, Ochre Slab and Doorpost.

After taking Sheila back to her friend's house, I met Stan at the pub.

Our last day in Cornwall that Easter, Stan and I went to Chair Ladder did one route and then drove back home to Manchester. This had been a very enjoyable weekend with Stan and I was pleased that our previous misunderstanding had been cleared up.

Wool and Anne bought a house in Glossop and started work in the area, so I started to see more of them. Over the next few months I climbed with Sheila and did the occasional route with Wool and various people from both the Alpha and the Black & Tans.

Martin continued to do new climbs in Wales doing The Skull on Cyrn Las with Arthur Williams and Jud Jordan, and in the Arrans, Martin, Arthur and Dave Little did the first ascent of Aardvark, a superb HVS.

Paul Nunn teamed up with Brian Henderson to do King Rat and Morangie on Goat Crag in Borrowdale and with Tom Patey and Brian Robertson the same pair did The Old Man of Stoer in Sutherland.

At Gogarth Richard McHardy and Pete Crew produced Ceilidh. Ingle and Crew found Interpolator and Boysen seconded Brown on Wen. A week later Martin went back to do two fine routes in the same day, Scavenger and Fifth Avenue, and was met at the top by Crew and Alcock who had just completed the first ascent of Central Park. In June Crew climbed with Brown for the first time to do Dinosaur; the first of many new climbs by this team.

Chapter 19
Alps and a Greek Odyssey 1966

As the summer holidays approached, I arranged to go to the Alps with Pike and Di, and as Sheila had done her Finals at University she completed our number.

Setting off in my van we drove to the Kaisergebirge in Austria and joined Wool, Anne and Pete Mason at the Stripsen Joch hut. There was quite a crowd of climbers in the Kaiser from our area that year, but the weather was bad and not much was done. The most memorable aspect of our time there was sitting in the hut with some German climbers listening to the Soccer World Cup final from Wembley on the radio. The commentary was in German and when England scored the winning goal it took us ages to get the Germans to translate the final result, they were so sickened off.

Wool and Pete Mason did one route, the SE Ridge of the Christasturm, and then went off to the Grossglockner hoping to find the sun.

The weather wasn't improving at all, so Pike suggested that we drive to Greece to climb Mt. Olympus. I was dubious about this idea, already having driven nearly 1000 miles. I didn't relish the thought of another 1,200miles as the only driver in a crowded van so we had a vote. Pike and Di voted to go, I voted against and Sheila abstained. That was that, we set off for Greece.

Driving through the Tyrol to the then communist Yugoslavia we reached the Adriatic coast at the town of Split. Taking one look at the azure sea and the clear sky, we decided to have a rest day. The weather was scorching hot as it was now mid August and the heat became almost unbearable after about 9am when the van became a tin oven! We chose to drive from late in the afternoons until early the following morning and then sleep until the heat drove us from our sleeping bags. Then until the afternoon we rested, swam and sunbathed before travelling on again in the cool of the evening. This process gave our journey a modicum of comfort. Usually the two girls slept in the van whilst Pike and I would doss down at the side of it. One morning I awoke to find that Pike had moved into the van. He told me that he wakened up in the night to find a massive spider crawling across his sleeping bag towards me. He decided to join the girls and leave me asleep reasoning that what the eye doesn't see doesn't do any harm.

Following the coast south through magnificent scenery we eventually came to the medieval town of Dubrovnik. After spending some time doing the tourist bit we were on our way again south, almost to the Albanian border. At that time Albania was a forbidden country, so heading NE to Podgorica then keeping only about 25km from the Albanian border we set off on minor roads to drive round Albania towards the small town of Pec. This drive we did during the day and it took us through some very scenic mountains where a cool breeze wafted through the van's open windows. Further on, descending into a deep and twisting gorge mainly on gravel roads with a tumbling river to our right, we overtook a Muslim man on horseback who was being followed on foot by two or three women carrying large bundles on their heads; he and his horse carried nothing! If ever we stopped the van, even in the mountains, we were quickly surrounded by women and children begging for money. The only way to get rid of them it seemed was to throw a handful of loose change down the hillside then jump back in the van and drive off at speed.

Arriving at Pec we found that it was market day so we spent some of the afternoon looking round the stalls where silversmiths displayed their wares of splendid jewellery. In a shop doorway a woman was sitting on the step, breastfeeding a baby and feeding bread to some chickens with her free hand. Most of the people looked very poor and didn't seem to have seen any foreigners before, particularly from a capitalist country. They stared at us through strange dull eyes. It was quite unnerving and we could imagine having our throats slit and being robbed.

Leaving Pec around about 5pm we crossed a bridge over a wide river and below us we could see crowds of people bathing. As it was a scorching hot afternoon and the water looked so blue and inviting we decided to join the noisy throng of bathers. Sheila was the first to get ready and she took the plunge as the rest of us were getting changed. As we ran to the waters edge eager to cool off we were met with shouts from Sheila warning us not to go in. She came out of the river covered in human excrement; it was an open sewer but this didn't seem to bother the locals, who were splashing about quite happily.

Back at the van Pike, Di and I changed back into our clothes while Sheila had a good wash in a nearby stream. After making a meal, in any of the preparation of which, incidentally, Sheila had been banned from taking part, we set off in the general direction of Skopje approximately 100 miles away to the SE.

After 50miles along a flat fertile valley we came to a crossroads at a town called Prizren. To the right (south) a short distance away, lay Albania. To the left the road went north to join the main road to Skopje, but that way would be a long way round. Straight ahead were mountains and a sign which read "Titograd" leading to the motorway to Skopje 11 miles away.

We decided to go straight ahead. A sign indicated that there were roadworks for 7km but we pressed on full of optimism, which was soon dashed when we realised that we had entered "The Twilight Zone." The road was in a terrible condition having trenches across it in places which we had to negotiate by driving across rickety planks. It was now quite dark; the road was narrow and unsurfaced and full of deep holes. We would have liked to have turned back but the thought of driving along that section again was unbearable and after all, the sign had said it was only 7km. After what seemed to be hours of driving at about walking speed we arrived at a fairly smooth section of road; it was still unsurfaced and was raised up on steep embankments on either side. There was a bright full moon shining by this time and below to our left we could make out the old road leading down to a ford crossing a wide shallow river. Our road suddenly came to an abrupt end overlooking this river and on the other side in front of us was an identical ramp to the one that we were on. The penny dropped; we were on a new bridge! The only snag was the bridge was missing. There was nothing for it but to turn round and drive down onto the old road and across the ford.

The girls were in the back and Pike was in the front with me. I said, "I'll get out to see how much room there is to turn round." I opened the driver's door and stepped out into the moonlight. After peering around at the edge of the embankment, I turned on my heel and almost bumped into a six foot six Frankenstein's monster look-alike standing next to me in the moonlight. I almost died of fright! Pointing down to the river crossing, I blurted out in my best Yugoslav, "Titograd?"

The monster nodded and I could swear I saw a neck bolt glistening in the moonlight; he repeated the word Titograd in a moronic tone. I thanked him, jumped back into the van and locking the doors asked the girls to pass me an ice axe out of the back whereupon the monster shuffled off into the darkness.

We discussed who he might be, and came to the conclusion that he was either a night watchman or a vampire.

Finally we managed to cross the river and were soon back on the main road again, where miraculously a tarmac surface appeared. I put my foot down and speeded up considerably, thinking that this must be the end of the roadworks. After 100 metres, in the headlights I caught sight of a concrete flagstone, longer than a car width, lying across our side of the road. I braked hard but hit it square on, we took off for a few seconds and then came into land like a Jumbo jet with a poor pilot. A bone-shaking crash rattled our teeth and everything else in the van. Visions of irreparable damage and being stranded in these mountains held captive by Frankenstein's police force flashed across my mind. But after an anxious inspection of the vehicle it was concluded that nobody made vans as good as Morris Motors and we set off again, but more cautiously this time.

We were now back on a gravel road, probably the original one before they had attempted to improve things!

At last, reaching the mountains proper, we started to climb a pass on switchbacks, crawling slowly because of the poor surface. At the summit of the pass was a viewpoint overlooking a canyon which appeared to be a sibling of the Grand Canyon in Arizona. Parking the van, all four of us got out to look at the moonlit view, which was spectacular!

Pike and I made our way to four steps which led down to a flat stone platform on the lip of the abyss. In the dark, Pike caught his foot on one of the steps and if I hadn't grabbed him by the scruff of his neck he would have been base jumping without a parachute. Obviously not fazed by his little stumble, he picked up a stone and dropped it over the edge; we counted eight seconds before we heard it crash into the river below. Pike gave a nervous laugh and we all headed back to the van. The road down the other side of the mountains to where it began to flatten out was an improvement and to our delight we eventually came to a good tarmac road. We passed through a small village and after turning a sharp left-hand bend we stopped at a little lay-by next to a stream on our right. Filling the kettle from the stream and lighting the stove, we brewed a mug of tea each. It was just about daylight, probably around 4am, and looking at the map we estimated that we had covered 60 miles in 10 hours; we were tired and thought," So much for the short cut."

Pike and I were sitting drinking our tea in the front seats the girls were in the back. Coming down the road towards us we could see a peasant on a pushbike, obviously on his way to work; he was riding with his hands in his pockets. He noticed the van and started to stare at us, turning his head and looking back over his shoulder as he passed by. He must have known the bend was there, but his nosiness got the better of him and carrying on in a straight line he crossed the grass verge and still looking back, disappeared down the 15ft deep roadside ditch. All four of us let out screams of hysterical laughter, spitting tea over the windscreen; the poor guy climbed sheepishly out of the ditch, remounted his bike, raised his hand to let us know he was OK, then rode away.

It was evening as we approached Skopje. As we drove towards the city on a dual carriageway we couldn't help but notice the great cracks in the road surface, a legacy of a big earthquake some years previously.

Hoping to find somewhere to buy a meal we parked up in the main square in the city centre and although it was only eight o clock on Saturday night, there was nowhere open. Gangs of teenagers were roaming round with nothing to do; it was a depressing place so we decided to move on.

Stopping to fill up at a petrol station on the outskirts of the city, we found ourselves behind a big American car. The American driver was arguing with the station operative who wanted payment in Yugoslavian dinar and was refusing to take American dollars. The American was saying in English to the Yugoslav who didn't understand," Forget your dinar, buddy, these are American Dollars, they're worth diamonds to you people." The garage man wasn't convinced and wouldn't fill the car. He filled our van though and we paid in dinar. We drove away to the sound of a loud American voice cursing all things communist and Yugoslavian. Although he was arrogant and impolite the American did have a point. Yugoslavia at that time seemed to be a very dull place and the inhabitants appeared to be suspicious of anything or anyone foreign. Apart from the landscape of the country there didn't seem to be much of anything to recommend it; there was no music or colour anywhere, the people didn't seem to be enjoying life and we couldn't wait to get to Greece.

We crossed the border into Greece at a small town called Bogorodica and immediately there was a dramatic change of atmosphere. The streets were lined with colourful shops, and lively music could be heard coming from the many bars and restaurants. It was very pleasant to sit in the sun drinking a beer and taking in the aroma of the barbecued goat's meat which was roasting on a slowly turning spit; this was more like it! We pressed on again and another 50miles saw us in Thessalonica.

While Pike and the girls went to the shops to buy groceries, I stayed with the van in a little side street. Sitting there on a low wall watching the world go by, I could see an old woman attired all in a black and with a black head covering sitting on a chair outside a house a little further up the street. She spoke to me in Greek and beckoned for me to sit on a chair next to her, then going into the house she returned with a large jar containing yoghurt and spooned some into a dish for me.

I spent an interesting half hour talking to the old lady in English whilst she talked to me in Greek. I don't think either of us understood a word of the conversation, but we parted the best of friends.

Another hour and a half of driving down the coast towards Athens brought us to a campsite adjacent to a lovely beach; we reckoned that this would be a good base for an ascent of Mt. Olympus.

Eating a meal at a roof top restaurant and enjoying the warm evening air and the view over the Aegean Sea, we became aware that a group of young Greek men were staring in our direction. Sheila and Diana were wearing mini-skirts and on leaving the restaurant, we were followed by the Greeks who had obviously never seen mini-skirts before. At the top of the beach next to the campsite, there was a roofed wooden structure, a bit like a bandstand with a small dance floor. Popular music came from a couple of speakers and young people were dancing; we joined in and were enjoying ourselves when the Greek stalkers arrived and started to make a nuisance of themselves. Remembering the Scotch club fight in Chamonix, we decided that discretion is the better part of valour and we returned to our camp. The girls slept in the back of the van and Pike and I bedded down in the sand, but had a bad night due to mosquitoes.

Next morning the two of us were covered in lumps. It was very hot again and none of us felt like going up Mt. Olympus so we spent the day at the beach instead. It was nice to relax after our epic journey and the warm sea was soothing to the mosquito bites.

The following morning Diana was quite ill, probably with food poisoning. She had stomach pains, sickness and diarrhoea. Both she and Pike said they would like to go back to the Alps and Sheila and I agreed.

We had driven 1200 miles from the Alps to Greece and had only stayed for a day!

In the afternoon, we were on our way back north, but this time we decided to take the main motorway up the centre of Yugoslavia through Belgrade and Zagreb.

Arriving on the outskirts of Belgrade at dawn we were surprised to hit a traffic jam which was several miles long, two lanes crawling along in first gear.

At last near a parked Police car, after filtering into the outside lane, we started to speed up. Looking around for the cause of the hold up we saw a dead body on the inside lane, it was absolutely as flat as a pancake, like when one sees a dead cat in the road. We concluded that it must have been one of the many people who walked along the side of the motorway on their way to work. He had probably been knocked down in the dark then run over many times by following cars, none of which, it appeared, had bothered to stop. On our entry to the city centre at a big traffic island which had a statue in the middle, probably of Tito, I noticed a red light on the dashboard. I pulled in at the side of the busy road and, lifting the van bonnet, I started to mess about with the alternator. When I pressed down on the alternator the light went out only to reappear when I let go again. Standing there puzzled, I knew that it meant that the battery wasn't charging but I didn't know why. I suddenly became aware that I had an audience, a car had pulled up and two men were standing beside me staring at the van's engine. I thought eh up, two more nosey beggars. Then one of them spoke, and pointing to himself, he said, "I fix, I have a garage, follow me," and jumping into his car he joined the rush hour traffic and sped away.

I quickly got back into the van and followed, anxious not to lose sight of his vehicle in the heavily crowded streets. He led us away from the city centre into a kind of shanty town area and finally came to a stop behind a row of wooden houses. We told him we came from Manchester. He said, "Ha, Bobby Charlton, Manchester United," then he went into one of the houses. I was beginning to worry that we had made a mistake because he came back with another man who looked as though he had just escaped from a lunatic asylum. I thought we could be robbed and murdered and no one would ever know. Then his wife appeared with some chairs and a little table and signalled us to sit down. She went back to the house but soon reappeared carrying a tray containing some strong Greek coffee and four small cups. There was also a large pot of jam and four spoons. The coffee was as thick as mud and tasted like it. Each mouthful was followed by a spoonful of jam. I thought, this must be where they got the saying about a spoonful of sugar helps the medicine go down, but we accepted their hospitality graciously and pretended to like the stuff. We were so convincing that the lady of the house went back inside to bring us some more.

The three men had started work on the van and were fiddling about under the bonnet. We thanked the lady for the coffee and while Pike and the girls set out to explore the area, I decided to have a sleep in the back of the van. I was tired having driven all the previous night, and planned to drive the coming night as well if the van was fixed.

I was rudely awakened by what sounded to be a jet aircraft going into a dive. The crazy- looking man was sitting in the driving seat with his foot to the floor on the accelerator and the engine was screaming as if to blow up at any moment. Leaping up, banging my head in the process, I yelled at him to stop. He pointed to his chest and said, "Bus driver." The other men looked at me quizzically. I waved my arms about signalling for them to cease work and at the same time shoeing away several small children who were endeavouring to strip the van of all the rubber window gaskets. At that moment, the others arrived back and I said, "Come on we're going." The men started to demand money for their work, even though they hadn't managed to repair the van; we gave them about two pounds worth of dinar for their efforts and quickly left.

Looking in the AA literature for the nearest Austin/Morris garage, we discovered there was one in Trieste, 400 miles away but on our route to the Alps. When night descended, we stopped in a lay-by, choosing to conserve the car battery by not using the lights. Some time during the night we were awakened by the sound of a motor-bike engine. It was a policeman with a rifle slung over his shoulder demanding that we move on, but after we told him we had broken down he shrugged and drove away. So much for communist roadside recovery!

Early the following afternoon we arrived at the garage in Trieste and leaving the van there to be repaired, we all went off to the local municipal baths for a well needed shower and change of clothes.

The car was ready when we returned and we paid the bill with AA vouchers, getting some cash back in the process. Back on the motorway we headed west, by-passing a very smelly Venice. A long drive brought us to Bergamo where we left the motorway and headed up towards Lecco. Climbing steadily into the mountains, we felt good being back in the Alps.

Crossing the border into Switzerland at Castasegna around midnight we were soon at the village of Promontogno. Deciding to drive up the gravel road towards the Sciora, in the dark I took the wrong track and on trying to reverse, the back wheel went into the ditch. Pike and I got out to weigh up the situation; it didn't look good. The back axle was on the ground and the wheel was hanging over a 3ft deep ditch. We were tired but set about rescuing the vehicle by using our tradesmen's ingenuity.

Searching the nearby woods Pike and the girls collected a pile of logs whilst I jacked the back axle up off the ground. Then placing the logs in the ditch up to the level of the underside of the wheel we constructed a rudimentary platform from which I could drive back onto the track.

We found a place to turn round and drove back down to where the track widened then, leaving the van at the side of the road, we took our sleeping bags and a groundsheet into the trees and settled down to sleep. After a few minutes we were up again, removing numerous fallen apples from under the groundsheet. We were in an orchard! At last, with relative comfort we fell into a deep sleep.

Early the next morning we found the right track and drove up to the trailhead (as the Americans would say).

Parking up near the wooden bridge and breakfasting near the rushing stream we looked forward to a relaxing day in the sun.

The morning was spent preparing our campsite by the river pitching the tents near the spot that Paul and I had occupied when we came to do the North face of the Piz Badile in 1962.

Later when all the work was done Sheila and I were sitting having a brew by the river when Di came to us saying that there was a guy near the van who said we couldn't park there, and that we would have to move.

I went to investigate. Sure enough there was a Swiss man with a badge which identified him as Forest Police. He told me that parking wasn't allowed there even though I pointed out that there was no notice to that effect. He said that we could camp there, but would have to take the van back down to the valley or he would have to give us a ticket and fine us on the spot. I protested strongly and let him know that we thought he was being too officious and that as there was plenty of room there for the van, what harm were we doing?

He shrugged and told us that it was the law and it was his job to enforce it. Very reluctantly Pike and I unloaded anything that we thought we would need at the camp, then got in the van and drove back down the twisting, stony track to the village of Promontogno. After parking on some spare ground near the village, Pike suggested that we go for a beer, which I thought was a splendid idea. We found a bar and entered a pleasant, cool and shady room with a stone floor and carved wood-panelled walls and ceiling. Buying a beer we sat down at a table next to some local men who we assumed worked in the forest. They greeted us by nodding and raising a hand; there was a nice atmosphere about the place and felt relaxed. The day was hot, and we were loath to start the long walk back up to our camp so we downed a few more beers. Then the door to the bar opened and in walked the Forest policeman. He joined the locals at the next table and they all chatted and laughed together. When we got up to leave he raised his hand to us in a friendly gesture and gave a look which said," No hard feelings." We nodded and stepped outside into the heat to tackle the three hour walk ahead of us.

Back at the camp the air was cooler and the girls had a nice meal ready for us.

The following morning after packing our sacks we began the steep walk to the Sciora hut. It is a beautiful walk and having done it three times before, despite its beauty I knew that it was long and hard. As for the others, this was their first time in the area and they didn't know what to expect. Meandering uphill through the forest, we came to a little wooden bridge over a tumbling stream where we rested and quenched our thirst.

Then we were out of the woods and on the open hillside with magnificent views of the Badile, Cengalo and Sciora peaks. A welcome cooling breeze reached us from the Bondo glacier. Soon we were at the hut and drinking coffee outside on the stone terrace.

At dawn the next day, leaving Di at the hut, Pike, Sheila and I crossed the moraine and scrambled up the terraces to below the North Ridge of the Badile. When we arrived at the lower part of the ridge we could see other parties ahead of us; there was quite a queue. Pike teamed up with two lads from Cambridge University who were climbing just in front of us and Sheila and I climbed together. It's funny but I never gave a thought to my bad shoulder until, some way up the climb at a little overhang on a strenuous crack, I felt it twinge. I had been doing all the leading and was carrying a sack. Stepping down, I tried to climb a wall to the right without success. My confidence had taken a knock again. By this time we had fallen well behind Pike and his team. I tried the crack again to no avail. It was something that I would have normally found easy, but for the fear of dislocating my shoulder again; it was probably only about grade IV. I wished that we had all stayed together. I would have been alright seconding Pike but he was now a long way ahead and out of sight.

There was nothing for it but to retreat so partly down-climbing combined with a couple of abseils we eventually reach safe, easy ground. After a tiring flog across three moraines we arrived back at the Sciora hut where we found a worried looking Diana. The north ridge was shrouded in cloud, and thunder could be heard in the distance. After reassuring her that Pike was probably by that time at the summit or already descending she felt a lot better.

There was a storm that evening which we watched from the hut before going to bed. Pike returned the next day enthusing about the ridge and we all walked down to our camp together. The day after we struck camp and Pike and I went down to retrieve the van.

After loading up we set off towards the Maloja Pass on our way to Chamonix.

Arriving at the Biolay campsite in Chamonix we were pleased to see some familiar faces. Eddie and Bill Birch were camping there and they told us all the news. They told us that there had been some horrendous storms and that a lot of climbers had been caught out in them, including some of our friends. Gerry Rogan and Al Hunt had done the south ridge of the Aiguille Noire de Peuterey and were hit by the storm just below the summit. After a bivouac they spent two days getting down the east ridge, but got back safely.

Bill Birch and Nogs had an epic on the West Face of the Blaitiere when Nogs was hit by stonefall and sustained a bad head injury whilst on the upper ledges. Bill fastened him on and then descended to Chamonix to get help. He then went back up with the rescue team and Nogs was brought down to the hospital in Chamonix.

Another epic which turned into a tragedy took place on Mont Blanc and involved two of our friends.

Richard later told me that he and Mo had taken the last telepherique of the day to the Col du Geant and had made their way up to the bivi hut at the Col de la Fourche. They were disappointed to find the hut was nearly full.

A large team of French climbers were getting a bit nasty with four British lads but turned their attention to a Belgian couple when Richard and Mo turned up. The other Brits were two teams, Willy McGibbon and Davy Ross from Glasgow and Jim McCartney, a big Scot, with Colin Spacey who was a Geordie. Mo and Richard and the other four were planning to do the Old Brenva route.

Next morning early, Richard and Mo awoke to find the hut empty. They set off crossing the glacier to the Col Moore and could hear the other four up above in the dark. As they ascended easy mixed terrain, the guys above them dislodged a large boulder which cut one of the ropes belonging to the Glaswegian pair. As dawn broke they caught up with the others below where the snow had become hard ice which would require much step cutting for approximately 600 ft to the top of the climb. The only alternative was to climb through a serac barrier to the right. When they reached the top the fierce wind and bitter cold struck fear into them and large hailstones pummelled them. After some discussion as to the best descent, it was decided to go over the summit of Mont Blanc and down to the Vallot hut. After only a few hundred feet the wind became really wicked and the majority favoured turning back to go to the Col du Midi over Mont Maudit and Mt. Blanc du Tacul. They were now in a white out and not sure where they were. Everyone was very cold, Richard's gloves had disintegrated and his hands had become worryingly numb. After traversing the north side of Mont Maudit and losing some height they were forced to bivouac on an open slope. After a terrible night buried in spindrift, three to a bivi bag, the descent was resumed, still in awful conditions and almost zero visibility. Reaching a huge snow slope which vanished downwards into the cloud the team ruled out a descent due to the vast quantities of new snow. Mo, Richard and Jimmy opted to go down a rock ridge to the left while the other three sat in the rocks reluctant to move, but eventually agreed to all keep together in two teams.

During this descent Richard nearly fell, Mo went to sleep at the bottom of an abseil and tragically, lower down, Colin Spacey, who had been showing signs of exhaustion, died from hypothermia despite frantic attempts to resuscitate him.

Leaving Colin's body tied to the rocks where it would be visible to a rescue party, the others eventually made it to the Col du Midi where some French mountain troops gave them food and hot drinks and some medical treatment before helping them to the telepherique.

Back in Chamonix Dr. Tom Patey was concerned about Richard and Mo's frostbite. He urged them to return home immediately for specialised treatment and gave them a letter addressed to Dr. Mike Ward at the London Hospital who had been the doctor on the successful 1953 Everest expedition. After a months treatment in hyperbaric chambers they escaped any amputations.

(For more details and a first hand account of this epic, read Alan (Richard) McHardy's book.)

Two months after their hospital treatment, Richard had the first of many epileptic fits. He thinks this may have been due to the hyperbaric treatment or perhaps something to do with his old head injury from the 1964 accident. He also admits to heading a medicine ball in the gym not long before.

On a lighter note, in the Oberland, Clive Rowland and the appropriately named Bob Toogood did what they thought to be the second ascent of the 7,000ft NE Ridge of the Scheidegg Wetterhorn, but which they later discovered had actually been the first complete ascent.

When we arrived in Chamonix, Richard and Mo had already left for London; it was still bad weather and another epic was in progress, this time on the West Face of the Petite Dru. Some German climbers had been caught in a storm and one of them was injured; they had been on the face for a few days and needed help. There were three local rescue teams, the Chamonix Guides, the Ecole National and the Gendarmerie, and they were arguing amongst themselves as to whose turn it was to be on duty. A successful rescue was eventually carried out without loss of life by an international team of amateur climbers, consisting of the American Gary Hemming, Mick Burke and the French alpinist Rene Desmaison and others.

After a few days in Chamonix Sheila and I decided that we had had enough but Pike and Di wanted to stay on. They said that they could get a lift home with someone else, so we offered Eddie Birch a lift and offered to take Nogs' rucksack and climbing gear in the van.

Brian Sullivan turned up on his motorbike specially to take Nogs home on the pillion whenever he got out of hospital and Bill Birch had already gone home.

Chapter 20
The End of an Era 1966-67

Leaving Chamonix and driving to Geneva we stopped for a couple of hours to look around and bathe in the lake. We ate at a restaurant and then resumed our journey northwards towards Dijon. By the time we reached the Jura Mountains, it was dark. Sheila was in the back of the van surrounded by our own luggage along with Nogs' and Eddie's stuff - rucksacks and camping gear etc. Eddie sat in the passenger seat in the front and I was driving. About two hours after leaving Geneva, the unlit and unmarked road was demanding a lot of concentration. Coming to a long straight section of road I could see lights in the distance which I assumed was a vehicle coming towards us; Sheila and Eddie were asleep. The oncoming lights were taking a long time to get to us. They appeared to be forging straight ahead on full beam. I thought, this is a really long straight, and drove on towards the oncoming car; I was doing about 60mph. As the gap closed between us and the other vehicle, I became dazzled. It was only when we drew level that I realised that the other car was stationary and was parked on a large patch of gravel next to a hotel and that the road curved sharply to the right. I went straight on. Crossing the road and on to the gravel patch, I could see that we were hurtling towards a six foot high wall which followed the road round to the right from the hotel. I knew that we couldn't stop in time. It all happened in a split second but it's surprising how quickly the brain reacts to situations like this.

Standing hard on the brake with my right foot, I shouted a warning to the others to brace themselves. Then putting my left foot on the dash, I suddenly remembered Barry Ingle saying that he cracked his head on the top of the windscreen when he had a crash. I quickly thrust up my left hand above the windscreen to brace my upper body and just before impact I spun the steering wheel to the right. It was all reflex.

There was one almighty crash as the left side of the van hit the wall then all the suspension collapsed.

The entire luggage had come forward almost burying Sheila and Eddie. I was worried that perhaps another car coming from our direction might suffer the same fate if he too was dazzled. People came running from the hotel to see what had happened. All three of us climbed out. I spoke to a man and pointed to the van saying, "Automobile kaput, automobile kaput." He told me that he was English.

I explained about the parked car's headlights and he got some one to switch them off. Miraculously we were all OK, shaken but not stirred, but the van was a write-off.

The Englishman was the hotel owner; he took us inside and gave us a coffee. He told us that he had retired to France and had bought this hotel. The gendarmes arrived on the scene but after a few questions went away satisfied it hadn't been anyone's fault. The owner of the offending headlights was allowed to leave.

The hotel owner said we could stay there for the night. We felt very grateful and thanked him profusely, expecting at least four star accommodation. He then showed us to his wash house at the side of the hotel and said we could sleep on the stone floor. I felt like saying, " We're your countrymen in need of a good nights rest, where's your hospitality?" But I didn't in case he kicked us out.

After an uncomfortable night sleeping with the washing machines, we awoke to another beautiful sunny day. My left shoulder felt very stiff from the crash but at least the right one hadn't dislocated. In fact, considering the force with which we had hit the wall, we had got off pretty lightly with just a few bruises.

Outside the hotel we looked over the wall where it tapered down to about 3ft in height and continued parallel to the road and round the bend.

The view gave us a shock. We were peering down a steep cliff which dropped several hundred feet to a river gorge. We'd had a very lucky escape! A year later, Tony Riley left the road at the same spot but his vehicle ran up a mound of gravel and came to a sudden stop undamaged but with the front wheels on top of the wall. This sudden stop caused the loaded roof rack to part company with the car; flying over the wall and plunging into the gorge below.

We learned from the hotel owner that we were near the small town of Poligny. Looking in the AA handbook we discovered that the nearest AA office was in Geneva, but on phoning them, were told that as we were in France the matter would have to be dealt with by the Lyon office which was approximately 150 miles away to the south.

We had the van towed to a garage in Poligny, then armed with several written questions in French to help me along my way, provided by Sheila who was fluent in French, I set off to hitch-hike to Lyon.

The plan was for me to get some money from the AA and arrange for the van to be returned to England. This had to be done because leaving the van in France would incur import taxes but also my insurance company required its return to the UK so that their own inspectors could assess the damage.

I got to Lyon in two lifts, the first in a car with a couple who spoke English and who dropped me off at the slip road of the motorway to Lyon. Then after quite a long wait, one of those funny French vehicles, a cross between a lorry and a pickup truck, pulled up. The driver said something which I took to mean, "Where to?" I said, "Lyon." He motioned for me to get in. I showed the driver the AA office address and he nodded and drove on to the motorway. It was an interesting journey, I didn't speak French, nor did he speak English. There were long silences interspersed with grunts and some pointing. I showed him Sheila's written notes but ceased doing this when we nearly had a crash, thinking one crash a week is enough! The old lorry wouldn't go very fast and it was very hot in the cab. I was beginning to think that I'd made a mistake by getting in, but by late afternoon we arrived at Lyon. I was wondering how I would find the AA office when suddenly for no apparent reason we screeched to a halt. I looked questioningly at the driver who pointed across the road, and when I looked, there was the AA office. The guy was a star. I could have hugged him, but you never know with the French! I got out and said "Merci" lots of times then waved as he drove away.

In the AA office, a gorgeous young French woman asked in perfect English if she could help. I was tired from the day's events, but immediately fell in love. She dealt with all the paperwork and asked all about our holiday and seemed concerned about our crash, but best of all, she forwarded me a load of money, a loan from the AA.

When everything was sorted out it was about 5.10pm, I didn't fancy hitch-hiking back so I asked her about buses or trains to Poligny. She told me there was a train due to leave at 5.15pm and taking my hand (I nearly fainted with pleasure) she guided me out of the building and down the street to the railway station where she got me a ticket and put me on the train to the lunatic asylum. I'm only kidding; she put me on the train to Poligny.

I thought about her all the way back and the journey flew by; before I knew it, I was back with Eddie and Sheila.

They told me that while I had been away, they had scrounged some very large cardboard boxes from a domestic appliance shop, and had packed the entire luggage in them. They had then tied the boxes in the back of the van and labelled everything to go to "Piccadilly Railway Station, Manchester, England."

I went to say goodbye to my van, and then suggested we go for a meal on the AA.

We ate at a nice little restaurant and by coincidence, Ron James and his wife were at the next table. They were passing through on their way home. It's a small world!

That night we slept on benches on the platform of Poligny Station and the following morning boarded the train for Paris.

Sheila had arranged to meet up in Paris with a girlfriend from Manchester University but that was three days off so Eddie and I decided to stay with her until her friend arrived.

Booking into a small hotel in the Latin Quarter of Mont St. Michel Eddie and I checked our bed for bed bugs; it was that kind of place. When Sheila came from her room we asked if she had done the same.

She didn't seem to think it was necessary saying that it was perfectly clean; that's students for you!

Our first day in Paris, we visited the Louvre, seeing the Mona Lisa and the Venus di Milo. Then we walked round by the Place de la Concorde and up to the Arc de Triomphe. On our walk, we saw a model of the new Air France aeroplane, Concorde.

The following day we went to Notre Dame and lazed about on the banks of the Seine before going to Montmartre where Eddie had his portrait drawn, a present for his mother.

The next day, the obligatory trip to the Eiffel Tower, then a wander round the streets looking for Pierre Alain's shop hoping to get some PAs. When we eventually found the shop, it was closed with blinds covering the windows. We couldn't even see any PAs never mind buy any.

On our last morning, after breakfast, Sheila accompanied us to the Gare du Nord, where Eddie and I boarded our train and waved goodbye.

Settling down on the train we were thinking, soon we shall be in Calais and not long after that, we'll be home. Half an hour went by and then the compartment door opened and the ticket collector appeared. He looked at our tickets and started to gesticulate, shouting at us in French. Not understanding what he was saying, we stared at him with blank faces.

A French woman who was in the same compartment explained that the train was in two sections, the front half went all the way to Calais and the back half finished at the next station. Apparently we were in the wrong half and we were told that our tickets weren't valid for the full distance; we would have to get off at the next stop to buy another ticket. Now we started to gesticulate and shout in English cursing the stupid French way of doing things; but he was adamant and when the train stopped he insisted we get off. The front half pulled away and left us standing on the platform. A woman in the ticket office spoke English but couldn't understand why we had got off the train, saying that our tickets were valid. She took us to the stationmaster, who agreed with her and said that there would be another train in an hour. Even now I don't know why we had to get off the train; there must have been some misunderstanding. Either that or the ticket collector didn't like the English, and after what we had called him, who could blame him!

There were no more problems after that and at Calais we boarded the Channel ferry for a night crossing. By the time we had bought some duty free cigarettes and had a drink there wasn't much left in our wallets, so on reaching Dover, I paid another visit to the AA.

This time there was no gorgeous French girl, not even a gorgeous English girl, but the man behind the desk made up for it by sympathetically loaning me enough for a full English breakfast and a ticket to Manchester. It was nice to get home.

A few weeks later, the van made it back to Southampton where it was scrapped and I didn't get anything for it in the way of insurance as I only had third party fire and theft. A week or so later all our luggage arrived in Manchester, everything down to the last knife and fork, nothing was lost; a testament to Eddie's and Sheila's packing skills.

We took Nogs all his stuff, and found him to be recovering well, and the rest of us collected our own.

Looking for work proved difficult without my own transport and I didn't have the money to buy another van. Eventually I got a job as a fitter at Craven Brothers, a machine tool manufacturer in Reddish near Stockport. Travelling to and from work entailed two buses each way and when going into Manchester to the Sports Guild at night I was now dependent on public transport or lifts from friends.

It was about this time that I started socialising with Roger Birch, Eddie's older brother. Roger was a foreman gardener at a Manchester park and was also a climber like his brothers; and like them lived at their parent's home in Stretford. He was the owner of a Ford van and would sometimes lend it to me when I needed a vehicle, or he would give me a lift home after a night out. Most weekends we either went to Wales, the Lakes or out into Derbyshire. Richard had stopped climbing temporarily because of his epilepsy and I still had the dodgy shoulder; but we all carried on going out.

One night at a meeting of the Cromlech Climbing Club at a pub in Manchester I met Vic Tosh. Vic came from Middlesbrough but was working in Manchester. He climbed with some of the Teesside climbers and I knew him vaguely from seeing him in Wales. Vic was older than me as was Roger, but he looked really young. As he didn't know many climbers in Manchester, he became one of our social group and a good friend. Vic was good company, always cheerful and jokey whereas Roger could be moody and grumpy; but we all got on well together.

Vic had been in the Royal Navy on destroyers and told me, "It was like being in prison with a chance of being drowned," and that he had spent most of the time being seasick.

The Alpha Club was changing. The Sheffield and Manchester sections began to grow apart and some members moved away to other parts of the country. Les Brown and family lived near Middlesbrough where Les worked for ICI. Baz Ingle, Dave Potts and Pete Crew were living near Llanberis and had a new circle of friends. Paul Ross lived in Keswick and my cousin, Barry Johnson and his wife Valerie, lived at Drigg in west Cumbria. A lot of the original Alpha had given up climbing altogether but still put in an appearance at club dinners.

The Sheffield section stayed pretty much the same as a unit apart from taking on some new members, whereas we in Manchester were, as stated previously, amalgamating with various members of the Black&Tans. Martin was doing new routes with various seconds, namely Dave Little, Arthur Williams and Jud Jordan.

The main event of the year was the club dinner, which brought everyone back together for a night. In late 1966 it was held at the Bull in t'Thorn on the Ashbourne to Buxton road.

On the Saturday of the dinner Roger, Vic and I climbed at Earl Sterndale, a nice limestone crag set in a sheltered little valley. It was a cold and damp October day and after doing a couple of VSs, which I led, I felt very pleased with myself and suggested we retire early to the dinner venue; the others agreed. The pub was a large old place with a big new extension built on the side. There was a good turn out of the lads, old and new members; and a lot of climbers from other groups. Stan Wroe was there and Little Mick (Burke). Also our old friend Pete Bamfield who we hadn't seen for a while, had turned up for the dinner; it promised to be a good do!

The function room which we occupied was separated from the public dining room by some trellis work and was visible to members of the public who were dining there, young men and women out on their first date together, not realising what was in store.

When the dinner was finished, the tables were cleared away and a disco started up. Dancing and drinking was in full flow; everything was fine.

I remember I was dancing with Anne Woolcock when Paul Nunn, thinking to liven things up, threw an uncoiled climbing rope on to the dance floor. Someone shouted "Tug of war" and the women left the floor hurriedly. Two teams quickly formed and battle commenced. Tanky was on the opposing team to me and was their anchor man.

They had some big lads on their side, an unfair advantage; we were losing ground. Ted Howard was our Anchor and thought desperate events require desperate remedies. Ted's remedy was to tie our end to the pub piano; this stopped our slide to defeat, temporarily. Suddenly there was a great crash and a jangling noise as the piano disintegrated.

We had lost. I'll bet the public diners enjoyed the floor show.

By 10.30 pm the barman was saying that they had run out of beer - he probably wanted to get rid of us. But not to be discouraged by this news the lads started on bottles, two per pint pot. This went on until the landlord decided it was time to close. The night ended peacefully and everyone sloped off to their tents or vehicles to sleep it off.

One thing that happened that night that has stood the test of time. It was the night that Richard met Barbara, his future wife; they were married the following year.

On November the 5th, the lads decided to have a bonfire at Millstone Edge. So on Saturday night after the pub we were gathered together in the bay below the Great Slab. We had a big fire burning and it lit up the nearby crag. Some of the lads decided to solo the Great Slab route.

After doing the route Pike descended to the base of the crag and walked back towards the bonfire but before reaching the circle of light cast by the blaze he stepped off a 3ft high step of rock. In the dark and having bad eyesight he hadn't seen it and had stepped off it into space narrowly missing landing in the fire; amazingly, he wasn't hurt, possibly due to the amount of alcohol he had consumed earlier. Someone said, "We nearly had a Guy Fawkes there."

On New Year's Eve 1966 a number of us were celebrating at the Manchester Sports Guild. Roger was there with an old friend who was over on holiday from Canada. Her name was Pauline Baldock. She had very black hair and brown eyes and as I chatted to her about Canada, I thought, what's this girl doing with Roger when she could have me? When I met her again later in 1967, she told me that her first impression of me was that she thought I was miserable.

Roger took Pauline home to her parent's house and the rest of us went to a party. I got a lift home from the party with John and Kath Gosling who told me they were going to live in Santa Monica, California, where John, who was a doctor, had taken a job doing research at UCLA. They gave me their address and said that if ever I went to California, I should contact them.

The next time I saw Roger at the Guild, he told me he was planning to emigrate to Canada and asked if I would like to go with him. I said I would but I didn't have any money. Roger said that he had a few hundred pounds and encouraged me to go with him; I said, "OK."

When Vic heard our plans, he too said he would like to go. So that was settled and we all went to Liverpool for interviews at the Canada Immigration office. All three of us were accepted and were told that the Canadian government would pay our fares to Toronto but we would have to repay this in instalments when we found jobs.

Vic started to go out with a girl from our group of friends. Her name was Penny and she lived in Bramhall where her next door neighbour was George Best, the Manchester United star. Vic and Penny started to get serious and this resulted in Vic cancelling going to Canada which left just me and Roger.

In February I went to the Rag Ball at Manchester University with a girl friend called Celia; The Kinks were the main group playing there. While we were dancing I felt someone prod me in my back. It was Sheila. I hadn't seen her for ages and she told me that she had been teaching but was going to Canada in April. I told her about Roger and me, saying that we expected to go sometime in May and that we were going by ship to Montreal and then on by train to Toronto. She gave me the address and phone number of a couple she was going to stay with in Montreal, saying that they would put us up for the night when we arrived there. Roger's friend Pauline had said we could sleep on her floor when we got to Toronto until we found a place of our own.

Our tickets were booked for May 10th on the Empress of England but we had a few things to do before then. I decided that as I was leaving the country, possibly for a long time, I had some unfinished business at Stanage to see to. So on March 5th, seconded by Jud Jordan and Eddie Thurrell, I did the first ascent of Titanic Direct HVS 5a, my first new route there for over four years and one that I'd had in mind since before first dislocating my shoulder. A month later with John Gosling leading, Mike Simkins, Wool and I did Buffoon with some aid. Nowadays this route is called Goosey Goosey Gander and is graded E5 6a.

Easter was early that year so borrowing skis again from Bob Brigham and hiring a car, Celia and I with Eddie Thurrell and his girlfriend drove to Aviemore for some winter sports. The weather wasn't very good although there was plenty of snow and we managed to ski on Friday and Saturday. On Saturday night we met Les Brown and Pete Turnbull who were there for the ice climbing and had a good night in the pub with them. On Sunday it was snowing heavily and we were messing about on the nursery slopes below Corrie Cass practicing turns. Perhaps because of the cold or perhaps because I put too much weight on my right stick, I dislocated my right shoulder again.

Eddie took off my skis for me and someone said there was a first aid post up at the Sheiling. Holding my now useless arm with my other hand I trudged through the falling snow to the sheiling 500ft up the hill. When I got there I was told that they couldn't help me and that I should go to the doctor in Aviemore. Back I went, down the hill, walking slowly and in great pain. Eddie and the girls drove me to the doctor's surgery where I had a long wait before seeing him. When at last I got in to see the doctor he said that we would have to drive to the A&E at Inverness.

The first thing I said as I came out of the anaesthetic was, "Great Balls of Fire." Don't ask me why.

A week before our departure Roger and I had a farewell party at Barry Jones's flat in Ashton- u -Lyne. It was a good night and we were able to say goodbye to all our mates. The next few days were spent in preparation, packing etc.

The day prior to going away, I was driving Vic's Dormobile with Vic in the passenger seat to my parent's house in Hyde. Vic was going to take Roger and me to Liverpool the next day to board the ship so he was staying the night at my home.

Driving along Mottram Road in Hyde, I saw a motorcycle speed cop in front of us. I said to Vic," There's Roy Fryer, he's one of the Alpha lads; I've not seen him for ages." I tried to pass him but the road was too busy so I followed close behind him hoping to attract his attention to enable me to say goodbye. There was a car parked on double lines and he pulled in to question the driver. I couldn't stop there, but I overtook him sounding the horn as I did so; he looked up and I laughingly gave him the V sign. My heart dropped. It wasn't Roy. The cop mounted his bike and followed us; he overtook us and signalled for us to stop.

Pulling in to the side I felt sick. He parked his bike and came towards us. I opened the Dormobile door, held up my hand and said, "Before you start, I'm sorry I thought you were a friend of mine; Roy Fryer, of Dukinfield Police." He looked at me and said, " I know Roy, he's with the Sale Police force now; clear off, and watch it in future." I didn't need telling twice.

The following morning, Vic and I loaded my stuff into the Dormobile and after saying goodbye to my parents and sister, drove off to pick up Roger.

The ship was at the Princess Landing stage and looked really big. We said goodbye to Vic and embarked on a new adventure.

Chapter 21
Canada - A New Beginning 1967

Roger and I found our cabin. It was smack in the middle of the ship, which would be good if we got any rough weather. We shared it with a lad called Keith from Oldham and a young man from Belfast whose name was Patrick. Patrick's girlfriend was on board in another cabin with some girls and she and Patrick were eloping to Canada to get married. They told us that he was a Catholic and she was a Protestant and that their parents wanted them to split up. They said that it was very dangerous to see one another in Northern Ireland and almost impossible for them to marry there. I thought this was a real shame because they were a really nice quiet couple.

Leaving Liverpool and sailing down the Mersey to the Irish Sea was quite an emotional experience, not knowing when we would see our home country again.

We headed north to Greenock where we were to pick up more passengers. The sea was nice and calm, being sheltered from the swell of the Atlantic by Ireland. We enjoyed that first day and evening. There was a party atmosphere in the bar where some scouse lads were playing Beatles songs on their guitars. We befriended three girls who were going out to work in Montreal and a young student who was going to Canada to work in the forests for the summer. His name was Charles Cumming- Bruce and he told us his father was the British ambassador to Spain. We all got along famously and looked forward to a pleasant voyage.

The following morning (Wednesday) after leaving a very misty Greenock, our ship sailed down through the Firth of Clyde and after passing the north coast of Ireland entered the Atlantic. Immediately we could feel the difference.

The Empress of England was an Ocean going liner with stabilisers that stopped any rolling motion but not the pitching.

As the land disappeared from view the wind got up. That night lying in our bunks listening to the creaking and groaning of the ship, punctuated now and then with a blast on the ship's siren, drifting in and out of sleep I dreamt about the Titanic.

Thursday morning, Roger and I enjoyed a good breakfast. The restaurant was almost empty. There was no sign of the scouse lads; their cabin was situated in the bow of the ship and took the brunt of the rough seas. By midday, it was announced that a force 10 storm was blowing and passengers were warned not to go on deck. As far as the eye could see, there were gigantic waves. The ship no longer seemed to be very big. Every time a wave passed under the bows the ship sailed uphill, see-sawed on the crest, and for a second the propellers came out of the water causing the whole vessel to shudder before plunging down the other side into the trough. This was repeated over and over again. There were no scouse parties that night!

Friday wasn't any better. Again the restaurant was completely empty except for Roger and me. I managed a glass of orange juice; Roger had a full English breakfast!

The waves were as big as the football stands at Old Trafford lined up to the horizon and as far as could be seen in either direction. This storm continued into the weekend. On Monday we entered the Gulf of St. Lawrence and the sea became calmer. Roger and I, with the three girls and Charles, went on deck. To the north, through a hazy mist, we could see land flecked with old snow. We were told that it was Cape Race, Newfoundland - our first view of Canada. It looked like a big plateau rising out of the sea but it eventually sank out of sight. It would be another 500 miles, a day's sailing, before we reached our final destination of Montreal. There was some emotion shown by the girls and it began to hit us all that this was the start of a new life in a new country. Until that moment it had been a holiday - now it took on a more serious aspect.

Not many people went on holiday to Canada in those days. There weren't the holiday flights available then like there are today, and of the people who did go there many were immigrants.

It was pleasant and interesting sailing up the St Lawrence seeing the small communities along its banks. Arriving at Quebec City, all passengers disembarked to be processed through customs and immigration; this took a few hours before we boarded the ship again for the final leg of the voyage. After passing under the Quebec Bridge a further 60 miles landed us at Montreal.

Montreal is a big bustling city so Roger and I took a taxi to the address that Sheila had given to us. She was in and expecting us. Geoff and Suzy came in from work and made us feel very welcome.

The next day we boarded the train to Toronto. After the first 80 miles we crossed the border from the mainly French Province of Quebec into the Anglicised Ontario; a further 270 miles of trees and lakes and we arrived in Toronto.

At that time Toronto was one of the busiest cities in North America and the financial and business centre of all Canada boasting a skyline to rival New York.

The day was hot and we were tired and feeling unsure as to which way to go. Pauline lived in the suburb of Downsview north of the city and about 11 miles from where we were in Downtown Toronto.

The city is built on the north shores of Lake Ontario, which our train had followed for the last 170 miles of our journey. All streets and avenues run at right angles to each other; streets go north from the lake and avenues run east to west. Lake Ontario is the smallest of the Great Lakes but is like a fresh water inland sea being approximately 200 miles long by 60 miles wide; it's BIG!

Eventually we found Pauline's place which was a one-bedroom flat, in the basement of a single storey house at 3, Northgate Drive just south of Wilson Avenue. The street looked as though it should be nice and quiet but there was constant roar of traffic. On investigation we found that there was a sixteen lane highway only a hundred yards away behind the next row of houses.

Pauline was at work but her landlady, a Scotswoman called Davina, was expecting us and let us in to the apartment. Pauline arrived soon after with a friend from work; the friend's name was Nancy and she was Canadian. The two girls suggested that we all go out for a meal, so off we went in Nancy's car, an enormous thing called a Pontiac Parisienne.

Nancy's husband Ken worked at the airport and was on a late shift. Both he and Nancy in time became good friends of ours.

Those first few days in Toronto I wasn't very happy, I wanted to be out west near the Rockies; Ontario was too flat for my liking and I felt I needed to see some hills.

I had initially intended to stay in Canada for only a year, long enough to save a thousand pounds, see the Rockies and the Grand Canyon and visit Yosemite, but had hoped to do this while working out west.

During that first week, Nancy took us all to see Niagara Falls which was very impressive, even though the town of Niagara was a bit scruffy and much commercialised.

Roger and I had originally planned to go out to Vancouver but now he wanted to stay in Toronto saying that we would stand more chance of finding work there; enabling us save up to go out west the following year. I only had about £30 whereas Roger had around £300; he was pretty much in charge. As it turned out, he was probably right as there was plenty of work in Toronto and I desperately needed a job. I got the first one that I went for and the following Monday I started work as an airframe fitter at De Havilland Aircraft Company in Downsview, just a few hundred yards from where Pauline lived.

Pauline and I got on well together right from the start. She was from Dukinfield, the next town to Hyde where I had lived back home, and we found out that we had both worked on the same street when we were in our teens. It was strange that our paths hadn't crossed before Roger had taken her to the Guild last New Year's Eve, because we had both frequented the same jazz club in Manchester in 1962. She told me that she had immigrated to Canada in 1964 and had stayed with her aunt and uncle for the first nine months before getting her own place and said that she now worked as a clerk typist at Federal Mogul.

At first we didn't seem to have a lot in common, apart from our backgrounds but we liked each other and started going out together.

Roger in the meantime had bought a car, a VW Beetle, and was working as a gardener at the Canadian Exhibition grounds down near the lakeshore. He and I moved into our own basement apartment, around the corner and a short walking distance from where Pauline lived.

Things were beginning to look up and although there were no mountains within 500 miles of Toronto we were soon able to pay off our boat fare to the Canadian Government and take a few trips to the nearest climbing areas.

Roger had started a long distance friendship with one of the girls we had met on the ship. Jenny lived in Montreal so most weekends Roger would drive the 350 miles to see her.

During that first summer in Canada, Pauline and I spent some Sundays at her aunty Jean and uncle Cliff's smallholding at Caledon East, about thirty miles NW of Toronto. They had a couple of acres of land set amongst some little hills with a small lake nearby where we could swim.

Jean was in her mid-thirties, a sister of Pauline's mother. We all got on well and enjoyed our times there.

Some weekends Pauline and I along with Roger visited the nearest good climbing area, Bon Echo Provincial Park, about 180 miles away towards Ottawa. There was a crag rising from the lake which had some good routes done by the Canadian Alpine club. There was also a campsite in the park but we camped near a small cottage further towards the top end of the lake where we rented a rowing boat from the cottage owner. This enabled us to visit other nearby crags where we did some new climbs of about VS standard. It was a beautiful area with abundant wildlife. Chipmunks cadged food from us and numerous squirrels coloured black, red or grey were everywhere as were racoons with their burglar-masked faces.

Birds that I had never seen before, bright red cardinals, blue jays and redwing blackbirds ate food from our picnic table and in the autumn, hundreds of geese went winging their way south for the winter. I was beginning to like Ontario.

One time when Pauline and I were at Bon Echo by ourselves, we rowed across the lake to the crag, and as we approached, we saw a racoon at the foot of a steep corner. He was trapped between us and the crag or so we thought but as we neared him, he set off to climb the corner and shot up it in fine style, his small hands grasping the holds. Near the top, reaching a narrow ledge, he looked down at us then ran along the ledge to disappear in the bushes and forest beyond. When our turn came to climb, I reckoned that the racoon had just done the first ascent of a very good severe.

Pauline had never climbed before but for my sake did some easy climbs or sometimes just held my rope. She had never camped before either but found that she enjoyed it.

Driving back from Bon Echo one weekend, out of the corner of my eye I saw a beaver swimming nearby on the surface of a roadside lake. We screeched to a stop but he slapped his tail on the water and dived out of sight. On inspection we found that the little lake had been created by the dam of sticks at its lower end and though we watched for a while the beaver didn't reappear from his lodge.

Sheila visited us in Toronto and said that she was travelling out to Vancouver in British Columbia and was hoping to get work there. She told us that she would let us have her address when she got established in case we needed a floor to sleep on sometime.

A climbing friend that I had known back home was Nev Crowther, who now lived in Windsor, Ontario. We contacted him and arranged to go away for a long weekend to the Adirondack Mountains in New York State. I had done the north ridge of the Peigne in Chamonix in 1962 with Nev but hadn't seen him since as he had immigrated to Canada some years ago; it was great to see him again.

Roger and Nev travelled in Nev's car whilst Pauline and I followed in Roger's VW. Driving east along the highway to Kingston Ontario, we crossed the Thousand Islands Bridge over the St. Lawrence river into the USA and then drove east through the Adirondack Park towards Lake Placid. Passing through a small town late at night, with traffic lights swinging in the wind above the middle of the road Nev just got through before they started to change; I followed him on the amber light and a siren started to wail. Checking my mirror I was horrified to see a cop car with lights flashing pulling out to follow us. Asking Pauline, "What should I do?" she replied," STOP." I stopped, and the cops pulled up some distance behind us. I waited, as anyone in England would do, for the policeman to get out - which they didn't. Instead, a loud hailer ordered me to get out and place my hands on the car; I obeyed without hesitation, then two giant police officers struggled out of the patrol car and with hands on their pistols, sauntered over to where I stood. With a cop on either side of me, I thought, this is how Mickey Rooney must feel when stood between John Wayne and Lee Marvin. I was asked where we had come from and where we were going. I told them that I was English living in Canada and that we were going climbing. They looked puzzled and said, "What do you mean, climbing?" I tried to explain but they didn't seem to understand and then one of them suddenly said, "What about the red light?" I panicked, thinking amber isn't too bad but red is serious. He asked me again but this time pointed to the tail light on our car; it wasn't working. I gave the light a bang with my hand and to my relief; it came on. The cops were satisfied and sent us on our way with a warning not to let it happen again. Catching up with Nev and Roger who had waited for us round the corner we explained what had happened.

Pitching camp at Baldface Mountain beneath the strangely named rocks of Poke-O-Moonshine, we at last managed to get some sleep.

That was a good weekend; we climbed, swam in Lake Champlain and drove up the road which leads to the summit of Whiteface Mountain above the ski resort of Lake Placid. Nev by accident ran over and killed a rabbit on the road back to camp and discovering its body to be intact, he skinned it and we ate it that night, much to Pauline's disgust; she did eat a little of it though. On Monday we drove back the 500 miles to Toronto.

The autumn arrived in all its splendour and there aren't many places more colourful than Ontario with its maples. We arranged with Nev to go for a weekend to the Shawanagunks, a climbing area in the Catskill Mountains of New York state. Whilst climbing there I saw some American climbers that I knew from the Alps, Dick Williams and Jim McCarthy, and an English lad by the name of Rob Wood whom I knew vaguely from home. He said that he was on his way to live in Calgary, Alberta. That was the last weekend away in good weather, and then all too soon the winter was upon us.

Roger needed his car to travel to work and back. I had to walk to De Havilland, which, although only being about three quarters of a mile, in the deep snow and 25 degrees below zero temperature, wasn't good. I wasn't prepared for such cold and walking up the road in jeans, tee shirt and little windjammer with a headband over my ears, I nearly froze. My work- mates used to take pity on me, stopping to pick me up in their big cars.

One Saturday Roger and I went down to the Scarborough Bluffs above Lake Ontario. These bluffs are a conglomerate of rock and clay and are about 200 ft high, reminiscent of Mam Tor in Derbyshire. Descending to the lakeside we got out our axes and ropes etc and prepared to climb. The frozen lake stretched away to the horizon covered in snow, an enormous flat expanse; the bluffs towered above us, frozen hard.

After much cutting of steps in the hard surface we emerged triumphant at the top. This episode relieved our frustration of having nowhere to climb in Ontario during the cold, cold winter weekends.

My relationship with Pauline had become serious and we found that we had a lot in common after all. We were both interested in the Indian wars of the west; we both enjoyed reading science fiction and had similar tastes in music and both liked the countryside. Sometime around Christmas I asked her if she would like to join Roger and me on our trip out west in the coming spring. She said that she would love to go with us. When I told Roger, he wasn't very pleased and said that he had changed his mind about the trip so Pauline and I decided to go on our own. We started to plan our adventure by studying maps and reading about places to see i.e. National Parks, battlefields, forts, canyons and mountains etc. It was a typical long cold Ontario winter. It started in October and spring wasn't expected until April, but I enjoyed the novelty of it - the clear cold sunny days with permanent snow on the ground and ice on the trees which tinkled like bells when the wind blew. We visited Niagara when it was 30 below zero; there were enormous blocks of ice below the Falls reaching halfway to the top; but the Falls kept on flowing.

Meanwhile back in Britain in 1967, Wool and Paul continued to work on the Borrowdale Guidebook doing numerous new routes in the process and in the summer went out to the Alps separately in their own vans.

They met up in Garmisch, Wool nearly getting wiped out on a long hill down into the town when he lost all the brake fluid. They did the Aukenthaler Route on the S Face of the Schusselkarspitze, and then went to the Bregaglia where they did the first British ascent of the N Ridge of the Cengalo before heading home to Cornwall.

Richard wasn't climbing due to his epilepsy and in July he and Barbara got married. After a honeymoon in Cornwall where he did some easy climbs he decided it was time to return to something harder; he teamed up with Tut (Paul Braithwaite), a climber from the Manchester Gritstone Club whom we had all known for years. Richard and Tut did Winking Crack at Gogarth together and this heralded Richard's return to form.

Les Brown with Ken Jackson did the first ascent of The Nazgul on the Central Buttress of Scafell and at Gogarth Pete Crew with various partners (mainly Joe Brown) did a dozen new routes.

Gerry Rogan climbing with Ingle and then Dave Alcock did around four new routes including seconding the first ascent of Nightride with Joe Brown.

Hugh Banner and Pete Crew produced a new Cloggy guide for the Climbers Club. Obviously Crew was having a busy year!

Pike and Di went with Tony Riley to La Barard where they did four routes which included the classic S Ridge of the Dibona and the Aiguille Vallon Les Istage.

On the N. Face of the Civetta with half the Alpha, Ted Howard and Pete Maddocks did the Torre Val Grande. Ted, in etriers on the lip of the big roof, looked back at Pete who said, "It's OK, I'm watching carefully." Ted thought that's odd, what does he mean? Later Pete explained that he had never done any aid climbing before! Some learning curve; but it wasn't a problem for Pete.

Les Brown and John Adams did the second ascent of the Gervasutti Pillar.

Martin Boysen and Nick Estcourt did the second ascent of the American Route on the S Face of the Fou cutting out a lot of the aid climbing. Martin said that the A4 crack was really a HVS/ E1 layback, a bit like the Right Unconquerable at Stanage; they also did a new route on the N Face of the Pic Sans Nom.

At the end of the year, in November, Martin, Pete Crew, Mick Burke and Dougal Haston went to Patagonia to try Cerro Torre. The expedition wasn't a success mainly due to the bad weather, but also because this was the first expedition for everyone involved. Inexperience at organising such a project created complications. For example, they found themselves carrying loads in good weather only to find that when the good conditions came they were too tired to climb.

About Easter 1968, I received news from home that Martin and Maggie had been badly injured in a car crash. They were returning home from visiting Whillans at his home in Crawshaw Booth and Martin and Maggie were passengers in the back of Mike Yates's car. Mike had pulled out of a road junction in Manchester into the path of a fast moving vehicle; they were hit side on.

Chapter 22
Way Out West 1968

Pauline and I bought our own car; it was a turquoise VW Beetle with 70,000miles on the clock. I got it from a workmate, Dave Jerrison, who was from Middlesbrough in England, and he assured me that the car was good even though there were holes in the door.

On Friday May 3rd 1968 both Pauline and I left our jobs and spent the weekend buying some gear and packing our belongings.

On Monday May 6th at 2.00pm we were married at Toronto City Hall; Nancy and another friend, Pam, acted as our witnesses. After a drink in the bar at the top of the 56 floor Dominion Centre, we said goodbye to our friends and set off in the Beetle for California.

That night we stayed in a motel in London, Ontario. The following day after crossing the bridge from Windsor (Canada) to enter the USA at Detroit, Michigan, we followed Highway 94 west. Passing through places with great names like Battle Creek and Kalamazoo we eventually crossed into Indiana near Michigan City, and then it was only 40 miles to Illinois where we picked up Interstate Highway 80. As we bypassed Chicago, the view was of corrugated shacks on either side of the highway, the homes of poor Blacks and poor Whites who had probably moved from the south in search of work. Then suddenly the landscape started to change to open country as we travelled west of Joliet. At Ottawa, Illinois, we decided to book into another motel for the night, having done 500 miles that day. Wednesday we got up at 7.30am, had breakfast at the motel then set off across rolling prairie on Highway 80 in beautiful weather.

Arriving at the state border with Iowa around midday, we stopped to fill up with petrol and decided to have lunch at the adjoining diner. When we came out again the car wouldn't start; we needed a push.

We were the only ones on an enormous gravel car park, except for a surly looking guy who was reading a paper in a little tin shack. I asked him if he would give us a push to get us started. He grudgingly agreed to push us with his pickup truck. Pauline and I got back in our car and waited. Looking in the rear view mirror, I saw the pickup approaching in a cloud of dust. Suddenly there was an almighty crash and we found ourselves moving across the car park at a fair lick. I let in the clutch and our engine sprang to life. The truck reversed back to the tin shack and the driver resumed his position behind his newspaper. As we drove away I heard a scraping noise and on investigation found that the rear bumper was hanging off. I circled back to the tin shack and pointed out to the "Good Samaritan" what had happened, and asked if he had needed to hit us at 30mph.

With a surly grin he said, "What's the problem, it started didn't it?" and then being the good chap that he was he gave us some wire to fasten the bumper back on. We were glad to get away and after a long boring drive through the flat wheat fields of Iowa, and passing Des Moines (whoever he was?) arrived at Omaha, Nebraska, across the wide Missouri.

We pressed on, crossing the Platte River and it was dusk by the time we reached Grand Island. Having driven 560 miles that day we were tired and treated ourselves to the luxury of a Holiday Inn. We smuggled our camping stove, pans and food up to our room and Pauline cooked our meal in the bathroom on a luxury marble surface next to the washbasin. Rising early we were on our way again by 8.30am following the Platte River valley for 240 miles to the town of Ogallala where we stopped to buy groceries and a camera for Pauline. On again into the North East corner of Colorado, where we wasted an hour trying and failing to find the Sterling Reservoir campsite. Fed up with messing about we pushed on south west down Highway 76 across the most desolate, dry plateau in the world. There we got our first view of the Rockies in the distance which at first looked like clouds on the horizon. The small town of Hudson 30 miles from Denver offered food and accommodation so forgetting about camping, we booked into the Lu Leta motel, which wasn't up to much, but it was home for the night.

Leaving at 9.30 next morning and driving through Denver to Golden, the road wound through a steep sided gorge and took us to

Idaho Springs. For the next 30 miles climbing steadily through magnificent scenery we arrived at the summit of the Loveland Pass 12,000ft above sea level. Large snow drifts lined the road reminding us that here it was still early spring. When we got out of the car to look at the view, after only a minute a cold wind blowing off snow- capped peaks, 14,000 ft high, sent us hurrying back to the warmth of the Beetle. An hour ago in Golden it had been sunny but here with the wind it felt like winter. It started to rain and sleet as we arrived at Dillon Lake 11miles west of Loveland Pass. Dillon Lake was a resort with cafes and log cabins etc and was surrounded by ski areas; we decided to stop for a late breakfast. There was one other person in the Café, a cowboy on his way west to Utah. The ski season was over and it wasn't yet warm enough to spend time at the lake, so the whole town seemed dead.

After our meal, feeling a lot better we drove over Vail Pass, 11,000ft, and descended to the ski resort of Vail. Another 80 miles further on through Glenwood Springs, we decided to spend the night at a campsite near the village of New Castle. There was no one else at the campsite so as it was a cold night we slept inside a wooden building with some washing machines for company. The heating had been left on because of the freezing weather so on our airbeds we had a comfortable night.

The following morning, Saturday May 11th, we were up and making coffee by 7 o'clock; the temperature was 15 degrees F. An early getaway saw us in Grand Junction in time for a delicious western breakfast. Moving on again through desert country we crossed into Utah and turned south to Moab with hot sun all the way. There we visited the Arches National Park.

This was a really fantastic place with red rock pinnacles and huge natural rock arches some hundreds of feet high. In the distance the snow capped peaks which must have been at least 50 miles away looked quite close, shimmering in the desert heat. This was the sort of weather that we had been looking forward to! Leaving Arches behind us, we drove south then east back into Colorado through some heavy thunder storms and booked into the Ute Mountain motel in the small town of Cortez at $5 per night! Sunday morning, setting off at 9am we drove a few miles up the road to visit the cliff dwellings of Mesa Verde National Park. There are over 4,000 archaeological sites preserved here, 600 of which are cliff dwellings. The best examples of these are located beneath an enormous overhang and make up a complete town with footbridges and ladders connecting the different buildings. Nearby is a large circular temple dedicated to the sun god. All these pueblo dwellings were centuries old and had been built by civilised Pueblo Indians called Anasazi who lived there from AD600 until AD1300 when they suddenly left and migrated to Arizona and New Mexico.

After an interesting morning we drove back to Cortez for a late breakfast cum lunch. Following highway 160 south west across the Ute Mountain Indian Reservation to the Four Corners (the only place in the USA where four states meet - Arizona, Utah, Colorado and New Mexico) we crossed into Arizona. The Canyon De Chelly National Monument was a place that we wanted to see, so heading south on US 191 through sandstorms and the red rock desert country which is the Navajo Indian Reservation, we filled up at a place called Many Farms and soon after arrived at Chinle, the Monument headquarters. Back in 1968 there were a few buildings there at the Canyon Rim but the whole place looked poor and fairly run down but I believe it's not like that now. The Canyon sandstone cliffs and towers were very impressive and I wondered if any of them had been climbed. I knew that one of these towers, Spider Rock, 800ft high, was sacred to the Navajo Indians and that climbing was forbidden but some climbers don't respect such things. Looking down into the canyon bottom we could make out some ranch-style buildings; it seems that the canyon supports a fairly large Navajo farming community. We would have liked to have stayed longer, but as the weather looked threatening and there was nowhere to stay on the reservation we decided to push on.

It was a narrow road across wild semi-desert and there was a strong wind blowing which whipped up great clouds of sand. I was worried about our old car but needn't have been; it just took everything that nature could throw at it. This really was the Wild West. At one point an Indian on horseback herding sheep suddenly appeared over to our right and raised his hand in a salute; we waved back and for a minute imagined we were back in the Old West. Driving across the reservation, the only traffic we ever saw were blue pickup trucks driven by Navajos; they all seemed to have them. All of the Indians seemed to be dressed alike in denim jeans and jackets and all wore cowboy hats; it was like a uniform.

The houses were all wood-frame buildings and a lot of them had traditional brushwood hogans (small igloo shaped huts) along side them, presumably where their parents or grand parents lived. Beer cans thrown from the pickups littered the roadside, a sad reminder of the main pastime of a people whose traditional way of life had been taken away with nothing to replace it.

Near Holbrook we joined US Route 66 of Chuck Berry fame and booked into The Sundown Motel where we bought our evening meal and looked forward to a comfortable night.

Over the next day, we visited the Petrified Forest and the Painted Desert, and then drove on through Flagstaff to the town of Williams where we camped at the National Forest campsite. As we were the only ones camping there, a notice that warned of bears in the vicinity worried us but we didn't see any. The next day, after breaking camp, a drive of 60 miles across the high Coconino Plateau brought us to the South Rim of the Grand Canyon. The weather was clear and the views north across the canyon were tremendous as were the views down to the Colorado River threading its way through the Canyon one vertical mile below us. The scale of this wondrous place is difficult to grasp and the clarity of the Arizona air made the 12,600ft San Francisco Peaks 80 miles away to the south, appear much closer. Driving on again from Desert View to Cameron with the spectacle of another Painted Desert to our left, we turned south back to Flagstaff and the comfort of a motel. No danger of marauding bears that night but when we went out to a bar for a beer a drunken Apache dressed in denims fell across our table. The bartender picked him up and phoned for a taxi to take him home to the reservation.

Breakfasting at a café at 8.30 next morning we decided to have one more day in this area and, having seen Burt Lancaster in the movie "Apache," decided to drive down Oak Creek Canyon where it had been filmed. The canyon was a bit disappointing. I can't remember seeing any overhead wires or pylons in the film Apache, and Burt's Indian shack wasn't there either! But at least the river was nice and clear.

From there we drove to see some more cliff dwellings at Montezuma Castle National Monument. This we really enjoyed because we saw lots of lizards. The sun was baking hot and ambling round the area we were feeling a bit tired until we saw a notice which read, "If you are lucky enough to see a rattlesnake, please report it to the Ranger." From then on we became miraculously alert, but we didn't see any.

After spending another night in Flagstaff we got up at 5.30 and had breakfast at a café. Today was going to be a long drive across the Mohave Desert to Los Angeles where we had arranged to stay with John and Kath Gosling.

When we fuelled the car across the road from the café, the guy at the pump offered to check the oil and tyres for us. As he checked the back tyres, I thought I saw him squirt something under the car. When he had finished he told me that we had a leaking shock absorber which he could replace for $40 saying that otherwise we would never make it across the desert.

It was then that I remembered Nancy telling us that when she and Ken had been to Arizona someone had tried to sell them new tyres using a similar story. I looked at another guy who was leaning on the pump and he nodded agreement keeping a deadpan face. Suspicious, I bent down and ran my finger over the "leaking" oil; it was as clean as new. I told him that I would take a chance and not bother having the repair. Then he proved himself a con man by telling me that all the engine oil could drain away and blow up the engine if I didn't have it done. I told him that I was an engineer and knew different. We left there wondering how many gullible tourists he manages to swindle each year.

We drove across the Mohave Desert on Route 66, the road ahead shimmering in the heat which even in May must have been approaching 90 degrees. Having no air conditioning the car was like an oven; even with the windows down it was almost unbearable. On reaching the town of Kingman the road looped south and crossed the Colorado River to enter California at the border town of Needles. Here, the car was searched by border guards looking not for drugs, but for fruit and vegetables. California's pest free agriculture had to be preserved and any veg being unofficially transported over the border was confiscated; that's how we lost our potatoes! Needles, because of it's location on the Colorado River, was a green oasis standing out against the desert backdrop. We decided to stop here for lunch, and on entering the diner the cold air conditioning almost made us want to put on sweaters but after becoming accustomed to it we found we didn't want to leave. Getting back in the car we wondered if we would survive the rest of the journey to LA.

Crossing more desert with stark looking mountains and glaring white dry lake beds on either side of the road and no traffic was frightening. What happens if you break down, especially in that heat?

After a while, we saw over to our left an enormous machine was carving out a new road parallel to Route 66. This road later became Interstate Highway 40, consigning the famous road and the song to the history books. At San Bernardino we ran into smog which had drifted up there from LA some 60 miles away.

Rush-hour traffic on the Santa Monica freeway was very frightening after the empty desert. Six lanes in each direction moving nose to tail at 60mph, and us not really knowing where we were going, prompted me to say, "If we ever get off here alive I'll never again drive on this road!" At the end of the freeway was the Pacific Ocean. We could go no further west without a boat, we were in Santa Monica at last. I found a phone box and called John and Kath and they came in their car to lead us back to their apartment; it was great to see them again. After we had unloaded our luggage our hosts took us to an English-style pub, "The Mucky Duck," where we had sandwiches, beer and a game of darts. John was about the same age as me and was tall and slim; I knew him to be a very good climber. Kath, a small attractive blonde was from Dukinfield, the same town back home as Pauline, and they knew each other's families. Both John and Kath made us feel very welcome, even giving up their bedroom for us so as not to disturb us when they were leaving for work in the mornings. Their apartment was on the first floor with a balcony and in the courtyard below was a communal swimming pool. Pauline and I spent the first day sunbathing and swimming until the others came home from work then we had a late meal and sat up drinking and talking till the early hours of the morning. John told me he had done some climbs in Yosemite and showed me some pictures of the Nose on El Capitan which he said hadn't yet had a British ascent. He asked if I fancied having a go at it with him. I told him I would have to do some other stuff first seeing that I hadn't done much climbing during the previous year and I was also doubtful about whether my shoulder would stand up to it. We decided to play it by ear.

Over the next few days we sunbathed, swam in the pool and did some sight seeing, driving round LA, Sunset Strip and Beverly Hills. Another day Pauline and I drove down the coast to Venice and visited Marine land.

On the Wednesday morning I took the car to be serviced ready for the next leg of our trip, and then the afternoon was spent by the pool. When John and Kath came home from work, John challenged me to a race down the pool. Diving in I dislocated my right shoulder again. John being a doctor tried to put it back in place but realising the pain it caused said that he would take me to the hospital where he worked so that I could have it done under anaesthetic. The hospital at UCLA is a teaching hospital so I was examined by a doctor and two students. After instructing the students as to what to do, the doctor left them to it. They tried all kinds of methods to put my shoulder back in place, even some methods which John said had been used by the ancient Greeks. But try as they might they couldn't succeed and after two and a half hours seemed ready to give up. I was beginning to despair and was in a lot of pain when suddenly, the doctor came back. He asked the two students if they had given me anything for the pain; they shook their heads and looked slightly embarrassed. The doctor shook his head and gave them a note to go for some morphine. I felt like shaking the lot of them but it would have hurt my arm so I didn't try. When they had left the room, the doctor removed his shoe and putting his foot into my armpit; he took hold of my right arm and gently pulled it across my chest. I said, "Keep going, I can feel it's going in." he applied more pressure and in it went. What a relief the pain was gone but as the two students returned a wave of nausea came over me and I threw up. John came to collect me and with my arm in a sling, we left the hospital. The first thing I said to John was "That's it, no climbing for me in Yosemite."

I stayed in all the following day feeling miserable and read Joe Brown's book "The Hard Years." One evening we visited Pauline's uncle Sid who lived there in Santa Monica and when we told him we were staying with a brain surgeon he invited us to go again on Sunday night but this time with John and Kath.

Saturday morning, we watched a butterfly hatch out of its chrysalis, a fascinating experience. Then we all went for a drive in John's car to Corona and a crag called Big Rock where some big blue bugs came out of burrows in the ground to fly at us like missiles. We went out for a grotty meal then back home to play cards; I lost again, still feeling miserable.

On Sunday my shoulder felt better so I discarded the sling.

Monday morning after a late breakfast Pauline and I set off to drive up the coast through Santa Barbara to San Louis Obispo, then along the scenic Highway 1 following the coastline known as Big Sur to Carmel just before Monterey, where we booked in a motel for the night.

The next day we drove round the famous 17 mile stretch of coastline at Monterey and spent most of the day looking at the many seals.

This bit of the coast is some of the wildest and most beautiful in California but is owned by the Del Monte family who charge the public to drive along the 17 mile section. After cooking a meal down by the sea we set off again and headed through the wine producing areas passing through Merced towards Yosemite National Park. It was beginning to go dark so as we wanted to enter Yosemite in the daylight, we decided to stop for the night at a rest area near Mariposa. A cold and uncomfortable night sleeping on the seats of the Beetle made us very appreciative of the dawn when it came. Breakfast consisted of a brew and a butty at 7am, and on a beautiful sunny morning we drove into Yosemite stopping below El Capitan and looking up in awe, trying to grasp the scale of this magnificent piece of rock. The sound of someone knocking in pegs drifted down to us and after peering searchingly for a while I managed to see two tiny figures high up on the Nose.

The rest of the day was spent setting up camp at Camp 12 and then sight seeing at Mirror Lake and Yosemite Falls etc.

That evening we visited Camp 4 to see if there was anyone there whom I might know and were surprised to see Little Mick (Burke) and Rob Wood.

They had just got down from making the first British ascent of the Nose; it was they that we had seen climbing early that morning.

A pleasant evening was spent drinking wine and catching up on events.

Mick had travelled up from South America on the train leaving Martin, Pete Crew and Haston who had gone back to the UK after the failed expedition to Cerro Torre. Mick hadn't heard about Martin and Maggie's accident and was shocked when I told him.

Back at Camp 12, we were just about to go to bed when John and Kath arrived and after a brew and a chat we all turned in.

After a late breakfast, we all had a trip up to Glacier Point to take in the incredible view of the Valley and then back at Yosemite village where Kath bought us a wedding present, a signed copy of an Ansel Adams' photo of the Nose of El Capitan.

Phil Gleason, an American climber friend of John's, joined us at Camp 12 and we had an enjoyable evening sitting round the camp fire talking and drinking. The remainder of our stay in Yosemite was taken up with John, Phil and I doing an easy route on a crag near the Lower Falls followed by the other two doing some bouldering. John got bitten on the hand by a scorpion and needed ice packs to reduce the swelling.

One evening while we were all sitting by the campfire, a large bear ambled through the camp causing panic all round and precipitating a mad dash for the cars. That night we slept in the car, feeling safer there because the bear was rampaging and crashing around almost until dawn.

On Sunday John and Kath packed their things and we all went to pick up Phil at Camp 4 and then drove up to the Mariposa Grove to see the Giant Sequoia trees which are very impressive. Saying a sad goodbye to John and Kath who were going home to LA, Phil, Pauline and I went back to the Village where I bought a Navajo rug for Pauline.

At noon the following day after calling at Camp 4 to say goodbye to Mick, Rob and Phil, Pauline and I drove west to join Highway 5 near Manteca.

Heading north through Sacramento we stopped to camp for the night at Shasta dam just north of Redding. The next day, driving north again to the oddly named town of Weed and passing the 14,162 ft snow capped Mt. Shasta we were at last in the Cascade Range of mountains.

This chain of mountains runs down from the Canadian border through Washington State and Oregon to northern California before merging with the Sierra Nevada and the lower mountain ranges west of the Sacramento Valley. The Cascades have some very high mountains, as high as any in the Rockies. They are heavily glaciated, even some of the lower ones amongst them, due to the high level of precipitation on the west coast. They are also home to some active volcanoes such as Mt. St. Helens which last erupted in 1980 causing widespread devastation when the top blew off the mountain and lowered its altitude by several thousand feet. Mt. Rainier in Washington State which is the highest at 14,410ft is very glaciated and reminiscent of Mont Blanc. Further north near, near the Canadian border, the cone-shaped Mt. Baker is another glistening white, dormant volcano as is Mt. Hood behind Portland, Oregon.

Leaving Highway 5 at Weed, we drove over the border into Oregon and the logging town of Klamath Falls where we shopped for food etc.

That afternoon after passing through the town of Fort Klamath we arrived at Crater Lake National Park. This is another mountain that has blown its top sometime in the distant past, leaving a large crater approximately five miles across which is filled to within a few hundred feet of the rim with a lake of turquoise water. At the centre of this lake an ash cone has grown up to form an island which is now covered with Pine trees.

When we were at Crater Lake it was early in the season and as the crater is at an altitude of 7,000+ ft there was a lot of deep snow surrounding it and the day was bitterly cold. As we left the National Park on a minor road the scenery near Diamond Lake and down to the towns of Steamboat and Glide was well worth the drive. Stopping in a lay-by overlooking the Steamboat River we cooked our evening meal before driving on to join Highway 5 again at the town of Roseburg where we booked in at The Town House motel.

That night we watched Senator Robert Kennedy on TV giving a speech at a big hotel in Los Angeles but as we were tired I turned it off and went to bed.

The following morning when I went to the motel office to pay, the manageress said, "Isn't it awful about Kennedy being shot?" Puzzled and wondering what she meant, I asked, "Who do you mean, John?" "No Robert, last night," she replied. What a shock it was, everyone that we met that day was in tears wondering how such a dreadful thing could have happened again to the same family. And when talking to Americans we got the feeling that not only was there a real sadness felt on all sides about this assassination but also there was a sense of shame that these things were becoming almost commonplace in the country they loved.

It took us two days to drive up the spectacular coast of Oregon to the five-mile long bridge spanning the mighty Columbia River, where we crossed into Washington State. The weather had deteriorated and by the time we arrived at the town of Aberdeen near the Olympic Peninsula National Park we had had enough. After another night in a motel we decided to push on to Canada and arrived at Sheila's in Vancouver at around 4.45pm, parking the car on the gravel road behind her apartment.

After a meal and an evening walk down to Stanley Park; we returned for an early night.

Cliff Dwellings at Mesa Verde, Colorado. 1968

Arches Nat'l Park, Utah, 1968

(L to R); Stewart Fulton and Donald Francis, Mt Baker Washington State 1968

Bon Echo Provincial Park, Ontario 1970

Central Buttress, Scafell, 1991 A Parker

Titanic Direct, Stanage, 2005

Chapter 23
Beautiful British Columbia 1968

Wakening early next morning to the sound of pneumatic drills and other machinery, I went out at the back to get something from the car; the car wasn't there and the road was all dug up. I asked one of the workmen about the car and he told me it had been towed away to "The Pound."

When we arrived at the Pound to pick up the Beetle we had to pay $6 to retrieve it and were given a ticket to take to the Police station to pay a fine. The policeman asked why we hadn't obeyed the warning notices about the roadworks and I told him that we had arrived late in the dark after having driven from Ontario. He said, "Oh, that's not very hospitable of us," and he tore up the parking ticket saying, "Enjoy your stay in BC."

I thanked him and beat a quick retreat. After a few days at Sheila's, Pauline and I set off again, this time heading east along the Canada/US border to Osoyoos in the Okanagan which is a fruit growing semi-desert area of British Columbia. The warm, dry climate is due to the area being between the Rocky Mountains to the east and the Coastal Range and the Cascades to the west. Any precipitation from the east falls on the Rockies and any from the Pacific is dumped on the other ranges before it can reach the Okanagan. There is some excellent rock-climbing in this area. Driving on through the towns of Rossland and Trail over about three minor ranges of hills and mountains, just before crossing the border into Idaho, we saw a large porcupine ambling across the road. Then in Idaho a black bear ran across the road causing me to think that the biggest danger from these animals is being hurt by crashing the car while trying to avoid them. That night camping at a National Forest campsite as we sat by our fire a large rabbit ran right up to us, peered at the fire then looked at us and ran away.

Our next visitor was an American man who was camping nearby. He strolled up to us and his very first words were," Hello I am Mr. Bighead, (I can't remember his real name, but that one fits) I am the president of the First National Bank of Pennsylvania." Then he paused, waiting for our cries of admiration. I said, "Hi, I'm Al Parker, an out-of-work fitter and this is my wife Pauline who is also not working." On hearing this he cleared off much to our relief.

Crossing the upper narrow strip of Idaho into Montana the weather became stormy so we booked into a motel at the small town of Hungry Horse near the west entrance to Glacier National Park.

That evening we went to look at the Hungry Horse dam which holds back a 40 mile long lake and looks like a mini Hoover dam but which has probably never been heard of outside of Montana or perhaps even outside Hungry Horse for that matter.

Calling in at the Angler's Bar back in town for a beer before our evening meal, we sat at a table listening to Elvis on the juke box. The only other customers were a middle aged couple standing at the bar talking to the bartender and they were obviously locals. When Pauline and I got up to leave, I took the glasses back to the bar thanked the bartender and said "Goodnight." The man standing at the bar, who looked like Robert Mitchum, asked where we were from. I told him, "Canada, but originally from England." He looked interested and said "London, eh?" I replied, "No, Manchester." He looked blank and said that he had only heard of London. Anyway that broke the ice and they insisted on buying us a drink. They told us they were called Bud and Norah; she worked in the restaurant in the National Park and he worked in the forest cutting lumber. Bud said that he loved Montana and wouldn't want to live anywhere else saying that in October when the salmon come up the river to spawn you could see as many as 100 eagles waiting to pluck them from the water.

As the night progressed more locals came in and we were introduced as folks from London, England. It developed into quite a party; we all got a little drunk and before leaving I gave Bud my penknife and he gave me a lighter. At 11o'clock we all said our goodbyes and left the bar. Pauline and I went across the road to the motel cooked our evening meal and went to bed.[2]

---

[2] In 1996, twenty- eight years later while on holiday in America we were again passing through Hungry Horse this time with our 18 year old daughter Lucy. We stayed at a motel which we thought was the same one as before but there was no bar across the road. Asking at the Post Office if Bud and Norah still lived there we

Driving into Glacier National Park and up the steep and narrow road of the Logan Pass we saw a bear at the side of the road. Near the top of the pass the road was cut through deep snow drifts forming 30ft high vertical walls on either side. The pass had just opened after the winter so we were lucky to be able to go that way and see such magnificent scenery. Crossing the Continental Divide and dropping down to Lake St. Mary we drove to the Canadian side of Waterton International Peace Park, which straddles the border between the US and Canada. In Waterton we saw bear, bison and moose but as the weather was wet and windy, we didn't hang around and drove on through the destroyed town of Frank. This town had fallen victim to a large landslide in the early 20th century when during the night of 29th April 1903 half of the mountain above the town had broken away in one enormous slab of rock and plunged down into the valley sweeping everything before it. Travelling at 120km/hour it crashed down towards the coal mining town of Frank burying part of the town. It shot 3km across the Crowsnest Valley going 130 metres up the opposite slope. In 90 seconds part of Frank was buried forever killing at least 70 of the inhabitants; what remains is now known as Frank Slide.

At the town of Fernie, BC, we spent the night in the car and next morning after breakfast drove up to Radium Hot Springs in the Columbia River valley. This area must have been originally settled by Cumbrians as there is a Windermere and a Grasmere in the valley. At Radium we branched off through Kootenay National Park back over the Divide to Banff National Park in Alberta. In 1968 Alberta, which is twice the size of Britain, had a population of one and a half million with probably nearly as many bears. At the campsite near Lake Louise it was cold and wet so we decided to sleep in the car again; it would also be more bear-proof! We had by now got this off to a fine art. Taking the backs off the front seats, I put them under the car and then started to fill the space between the front and back seats with gear from the car boot. An American woman who stood watching in amazement asked me what I was doing. I told her we planned to sleep in the car on airbeds. She said, "Gee, what are airbeds?" When I explained that they were inflatable beds, she said, "I'll go get my husband then we can both watch." Off she went to their double-decker sized camper vehicle which was parked next to their house-sized tent and returned with her

were told that Bud had died five years previously and Norah had moved to live in Helena (they thought) with her sister.

oversized husband and children to watch me inflate our beds. When I produced the airbeds they all moaned in disappointment.

"Oh, you mean air mattresses." I think they must have been expecting a four poster bed or something. This little episode made me realise that generally when talking to some Americans, no matter how nice or friendly they may be, they don't seem able to put two and two together. Anyway they went away puzzling why we called them airbeds; it's a good job I hadn't said lilos.

We spent the next few days exploring the Banff / Jasper area and saw lots of wildlife, bears and elk at the roadsides and chipmunks and squirrels at our campsite, but the weather wasn't good considering that it was mid June. After a visit to the Columbia ice field where we went on to the glacier, a first for Pauline, we decided it was time to head back to BC. The following day we set off and drove over the scenic Kicking Horse Pass on the Trans-Canada Highway 1. After crossing the Columbia River at Golden then passing through Glacier National Park and Mt. Revelstoke National Park with mountains all the way, we came to the town of Kamloops. From Kamloops we followed the winding Thompson River Canyon to its junction with the Fraser Canyon and arrived at Vancouver in heavy rain to stay at Sheila's place again.

The time had come to look for somewhere to live and somewhere to work. The first problem was easily solved; we found a basement apartment at West 13th Avenue. It was quite spacious, fully furnished and cheap. We were told it wouldn't be available until the next week so off we went to camp at Alice Lake near Squamish. That was a very wet week and we were pleased when the time came for us to return to Vancouver to move into our new home.

I knew that some of the Langdale lads lived in Vancouver, so looking in the phone book I found Pete Shotton's number. I called him and he gave me his address and invited us round. When we arrived at Pete's he was sitting on the wall outside and although I hadn't seen him for a few years he just nodded and said, "Hi, Al, come on in." It was as though he'd seen me only last week. He introduced us to his wife, Joan, who already had the kettle on. Pete, who was also a fitter, told me that he had been out of work for months and that jobs in engineering were few unless you were very lucky.

Pete told us that Donald Francis and partner Sue lived nearby with their young daughter Joanne. Also in Vancouver were Comic Pete and his wife Del. Comic worked in a small engineering works; he was one of the lucky ones. Stewart Fulton was looking for work and Roger

(Dodger) Marshall worked for the Vancouver Sun Newspaper. Pete told us that they all met for a drink on Saturday nights taking turns at each other's apartments. He suggested that they all come to us next Saturday for a reunion get-together. How could we refuse? They came early on Saturday evening with stacks of beer and stayed until 10am on Sunday.

Pauline found work at British American Oil as a clerk / typist but even though I tried hard to find a job, there was nothing available in engineering. I went for various interviews for other types of work but having a trade went against me, the reasoning being that I would probably quit as soon as something came up in my trade.

Donald was an art student and spent a lot of time at the beach. I looked for jobs in the mornings and joined Donald in the afternoons. One day we walked to the top of the Lions, the two mountains which are plainly seen from Vancouver. This entailed a massive slog up steep forested slopes but it was worth it for the summit views.

One day I noticed in the phone book that Mirlees Diesel Engine Co. had an office in Vancouver. I had worked for Mirlees back home in Stockport so I went to the office to see if they had any work. I was offered a job installing some engines at a power station at Dawson Creek 700miles north of Vancouver. I was told it was a 6 months contract living on site without married accommodation. I turned the job down as we had only been married for two months and spending the winter in the frozen north away from Pauline didn't appeal. The chap at the Mirlees agency told me there was another guy living in Vancouver who had worked at Mirlees. His name was George Galley and he had his own business down at the docks overhauling ships' engines. George and I had done our apprenticeships together at Ashton National so I was keen to see him again and after all he might have some work for me.

When I walked into George's workshop, he nearly fell through the floor with surprise. He was pleased to see me but said that it was a quiet time for him at work and he couldn't help me. George was about 5ft 6" tall with shoulders almost as wide. He had always been a drinker and a fighter when he was young but told me he was now settled down and married to a Canadian girl and they had a baby.

The Langdale lads had settled into a kind of bored stagnation and didn't seem to be motivated to do anything except drink. For once, probably because we were new on the scene, I found myself to be the driving force. I did a climb with Stewart at Squamish Chief which at that time hadn't been developed much but there were obvious possibilities and I wished that my shoulder had been fixed. We also climbed at the crag at Lighthouse Point just north of Vancouver; this was a sea cliff in a beautiful setting and was approached through a grove of enormous Douglas firs.

One weekend, Donald, Sue and Joanne, and Pauline and I went down to the Mt. Baker area in Washington State. The weather was beautifully sunny and very hot. On Saturday night at a place called Hannegan's Horse Camp lying outside in our sleeping bags we fell asleep counting hundreds of shooting stars as the Earth passed through a meteorite shower. On the Sunday in the heat of the day we walked up a long trail to the scenic Twin Lakes. When we arrived at the lakes feeling hot and very sweaty the clear azure water looked irresistible, so stripping to our underwear we all leapt in. Impetuous fools! Our hearts almost stopped. It was like being stabbed by a thousand knives as soon as we touched the water; we couldn't get out quickly enough. In our desire for a cooling swim we had failed to notice the snowfield that swept into the opposite end of the lake. Afterwards we lay in the hot sun feeling the life returning slowly to our frozen limbs and our teeth ceased to chatter. This part of the North Cascades is very beautiful. The views of Mt. Baker, white against the dark blue sky and the glaciers and rocky ridges of Mt. Shuksan, made us determined to come back as soon as possible to explore the area more thoroughly.

Some weeks later we were all back there again, camping at the Silver Firs Campsite, but this time with Stewart, Comic Pete and Del, who was 9 months pregnant. Comic was in a miserable mood, he'd had an accident at work which had taken the top off his right thumb. This bit of thumb had been grafted into the middle of his palm to keep it alive until it could be stitched back on permanently.

Comic sat at the camp picnic table moaning and contemplating his thumb while Del who was about to give birth at any moment, erected the tent, unpacked the car and cooked their meal. Comic's mood wasn't made any better by the fact that before leaving Vancouver, Shotton had told him he would be allowed to take two 12 packs of beer across the border. When he and Del reached the US border they were told they could only take one 12 pack into the States. Refusing to let his beer be confiscated, Comic sat in the car and drank 12 bottles of beer; then Del drove them to join us at the campsite.

Donald and I wanted to do the magnificent looking Mt. Shuksan which, although only 9,127ft was heavily glaciated. On Saturday afternoon with Stewart we reconnoitred the approach and well before dawn the next day, Donald and I set off to walk the four miles along a wooded ridge to Lake Ann.

The morning was very dark, without stars and cloudy, but we were optimistic that the weather would improve. Lake Ann lies near to the start of the route which we planned to take up the glacier to the summit of Shuksan. The trail through the forest was hard going and I wondered what creatures were watching us beyond the limit of the light cast by our head-torches. Donald said with authority, "Don't worry about bears, they'll be scared of us." I wasn't so convinced but Donald assured me that he was an expert.

It was just about dawn when we reached Lake Ann. The rain was pouring steadily and we couldn't see Shuksan at all. Stopping on a little rocky knoll to talk to a couple from Seattle who had spent the night there at Lake Ann, we learned that they too had been planning to do the same route as us. They were of the opinion that the weather would get worse before it got better and had decided to return to the road.

Still optimistic we decided to hang on for another hour or so but when it started to snow, thunder and lightening we decided to bale out as well.

Back in Vancouver, there was still no sign of any work for me, and as our original plans had been to save enough money to set us up on our eventual return to England; we started thinking about going back to Toronto where I was sure to get work. We didn't really want to go but felt that we had no option.

Pauline phoned Davina, her ex-landlady in Downsview, who told us that they had redecorated the apartment and added a bedroom and were about to advertise it for rent. Making a quick decision, we asked her to save it for us and we would be back in two weeks.

Pauline resigned her job at BA and we started to pack our things and transfer money etc. The lads and their wives and partners arranged a farewell do for Friday night but as the week progressed all the women dropped out one by one.

On Friday night, Shotton, Donald, Stewart, Dodger and I hit the town.

It was a real pub crawl; where we went or how we got back home is not clear, but I do know I didn't get home until about 3am.

Stewart came round next day to repay $20 that I had loaned him and to say goodbye. That was the last time that I saw him. I heard from Donald a year later that Stewart who was an electrician had been electrocuted at work and had sadly died; he was a good guy and both Pauline and I liked him a lot.

On Sunday 15th September we left Vancouver and drove south over the border to Everet in Washington State. Turning east on Highway 2, I noticed that the car had started to mis-fire.

At Wenatchee the following day we took the car to a VW garage where they told us that we probably had a burnt out valve which would be expensive. I decided to continue on only 3 cylinders; our top speed was now 45mph on the flat! Driving on through Idaho and over the Bitterroot mountains we stopped for the night at Missoula, Montana.

Next day it was on again through Butte, a scruffy town which is home to one of the world's largest open cast copper mines then on Highway 90, through Bozeman following the Yellowstone River to yet another motel at Laurel near the town of Billings. As we weren't far from the site of the Custer Massacre at the Little Big Horn, we decided to pay it a visit.

On a beautiful September afternoon, walking round the battlefield with no one else there and with views to the distant Big Horn mountains, it was easy to imagine that fateful day in June 1876.

Over the next few days we drove across South Dakota, visiting the Badlands on the way. Turning north to Minneapolis where on the Freeway we could only just make the minimum speed of 45mph, we chugged our way to the State of Wisconsin. There was still over 300 miles to the Canadian border at Saulte Ste. Marie and it was dusk. Passing through dense forest on either side of the road, towns became few and far between so we thought to stop for the night at the next place along the way but were disappointed to find that there was no accommodation there. It was 107miles to the next town and darkness had fallen. Pushing on, hoping that something would turn up, we suddenly saw a light in the woods to our left. Driving back, to our relief, there was a bar, lit up and open with cabins for rent. I parked the VW, left Pauline in the car and went into the dimly lit bar to enquire about accommodation. There was a woman serving at the bar and three men sitting on high stools drinking.

Approaching the bar, I received suspicious looks from all present.

One of the men turned out to be the owner and he told me he would rent us a cabin for $8 for one night. This was expensive but I thought we didn't have a choice so I agreed.

He took our money and showed us to our cabin, where he had to kick the door open as it was jammed due to the dampness. In the corner of the room a pile of unwashed sheets met our gaze but the bed itself was made up and looked reasonable. The room felt cold and damp and after only five minutes in the bed the damp struck through to our bones. I decided to ask for our money back, planning to leave and drive on.

The door was jammed and wouldn't open so after a struggle with the sash window I managed get an opening of about 20 inches at the bottom; outside it was approximately six feet to the ground. I went through feet first and strained my back. Re-entering the Bar I said, "We can't sleep in there, it's damp, we want our money back" The owner said in an angry voice, "What do you mean it's a dump?" I said, "You misunderstand, it's damp, wet!"

He replied, "Well, it's been raining a lot lately; no, you can't have a refund." I decided not to argue as we were miles from anywhere, up in the northern woods of Wisconsin and we suddenly felt vulnerable. The Bates Motel in Psycho came to mind. Back at the cabin with the tent on the bed to lie on it was tolerable. At dawn we were on the road again and after a couple of hours were back in Canada. Four hundred miles later we arrived back in Toronto, having travelled a total of 14,000 miles since starting out in May.

Chapter 24
News from Home

While Pauline and I had been driving all over North America, during 1968 the lads at home had been busy as usual.

Wool had been with a group from the Rucksack Club to the Karakorum. The expedition planned an attempt to climb Malubiting. The expedition was unsuccessful and everyone more or less gave up after Brian Ripley lost his life.

Tut Braithwaite did the Bonatti Pillar with Dave Barton and then teamed up with Richard McHardy to do the Gervasutti Pillar and the Sentinel Rouge on Mt. Blanc. In Britain, Richard did Tiger Traverse at Cratcliffe seconded by Eddie Birch who had a foot in plaster, then on Cyrn Las on Snowdon Richard made a solo ascent of The Grooves with the Overhanging Arete finish. At Gogarth, with various partners he did The Strand E2 5b, T Rex with the true finish E3 5c and Mammoth E5 6a. These routes along with Pterodactyl E3 5c and Great Arete on Llech Ddu E4 6a were mostly second ascents. During this period and continuing into the following year he did eleven Girdle Traverses including Cloggy Pinnacle E3 5c, Castell Cidwm E3 6a, Far East on Cloggy and Plexus Buttress.

Richard became competent at solo climbing doing many routes this way, the following being but a few : Vector at Tremadog E2 5c, Woubits at Cloggy E2 5b, a long and lonely solo, and in Scotland Carnivore E2/3, Zero Gully Ben Nevis and Pumpkin on Creagh Meaghaidh. He also soloed Cenotaph Corner which sometime later when leading he fell off. When he led T Rex, he took a fall of over a hundred feet with most of his protection pulling but went back up and finished the climb!

Martin Boysen wasn't climbing because of the car accident.

In June Dave Potts and Barry Ingle did the first ascent of Route 68.

Pike went to the Dolomites and did three routes in the Sella Towers and the Pilastro on the Tofana and back home Dream of White Horses.

Crew and Ingle did Exit Chimney at Gogarth and Brown and Pete Crew did Spider's Web.

Les Brown left Middlesbrough to go and live in Stirling in Scotland, where having a good eye for a line, he proceeded to produce new climbs on Creag an Dubh Loch, Ben Loyal and other places.

Ted Howard, Clive Rowland and Bob Toogood did the first British ascent of the West Ridge of the Salbitchen. Ted, reaching the crux pitch which he was to lead, couldn't relate the description to the great hanging flake above, but just went ahead and did it anyway. The description turned out to be Trespasser Groove on Esk Buttress in the Lakes; the British translated guidebook had been mis-bound.

Ted Howard reckons that the best route by far that he ever did in the Alps was the Gugliermina N.E. Face overlooking the Freney glacier.

He and Al Wright were hit by a huge storm - three days with an enforced hanging bivouac; he enjoyed every minute. The man is a glutton for punishment!

John Smith who had been very active on rock throughout the sixties, climbing in most areas of Britain, continued to repeat some of the harder routes put up by our generation. In 1968 he did Mousetrap, Red Wall and Sind on Anglesey and Dream of White Horses, Park Lane and many others.

Then as usual at the end of the year, John organised the Annual Club Dinner. This for the second time was held at the Bull in t'Thorn on the Buxton – Ashbourne road; I think it had changed hands since the tug-of-war episode. On this occasion the after dinner activities were as lively as ever with dancing and a jousting match. This game was very rough, with smaller guys riding on the backs of the big guys battering away at each other until one side gave way. The pub ran out of beer again, so everyone retired to the car park, where suits of armour and swords which had decorated the inside walls of the pub were used in a real life battle. A good time was had by all!

The next year 1969, Martin and Maggie were out of hospital and for a while Maggie had to wear a calliper on her leg. They spent Easter in Skye and took their holidays at home that year. In Skye, on The Great Prow of Blaven, Martin and Dave Alcock did the excellent Jib HVS and Bargain Offer also HVS; thus announcing Martin's return to climbing after the accident. This was followed by Black Shadow E2 on Dinas Mot with Dave Alcock.

Pat Fearnehough compiled and edited the Fell and Rock Club Guidebook to Great Gable, Wasdale and Eskdale; which came out that year.

Paul had taken on the task of producing the Guidebook to Northern Limestone for the C.C. and this was finished in 1969.

Pete Crew produced the Anglesey Guide to Gogarth for West Col and with Joe Brown spent five days climbing the route Pergyl followed by Red Haze. They also did Touse Wall on Craig-Y-Rhaeadr; and this was possibly Pete's last route before giving up climbing.

Dave Potts who had been an Alpha member for most of the sixties joined Les Holliwell on the first ascent of Wonderwall E3.

The Sheffield section of the Alpha had started a tradition of having club meets in Sutherland at Spring bank holidays, camping at Sheigra or Oldshoremore campsites north of Kinlochbervie. The buttresses of Foinaven were explored and many fine climbs were pioneered mainly by Paul Nunn, although Patey had been there in 1962. Paul accompanied by Clive Rowland and Bob Toogood did the first ascent of Dialectic 980ft E2. And Ted Howard and Clive climbed the 920ft VS Chengallo.

At the remote Sandwood Bay north of Sheigra, stands the sandstone sea stack of Am Buachaille (The Herdsman). This stack had been climbed in 1967 by Tom Patey, John Cleare and Ian Clough.

In 1969 a number of Alpha lads made an epic second ascent of this stack.

Pike, Clive, Paul, Tony Riley, Trevor Briggs, Dave Peck, Ted Howard and possibly a couple of others were involved. Paul swam the 30ft wide channel to reach the stack, fixed a rope and brought the others across.

All reached the summit but Ted's rope got chopped in the process. This was used as a belay point around the top of the stack and was still there 15 years later. After the abseil, with all the team gathered on the shelf at the base of Am Buachaille, Clive set off trailing a rope to swim back to the main cliff. Whilst the ascent had been taking place the tide had come in covering the fixed rope by some depth making it difficult to hold on to. Clive lost his grip on the rope and was almost swept out to sea in the strong current but managed to make it back to the mainland. When all were safely across, cold and wet, they found themselves cut off from the ascent route by the tide. Dave Peck made what the rest of the lads described as an heroic lead, up a 200ft mud filled groove to the top of the cliff. This according to Ted was "Gladiatorial stuff, honestly."

In the Alps, Richard and Tut had a good season doing the Gervasutti Pillar, North Face of the Dru, North Face of the Triollet and the first British ascent of the Croz Spur on the Grandes Jorasses. The season was rounded off nicely with an ascent of the Route Major on Mt. Blanc with some of the other lads, Paul Nunn amongst them.

Ted Howard and Bob Toogood did the Eperon on the Brenva Face soloing the lot through the night and finishing in a snow storm. Near the summit of Mt. Blanc they stumbled on two Japanese climbers lying under a bivvy sheet with their feet sticking out. Ted lifted the sheet and asked where the Vallot hut was. Following a pointed finger Ted and Bob ploughed on over the summit and down, falling on an empty aluminium hut. The two Japanese had followed them down. A little later at dusk, 22 people staggered in out of the blizzard. It was very cramped in the hut so the next day Ted, Bob and the two Japs decided to go down and not wait out the storm as they were all out of food. Out they went and the 22 French followed them down over the Dome de Goutier, no visibility, down and down until suddenly the ground rose up in a ridge - the Aiguilles de Bionnassay. They turned everyone round, the whole 22, and went back up the Goutier; there were by now a lot of near exhausted people. Cutting blindly across the Dome and down, they literally banged into the Goutier hut. The French never said a word then or later; they just went off by themselves. The Japanese, on the other hand, bought Ted and Bob an egg meal, the whole works as a sort of thank you!

Back in Chamonix this led to an epic party with other Japanese and British climbers; the rounds were 19 beers each time. The two Japs insisted that Bob and Ted sleep in bags in their tent and next morning woke them up to a cooked breakfast!

Back home Richard did the first free ascent of Hanging Crack at Dovestones seconded by Tut, and Syringe on Gogarth E3 5c with Dave Jones.

On Great Gable again with Tut, Richard led the first ascent of The Vikings E3 5c, the hardest climb in the guide at that time and thought by some to be E4.

After the 1968/9 winter in Toronto, we had some more weekends away at Bon Echo and a weekend with Roger at the Gunks in New York State.

Roger by this time was living in Washington DC, working as head gardener at the British Embassy. I was working at General Electric in Scarborough, Ontario, on steam turbines and Pauline worked at an electronics company not far from where we lived in Downsview.

We had invited Pauline's parents to come over for a holiday in July/August for a month. We also received a letter from Wool and Anne to say that they were emigrating to Canada and they asked if they could stay with us en route to Calgary.

Things were looking good; we had something to look forward to. We started making plans to take Pauline's mother and dad out west. Roger lent us his big American car for a month and he had our Beetle.

The holidays arrived and I met my in-laws for the first time. Allowing them a couple of days to get over the jetlag we then set off to drive west, taking the same route that Pauline and I had taken the year before.

In a motel at Kalamazoo, we watched with the rest of the world when Apollo 11 crew Neil Armstrong and Buzz Aldrin made the first Moon landing.

Passing Chicago we joined Highway 80 west and followed it out to Fort Laramie, Wyoming, then on to Shoshoni where, silhouetted against the sunset, we saw a small bird riding on an owl's back pecking at it, presumably because the owl had stolen its young.

Next day we drove over the Tagwatee Pass and arrived in the Grand Teton National Park in a thunderstorm. It reminded me of the film Shane which had been made in the Tetons.

We camped for a week in the Tetons, doing some good walks and visiting Yellowstone National Park 20 miles to the north.

On our way back east we stopped again at the Little Big Horn Battlefield as Pauline's dad was, like us, interested in the Indian wars of the west.

Our drive back took us through Deadwood City, the Black Hills and Badlands of South Dakota. It had been a good trip covering over 5,000 miles but we had to get back in time to meet Wool and Anne who would soon be arriving in Canada to stay with us.

We met Wool and Anne at the airport and took them back to our apartment. It was great to see them again and catch up on events back home. Pauline's parents stayed for a few days at Pauline's aunt's house to give us some time with our friends. Anne and Wool stayed about a week and we took them to see Niagara Falls. They had decided that they wanted to go to live in Calgary and as some people did in those days, they contracted to deliver a car from Toronto to a customer out west; this meant they had free transport to Calgary. We were sorry to see them leave and about a week later we also had to say goodbye to Pauline's mother and dad. This left us feeling a little homesick but we comforted ourselves with the thought that we would be going home to England the following summer.

In September Pauline and I returned Roger's car by driving to meet him for a weekend in the Gunks. He was with some American climbers and they couldn't understand why Roger had an American accent when we didn't, and yet we were all from the same city in England.

It seemed strange to be driving the Beetle again after the luxury of a Ford Falcon but it was nice to have our own car back.

Just before Christmas, the union contract at General Electric was due for renewal and this usually meant there would be a long strike. Because we were saving to go home I felt I couldn't afford to go on strike so I changed my job. I got work at Howden and Parsons, again on steam turbines. Parsons originated in Newcastle-on-Tyne and most of the staff at the Toronto plant were immigrants from Newcastle. One day I was working with a Geordie lad called Jimmy Lavery and we got talking about our respective interests. Jim was a keen skier and when I told him I was a climber he said that he used to climb back home in Northumberland and the Lakes. When I asked who he climbed with, he told me "Geoff Oliver and Eric Rayson." I knew them both, in fact Geoff Oliver had become a member of the Alpha and I knew Eric from climbing in the Lakes; it's a small world.

General Electric didn't strike after all so I had changed my job unnecessarily but never mind I had met Jim and we became good friends.

The winter passed uneventfully. We were saving hard and looking forward to going home. All my workmates thought I was mad to want to leave Canada, but all the work was in the east and the mountains were 2,000 miles away out west and I wanted to live near the hills.

We booked our passage on the Empress of Canada to sail from Montreal on June 6th - D day.

In early Spring Jimmy and his Canadian wife Gerry, went with us for a weekend to Bon Echo. Jimmy and I were intending to climb but there were no boats available to take us across the lake to the crag so we had to be content with a weekends camping.

In April bad luck struck. I dislocated my shoulder again, this time at work. I had to take two weeks off and this would reduce the amount of money that we wanted to take home to England but it couldn't be helped. Then came blow number two; Parsons went on strike.

The boss from Pauline's old firm Federal Mogul offered me a few weeks work helping their company to move premises so this helped, and I managed to get Jimmy on there as well. The time came to say goodbye yet again. Pauline and I boarded the ship at Montreal and set sail for home. Surprisingly, we were very pleased to hear the scouse accents of the stewards on the ship; one of the waiters in the bar even remembered me from three years earlier when he had worked on the Empress of England.

The voyage home was rather boring. The Atlantic was dead calm and it was thick fog all the way across. The only memorable event was when we saw dolphins at the bow of the ship leading us home. Approaching Britain from the south west I was hoping to see the mountains of Ireland but the fog was too thick. The Mersey river pilot was picked up off Anglesey and there again the fog prevented us from seeing any land.

The first land that we did see was when we heard the ship drop anchor mid-Mersey and going on deck we saw the lights of Liverpool and the Liver Building welcoming us home.

Next morning, June 14th 1970, after breakfast the ship docked at the Princess Landing Stage and Pauline's mother and dad were there to meet us with their car.

Chapter 25
The Winds of Change 1970

The climbing world had changed a lot during the three and a half years that I had been away in Canada.

The Alpha had started to slip from the top of the pile and the club itself had started to fragment. There were new kids on the block waiting in the wings ready to take over, spearheaded by Pete Livesey and Ron Fawcett. The evolution of better protection was helping to advance the standards to another level.

The Alpha which had been the main driving force in the sixties had started to level out, and by taking on new members from their own generation instead of new young members had set the club's decline in motion, similar to the Rock and Ice ten years earlier.

The club itself seemed pretty much the same, except that now, some of the lads had become very experienced mountaineers as well as being good rock climbers and there were more opportunities for them to go on expeditions to the greater ranges; this meant that new climbing partnerships were formed. Natural migration to live in other areas, and family and career commitments, contributed to the erosion of the solidarity of the club. Members developed a wider circle of friends as is natural and drifted away, but as is the case today, were always pleased to see each other whenever their paths crossed. The Sheffield section took the longest to change but did eventually follow this pattern of disintegration which will inevitably lead to the extinction of the Alpha. When I arrived back in the UK, there were some new members, friends of the Sheffield section, who had been known to the rest of us for a long time. These were Jack Hesmondhalgh from Carlisle who was a friend of Pat Fearnehough, and three others from Sheffield, Alan Maskery, R Olivant and Ben Wilson.

In 1970 Pike and Dianna had gone to live in South Africa so weren't around when we came home from Canada but they returned disillusioned before the winter; it was good to see them again.

Club meets had been resurrected but really the Alpha had split and the annual club meet in Sutherland consisted mainly of Sheffield Alpha and my cousin Barry Johnson with his wife Valerie.

Paul Nunn, Tom Patey, Clive Rowland, Fred Fuller and Spud (Dave Goodwin) another new member all climbed a sea stack, The Maiden at Whiten Head. This ended in tragedy on the descent, when abseiling off 130ft to the base of the stack; everyone was down except Patey who was last. Part way down, he somehow became detached from the rope and fell 100ft to his death. A first hand account is given by Paul Nunn in his book "At the Sharp End"

During 1970 Richard was still climbing with Tut Braithwaite and led the first free ascent of November on Cloggy.

Richard, Paul, Tut, Hamish MacInnes, Chris Woodall and a journalist Pete Seeds all went to the Caucasus Mountains on what was a generally unsuccessful expedition.

Martin, now fit again, went with Bonington's successful expedition to Annapurna South Face thus launching his Himalayan career.

Pauline and I bought a house in Old Glossop in Derbyshire and Richard and Barbara bought a house on Sheffield Road in Glossop.

The 1970 club dinner was held at the Wasdale Head Hotel.

Clive and I did a winter ascent of Grooved Arete on Pike's Crag but after this dinner which was a fairly civilised affair, club dinners became more and more infrequent, going from intervals of five years to even longer apart. This was another sign of the club's decline.

Early in 1971 John Gosling arranged for me to have my shoulder operated on by a surgeon whom he knew at Withington Hospital. The surgeon's name was Oliver Cowpe and he had been an MUMC member in the 1940s. Being a climber himself he knew what was required and the operation has proved to be a great success.

Anne Woolcock separated from Wool, and came home from Canada to live and work in Glossop. One evening she turned up at our house with a friend who had recently returned from Canada. His name was Ian Heys. Ian belonged to a group of climbers from the Burnley area and had a twin brother who was also a climber. That night of our meeting, I had my shoulder strapped up and Ian had a broken ankle in plaster; what a pair! Anne and Ian started going out together and the four of us became good friends; and we still are today 40 years later.

While recovering from this shoulder operation, I went to Stanage on a summer evening with Richard who was soloing everything in sight. I still had my arm in a sling so I sat and watched him. He was climbing well but fell off near the top of Millsom's Minion and fell 50ft onto rocks and broke his right femur. Perhaps he had had a petit mal fit - who knows?

After 12 weeks in traction he mounted his pushbike to come to our house. The chain came off and so did Richard, breaking the same bone again. About this time Ian and Anne bought a house near to us and Ian commenced renovating it.

When my shoulder was strong again, Ian and I started to climb together and I soon found out how good he was. He had done most of the hard routes of the day in Wales and the Lakes and with his friends from Burnley had climbed extensively in Yorkshire; although you wouldn't have known it as he is a modest sort of chap.

There were still a lot of routes in Derbyshire that he hadn't done and climbing with him served to build up my confidence again, at least on gritstone.

Climbing both days every weekend and taking our holidays in the hills we got a lot done. Over the next four years we climbed in the Lakes, Wales and Scotland. We had two trips to the Bregaglia where I had three retreats, but Ian did the Cengalo N Ridge; it was a good four years. Our training for the Alps in 1974 consisted of doing the Marsden- Edale with 10 climbs on the way - a hard day! We also did a walk from Grasmere to Wasdale taking in Deerbield Crack, Stoats Crack on Pavey, Nocturne on Gimmer, Bowfell Buttress and Bridge's Route on Esk buttress. We had intended finishing with Botterill's Slab, but by the time we got to Mickledore it was too late and we were too tired; so we descended to Wasdale where we were met by the girls. This jaunt was 12 miles with 1800 ft of climbing and had taken 12 hours, with heavy rain at the start and hot sun later in the day. In 1975 Anne and Ian got married and moved to live in Anne's native Cumbria. They still live there and have two grown up daughters, both of whom are climbers.

After Ian left Glossop I started climbing with various local lads. One of these was Mike Blackwell who lived round the corner from me. Mike knew some of the Alpha lads and at one time had been a member of the Manchester Gritstone Club. We did some good climbs together.

One day I was driving towards Crowden alone when I saw four young lads with climbing ropes trying to hitch a lift. I stopped and said I would give them a lift if I could climb with them; they agreed and got in the van.

That day on Shining Clough was an eye opener. One of them didn't even know how to tie on the rope; I had to show him. Despite this they were all good climbers. Their names were Gabriel and John Regan, Loris Doyle and James Moran. Gabriel and James a few years later went on to do many hard new routes. Here were some of the new kids on the block!

Richard moved to Scotland but before he went he did two outstanding new routes in Derbyshire. One was Edge Lane E5 5c on Millstone Edge and the other was The Glorious Twelfth E2 5b near Kinder Downfall. The day after, Paul Nunn did The Bloody Thirteenth E1 5b on the same crag.

I started climbing with the Black and Tans again and was invited to join their club and from 1976 to 1980 at various times I climbed with Dennis Carr and Eddie Thurrell then later with Ted Rodgers, Les Brown and Graham Fyffe. With these different partners I did 14 new climbs in the Kinder Ravine (Shotgun Groove and Hard Times etc) plus ten elsewhere (Banshee E1 at Tintwistle Knarr and Satyr E4 5c at Shining Clough) and nine more on Stanage which included Missing Link E1 5c and King Kong E3 6a.

In 1977 our daughter Lucy was born and I slowed down a bit on my climbing. From 1980 until 1982 I climbed with Tony Young and sometimes my old friend Les Brown. Once while climbing in the wet at Hen Cloud with Les, I fell off when leading the top pitch of Encouragement E1 5b. I had one runner which held me but I caught Les in the face with my foot, sending his glasses spinning down the crag. I asked Les if he wanted to continue and his reply was, "Get back up there and finish it, now you've broken my specs," so I did as I was told. Later, I said, "We're quits now for when you fell on my head from Goliath's Groove all those years ago."

In 1982 with a friend from work, Eric Pate, I opened a climbing shop in Glossop; we called it Peak Gear. I applied to join the union for Alpha shopkeepers.

During 11 years that we had the shop I started to do some guiding to supplement my income which was meagre. The guiding helped to bring in some good customers to the shop and one in particular was a Dr Barry Chopping, a GP from New Mills. Barry took to climbing like a duck to water, we became good friends and climbed regularly together. From being a complete novice, Barry finished up leading climbs like Cenotaph Corner and the Grooves on Cyrn Las - not bad for a man who started in his forties. Another regular visitor to our shop was an ex- professional rugby player, Ken Dee. Nobody knows how old Ken is, he won't tell anyone, but he does well for an old man. He is a big strapping chap who when I first met him in 1983 must have been about 50 but would never admit to it.

Years ago Ken worked at the Clachaig pub in Glencoe and climbed with the locals there; he is good company on the hills and has an endless supply of corny jokes. His favourite mountain is the Matterhorn which he has climbed several times. Anyway Ken and I became big mates and from 1983 until 1992 climbed everywhere together.

On Kinder Great Buttress we did some of the best new routes I've ever done: Don't Look Back HVS with three pitches and The Go Between E1 5b. We also did the very hard 90ft route The Gallows E3 6a and "Hair of the Dog" HVS 5b.

In 1991 I fulfilled an ambition when I did CB on Scafell with Ken and Barry Chopping. Then the shop started to lose money as there was too much competition from the big boys so in 1993 we decided to close. At the age of 53 I found myself out of work, but eventually after working as a handyman and a builder's labourer for other people, I set up on my own doing joinery and general building work (my Dad had been a joiner and I had inherited his tools). This I continued to do until I retired 12 years later.

From 1993 I climbed with various local climbers, namely Keith Ashton and Gabriel Regan with whom I did Eireborne E1 5c at the Knarr and also with Malc Baxter doing some good new routes, mainly on Kinder. In the nineties Pauline, our daughter Lucy and I had three big trips around Canada and the USA visiting our old stamping grounds. We visited the Grand Teton National Park three times; staying at the climber's Ranch in Jackson Hole which provides excellent cheap accommodation and is run by the American Alpine club. The Ranch is an ideal base for climbing and walking in the Tetons and has great self catering facilities.

Since the Millennium, I have climbed with various people - Les Brown, Stephen Barber and Karl Atherton - but I climb very rarely these days. I still enjoy regular hill walking which I find very enjoyable and have taken my holidays in Britain, Spain and once to Kalymnos.

Epilogue
Looking Back: The View From 2010

Of the original members of the Alpha Club, <u>Keith Taylor, Dave Upton,</u> <u>Tony Hunt, Dave Sandall and Pete Baldwin</u> gave up climbing in the late fifties and early sixties. Nothing is known about where they are or what they did since then.

<u>Pete Bamfield</u> gave up climbing in the early sixties. He became a double base player in a jazz band and took up cycling. After marrying he realised his teenage dream of buying the farmhouse below Castle Naze in Derbyshire where he lived until his wife Mary became ill with cancer. They then moved to Mary's hometown of Cardiff where Mary died in 2007. Pete, after beating cancer himself, cycled west to east across America. He still lives in Cardiff and is retired.

<u>Bob Brayshaw</u> was an early star of the Alpha and could have been a great climber, but he gave it up when he married around 1962.
No one has heard from him since then.

<u>Les Brown</u> moved to live in Mellor near Stockport in the 1970s. He has been consistently active down the years, climbing all over the World - the Bugaboos in BC Canada and at Leavenworth in Washington State where with Pete Turnbull he did the classic Outer Space. In the 1980s he went to Huandoy in Peru with Al Wright and Trevor Briggs. That same decade he pioneered approximately 60 new climbs in the Costa Blanca, mainly with Claude Davies and Joe Brown (no relation).
With Pete Turnbull he made an ascent of the Diamond Couloir on Mt. Kenya. In 1990 with Trevor Jones he discovered Jabel El Khest in the Anti Atlas Mountains of Morocco and subsequently with Joe, Claude and others has done over 80 first ascents there. What a man!
In 1995 with his wife Margaret they walked from Bordeaux to Mt. Blanc summit 1250km in 6 weeks. Sadly Margaret died in 2005.

Les continues to live in Mellor and still climbs at a good standard at the age of 73. He has two grown up daughters and a son.

Pete Crew gave up climbing about 1970 to pursue his other passion, archaeology,
He was a dynamic climber but couldn't sustain his interest. He lives in North Wales.

Alan Ellison went off the scene in the early sixties and nothing is known of where he is now or if he still climbs.

Andy Garvey was another to give up climbing when he married although he carried on hill walking. His wife died in the mid Noughties. Andy lives in Dukinfield Cheshire and is active in the local walking club; once or twice recently he has also accompanied some of the lads on walks.

Al Goodwin, Stan's younger brother moved to Australia and keeps in touch with Stan.

Vincent Stanley Goodwin (V.S.Goodwin), gave up climbing in the mid sixties but continues to enjoy walking to this day. He lives in Stockport and plays Spanish guitar for a hobby.

Ted Howard first went to the Himalayas in 1975 with Don Morrison's team. They failed on the Ogre.
Ted continued to climb in Britain and the Alps. Then in 1987 he led an expedition to Latok 2 with Paul Nunn, Bill Barker, Joe Brown, Mo Antoine and others. They were stopped by a continuous storm 900ft from the summit and were lucky to get off without injuries. Ted led trekking parties in Baltistan. Saychun Glacier to K6, K7, Gordora Peak, Leyla, Masherbrum, Trinity Peak past the Kashmir borders to China.
He also took private treks to Nepal round the Annapurna Massif, the Annapurna Sanctuary and South Face base camp. Other treks were the Kudi to Pokara ridge trek and the Yalung peak to the Tibetan border.
He took a second expedition to Latok 2 in 1992 which included Paul Nunn, Clive Rowland, Tony Riley, Malcolm Cundy and Pete Jackson but bad weather and apathy put paid to it.
Since 1994 he has climbed generally in Britain with visits to the Alps and fairly recently at Ailefroide with John Smith, Dave Goodwin, Pike and Willis Ward.
Ted and his wife Sheila now live in Scotland at Muir of Ord.

<u>Barry Ingle</u> still lives in Wales with his wife Pat but spends a lot of time in France where they have a house in the Dauphine. He still climbs occasionally and tends to prefer sport climbing.

<u>Dave Potts </u>lives in North Wales and is one who came into the Alpha at about the same time as Crew and Ingle. He was a regular figure on the Llanberis scene and in the seventies climbed with the Holliwell brothers.

<u>Martin Boysen</u> went to Arctic Norway with Clive in 1973 where they did the first ascent of Fortress Peak by the easiest line and then a Face route on the same peak a 1500ft first ascent. In 1974 he did the first ascent of Changabang (Himalaya) and in the same year worked on the Clint Eastwood film "The Eiger Sanction." This was followed in1975 with an expedition to Trango Tower where he thought he was going to die when his leg became stuck in a wide overhanging crack high on the face. It took hours of frantic effort to get free and caused the attempt to be abandoned (see Martin's own account of this episode in the book "The Games Climbers Play" from an article in Mountain 52, 1976). Straight after this he joined the successful Bonington Everest SW Face expedition but this was marred by the death of Mick Burke who disappeared near the summit after presumably reaching it.

The following year he returned to Trango with Mo Antoine, Joe Brown, Mal Howell, Jim Curran and Tony Riley and this time succeeded in climbing "The Fissure Boysen" and reached the summit; another first ascent.

This was followed by a working holiday in the Bregaglia looking after Fred Zimmerman and Sean Connery whilst making the film Five Days Last Summer.

In 1978 he went back to South America on an expedition to Torre Egger.

He went back to the Himalaya in 1979, this time to the West Face of Gasherbrum 4 with Mo Antoine.

In 1980 he climbed Ama Dablam in Nepal with the American Tom Frost while making a film.

Another expedition in 1981Martin with Rab Carrington, John Yates and Cho Brooks went to climb Latok.

Since then Martin has continued climbing at home and abroad but says he has given up big mountains for the safety of British climbing.

He now climbs mainly with Rab Carrington and at the age of 67 still ventures into the E grades. He lives in Hale near Altrincham Cheshire with his wife Maggie. They have a daughter Kate and grandchildren.

Malcolm Cundy (Pike) continued Alpine climbing for a few years doing routes like the Old Brenva on Mt. Blanc and the Traverse of the Drus before trying his hand at Alpine winter climbing. His daughter Zara was born in 1971 and in 1975 they moved to Appleby in Cumbria.

He took Leo Houlding to the crags when Leo was nine years old.

Pike has continued to climb at home and abroad until knee trouble prevented him doing so; he is a keen mountain biker and has also dabbled in fell running.

Brian Barlow gave up climbing in the early sixties. Brian was a good climber and one of the original Alpha Club but he was in love with motor bikes. He worked on the racing team for Reynolds Chains visiting all the big races. He is a skilled engineer and formed his own company.

He lives in rural Derbyshire and still rides motorbikes and has passed this passion on to his son.

Another keen biker is Bob Beesley. Bob still climbs occasionally mainly abroad because in his own words, he's not keen on the cold and wet of Scotland where he now lives. He owns several bikes including a 350cc BSA Gold Star which must be getting on for 50 years old and a Vincent Black Shadow 1000cc.

He lives near Aviemore with his wife and has a grown up daughter.

John Moss went to Calgary Alberta in the late sixties and climbed with the Calgary Mountain Club mainly in the Rockies. With Oliver Woolcock (Wool) he did such routes as N Face of Mt. Temple (second ascent) and N Face of Mt. Edith Cavell (third ascent). With Brian Greenwood, Wool and Chris Jones, he did the first ascent of the East Face of Mt. Hungabee.

He was last heard of in South Africa where he was a lecturer but will probably be retired by now.

Paul Ross is a prolific new router wherever he goes. He moved to New England in the seventies to open a climbing school and did many new climbs there. He did the Salathe Wall in 1973 with Richard McHardy and George Homer. He returned to England for a while but was lured back by the climate and climbing in S West Colorado where he now lives.

Tony Riley lives in Cumbria where until recently he had a photographic studio in Keswick. He has had 12 Alpine seasons has been cameraman on eight Himalayan expeditions and has been involved extensively in film and TV work: Five Days Last Summer, The Highlander, Everest NE Ridge, Everest 1990, Lakeland Rock and A Great Effort, with J Curran which won first prize at Trento Film Festival 1977. Three Himalayan films- Trango, Barnaj 77 and K2 Savage Mountain BBC1979. Then Old Man of Hoy, The Bat, Don Whillans' Last Climb and many more!

Tony has also exhibited his work at many venues across the UK.

Due to ill health Tony has recently had to cut back on his workload.

Barry Pedlar went off the scene in the early sixties and his whereabouts are unknown to the author.

Dave Peck lived for many years in Scotland in the Glen Affric area.

Like some others from the Alpha, Dave has spent many years in fell running with a special interest in long distance mountain runs. Recently a hip replacement operation forced him to become less active.

Clive Rowland has been on several expeditions, most of which are listed below:

Sheffield expedition to the Ogre in 1971

1973 Arctic Norway with Boysen to Fortress Peak.

1975 with Doug Scott to try Sospunbrakk, Karakorum, and failed but reconnoitred the Ogre finding a good place for Base camp.

In 1974 he went to the Pamirs with Nunn, Doug Scott, Guy Lee and Tut and did a new route on Pic Lenin. He went to the Ogre again with Scott, Bonington and Mo Antoine. After Bonington and Scott had been to the summit they were both injured on the descent. Bonington broke two ribs when abseiling - one rope was too short and he went off the end. Scott slipped on some ice and penduled into a corner, breaking both legs.

All this happened about three to four hundred feet below the summit.

Clive and Mo went up to get them but the weather closed in and all four were trapped in a snow cave without food for seven days. Clive and Mo helped the injured pair back to base camp and probably saved their lives.

In 1978 Clive and John Smith opened a climbing shop in Inverness.

1982 Clive soloed Red and Black Cuillins in a day.

1986 he did the Cassin route on Denali, Alaska in five days with J Brown, Mo, Davy Jones and J Fitzgerald. Also in 1986 he went to Everest NE Ridge where he got to 26,000ft before bad weather put an end to it.

Clive closed his shop a few years ago and now lives in Nairn, Scotland with his wife Fiona. They have a son and daughter; the son is a keen climber. Clive doesn't climb nowadays due to old injuries but is a keen hill walker.

<u>Jim Smith</u> married Richard's cousin Margaret in the mid sixties and family commitments took him away from the climbing scene.

Jim has been a keen walker and has attended most club dinners through the years. He lives in Droylesden, Manchester and is a popular figure at any reunion.

<u>Tanky Stokes</u> closed his shop in Sheffield when he retired but carried on organising the Marsden to Edale Fell race which he had sponsored and set up when the shop was still open; it bears his name "Tanky's Trog." Not a bad legacy for the old beggar. He still lives in Sheffield and is still a Youth at eighty!

<u>Gerry Rogan</u> emigrated to Canada in 1972 and climbed extensively with the Calgary Mountain Club which had its fair share of ex-Brits. With Jack Firth he climbed some frozen waterfalls but did his first big climb in Canada with Jon Jones, this was the Minaret, in the Bugaboos on the south Howser Spire; this was a new route. With the same partner he did the Becky/Chouinard on the west buttress of the South Howser Spire and the North Face of Mt. Robson. In 1974 he went with Bugs McKeith and George Homer to the Devil's Thumb which is situated on the Alaska pan handle and is one of the peaks on the Stikine Ice Cap. They ascended the East Ridge and at that time this was only the third ascent of the mountain. Other new routes he did in Canada were the east face of Mt. Bident in the Valley of the Ten Peaks with Jack Firth; Tout Ensemble on Mount Eisenhower (now called Castle Mountain) with Jon Jones, Rob Wood and G Homer; Sniveling Gully, an ice climb above the Banff /Jasper highway with Bugs McKeith and George Homer; Rogan's Gully on Mt. Cascade with McKeith and named by him; Bloody Fingers graded 5.11a on Burstall Slabs with Jon Jones in 1990; Christmas Present, an ice climb on Mt. Rundle with Jack Firth and Greg Sphor.

Gerry moved back to Europe in 1991 and except for a holiday in the Dolomites and the Verdun Gorge he did virtually nothing. He moved back to Canada in 2007 and climbed at Skaha Bluffs with Jon Jones.

Last heard of he was living in Holland - a bit of a change from the Rockies!

<u>Dave Sanders</u> went off the scene in the early sixties but reappeared at Margaret Brown's funeral. He has kept loosely in touch since; he is married and retired and lives in Greenfield near the Chew Valley.

<u>Arthur Williams</u> moved to live and work in North Carolina during the Sixties. He has been home on holiday a couple of times since, but still lives permanently in the USA.

<u>John Smith</u>, in 1973, led Trevor Briggs up Cenotaph wearing one of Trevor's PAs, as by mistake he had left one of his own at home.

They also did Shrike the same year. In 1975 John, Les Brown with Trevor and his non- climbing brother Graham went to the Vercors.

Les and John did the South West Face of Mont Aiguilles then drove to the Calanques. The following year John and Trevor did the North Ridge of the Piz Badile ended up in a massive snowstorm and had to bivvy in the summit hut; an epic descent followed. John then took a party up Mount Castellane (a snow peak) as Trevor didn't want to climb again. In 1978 John and Clive Rowland opened their climbing and skiing shop in Inverness.

Apart from skiing, he didn't go to the Alps again until about 2004, when after meeting up with Pike and Di, he did Aiguille L'Index, Petit Aiguille Verte, Cosmiques Arete etc. John continues to climb and walk but says that to him it's the friendships and camaraderie that really counts.

He now lives in Bath with his wife Heather; they have two grown up daughters.

<u>Mike Richardson</u> after first going to the Alps in 1964 found that family commitments precluded any further Alpine climbs until 1976, when he did the Cassin Route on the Piz Badile with Al Wright. In 1999 Mike was struck down with a serious illness which caused a great loss of strength; consequently he hasn't touched rock since.

Mike lives in Mexborough and is a keen twitcher and photographer.

<u>Pete Maddocks</u> is one of the great unsung good climbers of the Alpha Club. Pete has been consistently active over the years and did much of

his climbing with Ted Howard. With Ted and Clive in the Oberland he did the N Face of the Vaudaspitz and the E Face of the Kingspitz.

When on the N Ridge of the Badile he had the unnerving experience of seeing a climber fall past him to his death.

In recent years Pete has been an instructor for youth groups at his local climbing wall. He lives in Leicester with his wife Edna.

Howard Rainer (Garth) stopped climbing in the early sixties and his whereabouts are unknown.

Brian Griffiths was an early recruit to the Alpha from the SUMC. He climbed mainly with the Sheffield section - Nunn, Woolcock, Al Wright and Richardson. Griff has been on various expeditions over the years to Alaska and other areas and I do know he's done the NW Face of Half- Dome in Yosemite.

He held the position of Treasurer to the BMC for many years but gave it up when he became ill. He's OK now though and still climbs at a high standard. He is married and lives in Hathersage in Derbyshire.

Oliver Woolcock (Wool) moved to Calgary in 1969. The following year he climbed in Western Canada, mainly in the Rockies. He did the second ascent of the N Face of Mt. Temple and third ascent of the Chouinard route on the N Face of Mt. Edith Cavell with John Moss. He did the first ascent of the SW Face of the N Howser Tower in the Bugaboos with Archie Simpson and Chris Jones. He also got into downhill skiing but after moving with work to Winnipeg where there isn't much in the way of hills, he took up water skiing in the summer. After that he was off to Vancouver for three years and lots of skiing at Whistler. His next move was to Edmonton and more skiing and after two years, Toronto (all with ICI). Skiing wasn't much good in Toronto so he took up sailing and scuba diving. Diving had a similar camaraderie to climbing. He became a Divemaster and assistant instructor.

After 10 years in Toronto he got fed up, quit his job and moved to Gabriola Island near Vancouver. Since then with his Canadian wife he has run a self employed business making wooden giftware and he also taught sailing. He now teaches sailing in the spring and autumn and goes away sailing for two to four months in summer. Has sailed south to San Francisco and North to Glacier Bay Alaska. He teaches instructors during the winter months.

Barry Johnson for many years has been a keen fell runner and in his capacity of sports centre manager at Cockermouth he started organising triathlons and other events. Barry is a qualified swimming coach and is an excellent swimmer himself. He has taken part in international triathlons and now works as a personal trainer. At the present time he has clients amongst fell runners in the national team, top rally drivers and anyone else who can afford him.

Barry has run the Everest Marathon numerous times and on his 70th Birthday in 2010, he ran and cycled the Lakes, Meres and Waters run in the Lake District in 22 ½ hours, including taking a swim in Windermere, Wastwater and Low water; he recently won the European Triathlon in his age group. Will he never stop?!

He has lived for many years in the Cumbrian village of Eaglesfield with his wife Valerie. They have a grown up son, Simon.

<u>Alan McHardy (Richard)</u> was one of the best climbers of his generation. As well as being a leading British rock climber, over the years he has built up an impressive list of Alpine ascents. Where do we start?

Alpine climbs 300 metres to 1000 metres of D superior and above: Eastern Austria- four routes, Kaisergebirge five including a first British ascent.

Dolomites: 24 routes all areas. Bregaglia 11 plus five slightly shorter ones, Grimsel, Furka, Handegg, 8 climbs plus five shorter ones.

Chamonix /Courmayeur: 56 routes including Croz Spur, Central Pillar of Freney and the Bonatti- Gobbi on the Eickfieler and many easier routes when guiding.

In America, Salathe Wall on El Capitan and Salathe Steck on Sentinell Rock in 1973. He did NW Face of Fairview Dome and a lot of lesser routes with Barbara in 1996; Cragging in Utah and some guiding in New England.

Cragging in Jordan, Spain, Majorca, Sardinia, Kalymnos, Naranges Bulnaze in the Picos de Europa etc.

Richard and Barbara moved to Scotland in May of 1975.

After summer, winter and Alpine tests Richard qualified as a full U.I.A.G.M. Guide in 1979, with Full Carnet in 1980. This was possible because he had been free of fits for six years. He started working offshore in 1988 to supplement his guiding work.

He had a fit in Katmandu in 1993 and had to give up his work Guiding and Offshore. He started a rope access training business which was very successful and with the right drugs became fit free again.

He has done the Haute Route twice but says that he is not a good skier.

Richard and Barbara live on the Black Isle and he is writing his memoirs.

Paul (Tut) Braithwaite) came to the Alpha club late mainly through his association with Richard. Here again is a man with an impressive record having done most of the routes that Richard did plus the Eiger N Face. Tut also did many first winter ascents of difficult British rock climbs.

He was originally in the Manchester Gritstone Club and was a familiar figure in the Manchester climbing scene.

He was on the Bonington Everest SW Face expedition and the Torre Egger expedition with Martin. He worked on the film Five Days One Summer and went on Doug Scott's expedition to NE Ridge of Asgard on Baffin Island as well as to Pic Lenin with Doug Scott, Nunn, Guy Lee and Clive Rowland in 1974. For many years he had a climbing shop in Oldham but sold this to concentrate on a Rope Access business. He lives in Delph, Saddleworth.

Willis Ward from Sheffield joined the Alpha as a young lad in the mid sixties when he climbed a lot with Paul Nunn helping on the Kinder Guide; he led Belial while still a schoolboy. Willis was an active climber until a serious illness curbed his activities. He still enjoys a day out and now lives in Redditch Warwickshire.

Bob Toogood mentioned a lot in connection with Ted Howard and others was a relatively new member of the Alpha and I don't really know him, except to know that he was a very good climber and successful fell runner.

Dave Goodwin (Spud) is another of the most recent additions to the club and is another that I don't really know much about. I do know that he is a friend of John Smith and is part of a group of the Alpha that have stayed close. To celebrate his 60th birthday in 2010, Spud climbed Mont Blanc with a guide.

Ian Hartle from Buxton climbed with us during the early sixties then emigrated to New Zealand where he now lives.

Al Wright an ex-Peak CC and SUMC member was recruited by Pete Crew to the Alpha. He has a good Alpine record and was an accomplished rock climber. He joined the club in the early sixties but now suffers ill health. He lives with Pheny his wife.

Geoff Oliver pioneered routes in the Lake District and elsewhere. He climbed with the Craig Lough club from Newcastle but through his association with Pat Fearnehough, Les Brown, Paul and others he became a member of the Alpha Club. Geoff is also a member of the Fell and Rock. He still lives in North east and is a keen horse rider.

That is the whole list of members past and present except for the few who are no longer with us.

Absent Friends

Brian Platt (Platty) My old mate, an ace motorbike rider, used to scare me silly. Brian was a very early member of the Alpha and a good companion. He stopped climbing when he got married in 1962 but he and Vera used to come to club dinners. After a long battle with cancer Brian died January 5th 1990, on his birthday, aged 50.

Ralph Harris (Rastus) My first climbing partner and a founder member of the Alpha Club. Ralph was a pleasure to be with on the hills or anywhere for that matter; he was clever and had a good sense of humour.

After roaming the world as a radio officer in the Merchant Navy he came back into the ordinary world and couldn't cope. After years of mental turmoil and sickness he took his own life. Apart from his close relatives, Pete Bamfield and his wife Mary and I were the only ones to turn up for his funeral; very sad.

Pat Fearnehough left school at 15 and started work as a fireplace fitter with Albert Jackson Fireplaces. The heavy work as a teenager must to some extent have been responsible for his power and strength on the hill. He did his National Service with the RAF, signing on for an extra year to enable him to make the mountain rescue team.

Pat was an outstanding rock climber and mountaineer.

On his way to Latok 2 in 1978 he was swept to his death in the Braldu River by a small landslide.

Paul Nunn was a writer and an editor of Mountain Magazine.

Paul was a good friend and a superb climber. When he was young and new to the Alpha he was one of its stars, confidently tackling the hardest climbs of the day. He was a lecturer at Sheffield University where he had been a student. Paul was well known as a climber and mountaineer and did a term as President of the BMC. He worked on guidebooks for the Fell and Rock Club of which he was a member as well as guides for the CC of which he was also a member; he also edited the Bleaklow 1971 and Kinder 1974 guides for the BMC.

In spite of his academic life he was a big, tough, boisterous hard-drinking character, very strong on the hills but considerate towards lesser mortals - if he liked them!

He was a veteran of numerous expeditions: Latok 2 1977 and1978, Barnaj 1979 and in the seventies he did many good new climbs in Scotland.

Two new climbs in the Albigna were added to his substantial list while working as the stand-in for Sean Connery in Five Days One Summer. He climbed in the Caucasus, the Pamirs, and Baffin Island where he did the first ascent of NE Ridge on Asgard. He worked on the film reconstruction of the first ascent of the Bat on Ben Nevis, The Bat and the Wicked, with Jim Curran, Tony Riley, Rab Carrington and Brian Hall. Between 1982 and 87 he went three times to the Karakorum, Gasherbrum 3 and Gasherbrum 4 and once to Everest.

In August 1995 Paul died on Mani Peak (Haramosh 2) in Pakistan when he and Geoff Tier were buried in an ice avalanche. Hilary his widow lives in Sheffield.

Trevor Briggs was one of the most liked members of the Alpha. He got involved with the club when working for Tanky in 1963. Trevor climbed extensively in Britain and was proud of being on the mass ascent of Am Buachaille in Sutherland. Climbing with John Smith he did Cenotaph Corner, Shrike and many others. He climbed at the Calanques and the Vercors as well as doing the North Ridge of the Badile with Smith in 1976. He was always a cheerful and friendly character. In 2008 he developed bowel cancer which gradually spread to other parts but Trevor put up a brave fight and had a positive attitude. This alas was to no avail; he died in April 2009 and is sadly missed.

Roy Fryer was John Smith's friend from Buxton; they joined the Alpha at the same time. Roy was a talented and gymnastic climber, one of the many to lead extremes. He became a policeman soon after getting married and his work curtailed his climbing. Some years ago he emigrated to Australia where he climbed on sea cliffs.

Soon after retirement he and his wife were involved in a head on car collision sustaining injuries from which Roy died.

<u>Hugh Banner</u> was for some reason never an Alpha member. This is surprising because for a long time when he first came to Manchester he was part of our crowd.

Hughie was the one who started the challenge to the Rock and Ice by doing early repeats of the Brown and Whillans climbs both in Wales and on grit. He was a local expert at Helsby, climbing with Bob Beesley and Jim O'Neill whom he nicknamed "The Wild-Eyed Irishman."

He married Maureen and they lived in North Wales where he used his engineering skills to start his own company, HB, producing climbing equipment.

Hugh was a keen motorcyclist but in the nineties he lost a leg in a bad smash up. His ingenuity had him designing a prosthetic leg in the hope it would allow him to climb again.

He was later struck down with a brain tumour which caused his death.

Author's Postscript

Recently I walked up to Laddow Rocks. Crowden Great Brook is a wild and beautiful place; it was there that I first started climbing so it holds special memories for me.

Sitting below Long Climb with the cool breeze in my face and the sounds of grouse saying, "Go back, go back," that's what I did; I went back in time. Back to when Ralph and I climbed here together as young lads dreaming of the time when we would follow in the footsteps of Frank Smythe, our hero.

In those days Laddow was a popular and well-used crag with many good climbs and a mountain atmosphere. Today it isn't climbed on much resulting in a lot of good quality climbs becoming overgrown with grass and heather, but the atmosphere is still there as are some classic climbs.

Memories were rekindled about our early days and the climbers whom we met, who took the time to teach us about rope work and to tell us about other places to climb.

Memories returned of those days with old friends when Richard was a beginner and a timid climber; who would have thought then that he'd go so far? Pete Bamfield making us all laugh by telling us that he sat looking in the mirror at home wearing his climbing gear, peg hammer in hand to practice looking hard. Platty, Pike, Les, Baldwin and Barlow - all these were original Alpha lads.

Then in later years climbing at Stanage with the club swelled by new members from Sheffield and other far flung places, before girlfriends and wives, when we were like brothers thinking it would last for ever.

Nowadays, whenever I look in Robin Hood's Cave I half expect to see some of the lads cooking a meal, perhaps Bob Brayshaw, Arthur Williams, Paul or John Smith, but they aren't there; just the memory of them.

On the original Alpha Club cards Pete Bamfield as secretary had printed:

"All club members should uphold the good name of the club by climbing safely and behaving properly whilst on the mountain." I like to think we did that even though we had some riotous times whilst off the mountain.

Writing this book has been a trip down memory lane. I hope my memory has served me correctly.

Al. Parker 2010

Alpha Nicknames

Ralph Harris	Rastus
Alan McHardy	Richard
Malcolm Cundy	Pike/Piecan
Brian Platt	Platty
Alan Parker	Al/Festy
Alan Goodwin	Young Al
Arthur Williams	Arthur Nirk
Oliver Woolcock	Wool
Ian Hartle	Willy Hurtle
Pete Crew	Crewy
Barry Ingle	Baz
Brian Griffiths	Griff
Bryan Stokes	Tanky
Gerry Rogan	Grogan
Howard Rainer	Garth
Dave Goodwin	Spud
Trevor Briggs	Twiggs

Glossary of Terms

Rope up: to tie onto rope.

Leader: first on rope with rope trailing behind, no rope above.

Second: next on rope climbs with rope above.

Through or alternate leads: Leader and Second change over at each stance

Stance: A ledge where leader can stop to belay.

Belay: An anchor point for Leader to tie into so as to be safe while taking in rope or for second to be tied to while paying out rope.

Pitch: distance between stances.

Running belay or runner: places for leader to clip rope into whilst climbing which are retrieved by second man when he climbs up to join leader at stance.

Belay plate: friction device which locks when placed under load. To help leader or second to hold a falling companion.

Friends: expanding camming device used as belay or running belay. Various sizes to fit various cracks.

Nuts: metal wedges of various sizes on rope or wire slings, used for belays or running belays.

Chockstone: stone jammed in crack, used as above.

Run out: distance of leader from his last belay point.

Abseil, Rappel or Rope down: method of descending by sliding down the rope.

Jumar or Prussik: method of ascending the rope hanging free of the rock by use of knotted slings or metal devices.

Karabiner or crab: metal sprung clip to attach rope to belays.

Pitons or pegs: metal pegs driven into cracks for belays or for direct aid to climbing.

Ice pegs, Ice screws: used on ice for the same purposes as pitons on rock.

Crampons: metal plates with spikes which are strapped to the soles of boots when moving over ice.

Ice axes and hammers: used in conjunction with crampons when climbing ice.

New routes: first ascents of climbs named and graded by first ascensionist; recorded for inclusion in guidebooks.

Bivouac or Bivvy: a place on a ledge or some part of the mountain to spend the night.

PA's: The original lightweight rock boots, made in France by Pierre Alain.

Climbing Harness: Webbing belt and leg loops to which climbing rope is attached.

Techniques;

Hand-jam: to place hand in a crack in a way that causes it to become secure enough to use as a hand-hold.

Fist jams: similar to above.

Finger jams: ditto.

Leg or foot jams: place in crack to use as hold.

Layback: to lean back on a crack and walk the feet up on an opposing wall.

Bridging: to bridge across a groove or corner with a foot on opposing walls.

Wedging: to place bent arm in a wide crack to hold body upright.

Chimneying: to climb very wide cracks with feet on one wall and back and hands on opposing wall, walking feet upwards then pushing up the body with hands.

Traverse: to climb moving sideways.

Tension traverse: to use rope to assist in climbing sideways.

Hand and Footholds: anything that is used to pull or stand on.

Glissade: method of sliding down snow slopes, hopefully in control.

Ice axe Brake: to force pick of axe into snow or ice to arrest a fall.

Features on mountain or crag

Ridge: junction of two faces.

Rib or Arete: type of ridge steep or otherwise, on the face of a mountain or crag.

Chimney: a wide fissure big enough to get inside.

Crack: fissures from finger width to leg width.

Groove: V shaped vertical or leaning feature sometimes with crack inside.

Corner: as above but a 90 degree open book.

Diedre: French for corner.

Dihedral: American for corner or groove.

Wall: flat face above 80 degrees angle.

Slab: as above but less than 80 degrees.

Overhang: jutting out section of cliff; beyond vertical.

Crevasse: a fissure on a glacier.

Icefall: a steepening on a glacier which causes a jumble of crevasses and Seracs.

Serac: a pinnacle or tower of ice.

Bergschrund: a wide crevasse where the glacier adjoins the face of a mountain.

Gully: a fault running vertically down a mountain side.

Couloir: French for gully.

Cornice: overhang of wind blown snow on a ridge or top of a face.

Avalanche: a falling mass of snow or ice.

Rock fall; a falling mass of rock and solid material or could be a single stone.

Grades in Order of Rising Difficulty

Moderate.
Difficult
Very Difficult
Severe
Very Severe (VS)
Hard Very Severe (HVS)
Extreme; E1, E2, etc, nowadays up to E10.
The above grades are for the overall climb
There are technical grades for sections of a climb
For example; 4a. 4b. 4c. 5a 5b 5c 6a 6b 6c etc.